CASTE, CLASS
AND EDUCATION

MAP OF KARNATAKA

MAHARASHTRA

ANDHRA PRADESH

Bidar

Gulbarga

Bijapur

Belgaum

Raichur

I N T E G R A T E D
A R E A S

GOA

Dakshina Kannada

Dharwad

Bellary

Chitradurga

OLD MYSORE

Shimoga

ARABIAN SEA

Chikmagalur

Tumkur

Kolar

Uttara Kannada

Hassan

Bangalore

Bangalore Rural

Mandya

Kodagu

KERALA

Mysore

TAMIL NADU

CASTE, CLASS AND EDUCATION

Politics of the Capitation Fee Phenomenon in Karnataka

REKHA KAUL

SAGE PUBLICATIONS
New Delhi/Newbury Park/London

To My Late Father

First published in 1993 by

Sage Publications India Pvt Ltd
M-32, Greater Kailash Market-I
New Delhi 110 048

Sage Publications Inc	**Sage Publications Ltd**
2455 Teller Road	6 Bonhill Street
Newbury Park, California 91320	London EC2A 4PU

Published by Tejeshwar Singh for Sage Publications India Pvt Ltd, phototypeset by Pagewell Photosetters, Pondicherry, and printed at Chaman Enterprises, Delhi.

Library of Congress Cataloging-in-Publication Data

Kaul, Rekha.
    Caste, class, and education : politics of the capitation fee phenomenon in Karnataka / Rekha Kaul.
        p.   cm.
    Includes bibliographical references (p.   ) and index.
    1. Higher education and state—India—Karnataka—Case studies.
2. Private universities and colleges—India—Karnataka—Finance—Case studies. 3. Education, Higher—Social aspects—India—Karnataka—Case studies. I. Title. LC179.I5K38   1993   379.54'87—dc20   92–43394

ISBN 0–8039–9472–9
        81–7036–331–4

CONTENTS

List of Tables   6
Preface   9
Acknowledgements   12

1. Caste, Class and Education: A Historical Perspective   15
2. Society, Polity and Education in Karnataka   38
3. Evolution of the Capitation Fee Phenomenon in
   Karnataka   84
4. Policy Towards Private Colleges   110
5. The Management Process   142
6. The Students   187
7. The Faculty   224
8. Conclusion   241

Bibliography   265
Index   272

LIST OF TABLES

1.1   State of Engineering Education in India between 1911 and 1940   24

1.2   State of Medical Education in India between 1911 and 1940   25

1.3   Arts vs. Professional Colleges, 1916–17   26

2.1   Number of Agricultural Landholdings and Area, 1985–86   44

2.2   Composition of the Karnataka Legislative Assembly by Caste: 1952–72 Elections   48

2.3   Distribution of Households by Caste and Size of Operational Holdings: 1961   49

2.4   Industrial Establishments, 1979–84   52

2.5   Selected Economic Indicators, Karnataka, 1980–81 and 1985–86 to 1990–91   54

2.6   Social Composition of Students Receiving College Education in 1916   60

2.7   Numerical Strength of Members of Various Castes and Other Groups Appointed to Various Government Posts in Mysore State during 1921–24   63

2.8   Pattern of Recruitment of Brahmins/Non-Brahmins in Public Services, 1918–27   65

2.9   Representation of Selected Castes and Groups of Castes in the Karnataka Legislative Assembly between 1952 and 1967   68

2.10   Percentage of Posts Held by Different Communities in March 1972   70

2.11   Position of the Lingayats and Vokkaligas in Medical Colleges, 1977–83   80

2.12   Position of the Lingayats and Vokkaligas in Comparison
        to Brahmins in Engineering Colleges in the State during
        1984–85   81
2.13   Caste-wise Distribution of Brahmin, Lingayat and
        Vokkaliga Students Admitted to Medical Colleges in
        Karnataka during 1988–89   82
2.14   Admission of Brahmin, Lingayat and Vokkaliga Students
        to Engineering Colleges between 1977 and 1989   82
3.1   Growth in the Number of Engineering Colleges in
        Karnataka   85
3.2   Growth in the Number of Medical Colleges in Karnataka   86
3.3   Production of Selected Industries (tons), 1935–41   95
4.1   Distribution of Seats in Engineering Colleges   121
4.2   Scheme of Phased Abolition of Capitation Fee in Medical
        Colleges Issued in 1981   124
4.3   Distribution of Seats in Government Medical Colleges
        (Mode of Selection)   126
4.4   Distribution of Seats in Private Medical Colleges (Mode
        of Selection   128
4.5   Distribution of Seats in Private Medical Colleges in
        1984–85   133
4.6   Break-up of Seats Available in 1987–88 under the
        Government Merit Pool, Cash Deposit and Management
        Quota in Private Medical Colleges in Karnataka   134
5.1   College-wise Figures in Respect of Government and
        Private Medical Colleges Regarding Annual Admission
        to M.B.B.S.   154
5.2   Intake in Private Engineering Colleges (Full-Time
        Courses)   156
5.3   Composition of the Management Board (K.I.M.S.,
        B.I.T.)   160
5.4   Composition of the Management Board (A.I.T.,
        A.I.M.S.)   163
5.5   Composition of the Management Board (S.I.T.)   166
5.6   Composition of the Management Board (J.N.M.C. and
        K.L.E.S.)   170
5.7   Composition of the Management Board (S.S.I.T.)   173
5.8   Composition of the Management Board (Islamiah
        Institute of Technology)   174
5.9   Composition of the Management Board (M.I.T. and
        K.M.C.)   176
5.10   Composition of the Management Board (M.S. Ramaiah
        Institute of Technology, M.S. Ramaiah Medical College)   178
6.1   Parents' Occupation—Initial Sample (I)   190

6.2   Parents' Occupation—Detailed Sample II   191
6.3   Income Levels—Detailed Sample II   193
6.4   Schooling—Sample I   196
6.5   Schooling—Sample II   197
6.6   Rural–Urban Background—Sample I   198
6.7   Rural–Urban Background—Sample II   198
6.8   Attitude of Students Towards Capitation Fee
       System—Sample I   203
6.9   Attitude of Students Towards Capitation Fee
       System—Sample II   203
6.10   Quality of Education—Sample I   207
6.11   Quality of Education—Sample II   209
6.12   Intake of Students in Engineering and Medical Colleges,
       1979–83   212
6.13   Intake of Students in Engineering Colleges, 1986–88   213
6.14   Students' Union—Sample I   216
6.15   Students' Union—Sample II   216
6.16   Future Aspirations of Students—Sample I   219
6.17   Future Aspirations of Students—Sample II   220
7.1   Reasons for Joining Private Colleges   229
7.2   Background of Faculty   230
7.3   Facilities for Teaching and Research   234
7.4   Teachers' Views on Capitation Fee   238

PREFACE

The book seeks to explore the extent to which the structure of education depends on the nature of society and the state. Focusing on the issue of capitation fee, it tries to show how educational institutions have often been used by various classes and social groups as channels for strengthening their political and social base and for economic gains. Viewed as such, the capitation fee phenomenon is seen as a manifestation of the interplay of caste, class and politics.

To understand these linkages, I have taken the specific case of the State of Karnataka where private engineering and medical colleges charge exorbitant fees. I chose Karnataka for a detailed study because the capitation phenomenon has been most widespread there. It was also in this State that the first such institution was established at Manipal. The State has an interesting caste–class–power configuration which provided an appropriate setting for my explorations.

Beginning with a critical examination of education under the colonial regime where higher education remained largely confined to the upper castes and upper strata of society, the book goes on to discuss the scant attention paid to skill generation or development of medical education during this period. After Independence, the narrow growth of education under the British was sought to be corrected through the setting up of a number of schools and colleges. However, state funding was still woefully inadequate. Private initiative came in as an alternative, but it gradually moulded education to suit its own needs.

A socio-economic and political profile of Karnataka provides the necessary backdrop for the study. The book attempts to establish the combination of forces responsible for the rise of capitation fee colleges in the State. The caste factor is seen as an important aspect. The capitation fee phenomenon unravels the new role of caste as an instrument of power. It is observed that it was largely the landowning dominant castes, the Lingayats and Vokkaligas, who sought to advance their own interests by setting up private professional colleges. Subsequently, other caste and minority groups entered the domain. Profit-making interests later surfaced and entrepreneurs also entered the field of higher education.

The State government's policies and its interventions at various levels, including legislative measures, are analysed because instead of curbing the growth of the capitation fee system, they have only succeeded in legitimising it. Also examined are government stipulations and the extent to which they guide the private managements in their functioning vis-à-vis admission policy, intake of students, appointment of teachers, maintenance of standards, and the like.

The book incorporates a detailed study of 19 private engineering and medical colleges. Data was collected from the managements, faculty and students through questionnaires and interviews. While detailing the dynamics of caste, class and power in these private institutions as seen through the management process, the book also presents socio-economic and political profiles of members of the management boards. The study of the students and the faculty provides some interesting aspects of the entrepreneurial character of private institutions, and at the same time notes that the system has been essentially catering to the affluent sections of society.

Finally, the book discusses the socio-political and educational implications of the capitation fee phenomenon—how it reflects persisting inequalities and the elitist base of the education system, how it seeks to reproduce the dominant caste–class and power structures, and how it leads to lowering of educational standards. To counter the serious consequences of the system, possible interventions—both at the level of the state and at the grassroot level—are outlined as corrective measures. Here, an attempt is also made to analyse the dilemma of the state with its ideological commitment to the goal of equality, and its tacit support to the capitation fee system owing to various dominating pressures from middle caste elites, sectional and minority interests and entrepreneurial groups.

I would feel satisfied if the book can contribute to the on-going debate on the inter-related issues of privatization of higher education and the state's responsibility for providing such education to all. The issue has been highlighted recently by the Supreme Court and the Andhra Pradesh and Karnataka High Court judgements regarding the charging of capitation fees by private colleges. It is hoped that the debate culminates in the evolution of specific policy measures that can lead to the emergence of some alternative to the existing distortions in the sphere of private professional education.

1 November 1992   REKHA KAUL

ACKNOWLEDGEMENTS

The people who willingly extended their help and cooperation in the writing of this book number so many that it is difficult for me to thank them individually. I would like to record my gratitude to each one of them.

There are some I would like to specially mention. Professor Manoranjan Mohanty, Department of Political Science, University of Delhi, was a tremendous source of inspiration. He patiently read major portions of the draft and helped me formulate the structure of the book.

I would like to express my sincere gratitude to Professor Krishna Kumar, Department of Education, University of Delhi, for his encouragement and constructive suggestions. Professor K. Raghavendra Rao, University of Mangalore, willingly spared time to provide clarity to the theoretical formulations of the book. I would also like to thank Professor Bashiruddin Ahmad, Vice-Chancellor, Jamia Milia Islamia, for his valuable comments.

I had fruitful discussions with many experts on Karnataka who helped me in my understanding of the region. These included Professor M.N. Srinivas, formerly at the Institute for Social and Economic Change, Bangalore; Dr. Amal Ray, also from the same institute; Professor James Manor, University of Sussex; Professor Chelvaraju, Vice-Chancellor, University of Gulbarga; and Dr. G. Ramakrishna, Dr. R.L.M. Patil and Dr. N. Jayaram, all at the University of Bangalore.

The Directors of Technical and Medical Education, Government of Karnataka, were forthcoming in making available the relevant official information. I am deeply indebted to Mr. K. Nazir Hussain, Planning Department, Government of Karnataka, for providing me with some of the latest statistics for the book. The District Collectors of Chikmagalur and Tumkur (1988–89) enabled me to gain access to the private colleges in their districts and assisted me on various fronts.

Sachidanand Murthy, Chief of Bureau, *The Week*, H. Kusumakar, Resident Editor (Bangalore), *The Times of India*, Anand Doraiswamy, *Deccan Herald*, and K.S. Latha of *Indian Express* provided me information on capitation fee colleges and the current political developments in Karnataka. Sujit Deb, Librarian, Centre for the Study of Developing Societies, Delhi, and Aruna Tandon of the Nehru Memorial Museum Library were very helpful in locating some of the necessary reference material for the book.

I am grateful to Mr. Victor Kaul for moral support and constant dialogue. Dr. Malathi Subramanian, University of Delhi, Subir Shukla and Hema Ramakrishnan read some portions of the draft and offered useful suggestions. My husband, Ranjan, was a continued source of inspiration and played the role of a supportive editor.

My children, Neha and Nikhil, endured through all this uncomplainingly, and were a source of joy and cheer.

1

CASTE, CLASS AND EDUCATION: A HISTORICAL PERSPECTIVE

The decision of the state [Karnataka] government to allow two more private medical colleges has come as a big surprise . . . . Those who have opposed governmental patronage to private institutions that trade in education by charging donations or capitation fee are aghast at the decision of the cabinet which reportedly approved two medical colleges in Mandya and Kolar sponsored by Adichunchanagiri Mutt and a backward classes organisation respectively.[1]

The mushrooming of capitation fee colleges has attracted widespread attention. As the above extract from a newspaper article published in 1985 testifies, the system has been proliferating not only in the State of Karnataka but in other states as well. This has happened despite several official pronouncements, legislations and the July 1992 Supreme Court Verdict to do away with the capitation fee system.

The term 'capitation' refers to large sums of money and deposits demanded by private institutions, especially medical and engineering

---

[1] E. Raghavan, 'Promoting Capitation Culture?,' *The Times of India*, Bangalore, 16 June 1985.

colleges, for granting admission to prospective students. Thus, the benefits of education in such institutions accrue to those who can afford it.

The first capitation fee college in India came into existence in the State of Karnataka in 1953, followed by a few more colleges in the early sixties. However, it was only in 1965 that the Estimates Committee of Parliament first drew attention to the capitation fee problem. Since then, the situation has-become far more alarming. Every government at the centre and various State governments have frequently voiced concern over the issue. For instance, under Chief Minister Ramakrishna Hegde, the Janata Party in Karnataka promulgated the Karnataka Educational Institutions Act (1984) which banned capitation fees. But, in a volte-face a year later, he stated that 'even if black money is utilised in setting up medical colleges, as some have said, it is a means to bring out black money',[2] anticipating as it were, the schemes of the Narasimha Rao government to convert black money into white! The Telegu Desam government in Andhra Pradesh, too, banned capitation in 1984. However, the final change effected was no more than cosmetic. In fact, the Janardhan Reddy government in July–August 1992 sanctioned the setting up of 12 private medical colleges and eight dental colleges in the State.

Such failure is disquieting. Why have governments time and again been unable to curb the growth of capitation fee colleges? What lies behind such helplessness?

A search for answers to these questions leads us to take a closer look at the very nature of the phenomenon. A distinct feature of capitation fee colleges is their caste- and class-based character. Thus, from our point of view, a key set of questions would be: To what extent and in what manner are educational enterprises of this kind used by social groups and classes as avenues to achieve their objectives of power, profit and domination? Is this, indeed, the major factor underlying the 'problem' of institutions that charge capitation fees?

That these forces are at the core of issues concerning higher education can be seen from a related and more recent example—the raging controversy that came in the wake of the V.P. Singh government's decision to implement the Mandal Commission Report.

[2] *The Times of India*, Bangalore, 18 October 1985.

The Report underlined the importance of education and opportunities for employment and social mobility. Caste and class groups, seeking to realise their respective interests, clashed over the decision to implement the Report. Students, writers and social scientists agitating against this Report,[3] have questioned the validity of the very policy of 'affirmative action as a means of dispensing social justice to groups which have been systematically prevented from access to means of social mobility by tradition and history'.[4] The position taken by political parties on the issue have been 'quite predictable in terms of caste strategy',[5] yet no party has taken an unequivocal stand against the Mandal Report. Once again, such ambivalence echoes the government's equivocation regarding capitation fee colleges.

Issues such as 'Mandal' and 'capitation' indicate that it is impossible to understand any social phenomenon in the Indian situation without delving into the close interplay of caste, class and political forces.

Caste, Class and Politics

Caste and class in Indian society and polity have been the subject of a long-standing and ongoing debate. A number of perspectives have been brought to bear upon the issue. Studies that emphasise the continuity of the traditional social structure have focused on caste as a central category of Indian society,[6] and have thus enhanced our comprehension of caste. Their primary concern has been to

[3] See M.N. Srinivas, 'The Mandal Formula' in Ashghar Ali Engineer (Ed.), *Mandal Commission Controversy*, Ajanta Publications, Delhi, 1991, pp. 130–34. See also Andre Beteille, 'Millstone of Reservations: Liberation with Caste Quotas,' *The Times of India*, New Delhi, 12 October 1991.

[4] D.L. Sheth, 'Changing Terms of Elite Discourse: The Case of the O.B.C. Reservation' in T.V. Satyamurthy, *Vocabulary of Indian Politics* (tentative title), Oxford University Press, New Delhi, 1992 (in press).

[5] Gail Omvedt, 'Twice-Born Riot Against Democracy,' *Economic and Political Weekly*, Vol. XXV, No. 39, 29 September 1990, pp. 2195–201.

[6] For details, see D.L. Sheth, 'Caste and Politics: A Survey of Literature' in Gopal Krishna (Ed.), *Contributions to South Asian Studies*, Vol. I, Oxford University Press, Delhi, 1979, pp. 161–97.

examine the social structure of 'little communities'.[7] Some socio-
logists have gone beyond a community and looked into the question
of status and power relations among different groups and sub-
groups of various castes. However, one of their failings has been
the inability to take into consideration the social basis of caste and
place it in the evolution of the growing agrarian class structure.[8]

Coming later to the field, political scientists began to measure
the influence of caste on voting behaviour and focused attention
on the resulting political alignments among various caste groups.
But their studies have been limited in that they have not taken into
consideration the overall economic structure. Yet another perspective has been that of the class-determinist analysts who do not
acknowledge the autonomy of other social categories. Marxist
theoreticians have explained caste behaviour as a manifestation of
class behaviour—a much debated issue in India—and have tended
to overlook cultural categories.

Still another view has been taken by some other scholars who
see a peculiar intertwining of caste and class. Francine Frankel has
spoken of multiple sources of power of which caste and class are
primary.[9] These have been treated by her as processes interacting
with each other and with increasingly powerful state institutions.
However, state policies facilitate the manipulation of communal
and caste loyalties to diffuse class polarization. Beteille has studied
how the political process initiates class formation in a caste situation.[10] Omvedt has observed that caste relations embody not only
class elements but also peculiarly caste-based relations of domination.
In the Indian context, according to her, the lower castes were
oppressed and poor, while the upper castes were propertied. There
was thus a large degree of convergence between a person's caste
and his/her class. Later, there was a broad correlation between
caste and class under British rule which witnessed a replication of
the 'main classes of the pre-colonial caste–feudal period'.[11]

[7] M.N. Srinivas, *India's Villages*, Asia Publishing House, Bombay, 1960.

[8] Manoranjan Mohanty, 'Prologue' in Gail Omvedt (Ed.), *Land, Caste and Politics in Indian States: A Project of Teaching Politics*, Department of Political Science, University of Delhi, 1982.

[9] Francine R. Frankel and M.S.A. Rao (Eds.), *Dominance and State Power in Modern India: Decline of a Social Order*, Oxford University Press, Delhi, 1989.

[10] Andre Beteille, *Caste, Class and Power*, Oxford University Press, Bombay, 1966.

[11] Gail Omvedt (Ed.), *Land, Caste and Politics in Indian States*, op. cit., p. 19.

Though this correlation has remained significant in the post-colonial phase, it has not been static. The intermeshing of caste and class has not fundamentally changed the socio-economic structure. But it has, at the same time, contributed to the rise of new forces in the countryside. Many intermediate castes linked with agriculture became economically and politically powerful. This variation in the caste–class convergence assumes significance in our study of the capitation fee phenomenon.

After Independence, land reforms broadened the base of the 'proprietary classes' comprising landlords and rich farmers. These reforms were mainly aimed at the abolition of the Zamindari system and the protection of tenants against eviction. They imposed a ceiling on landholdings, but only the rich peasants who could pay compensation acquired ownership rights. Thus, land was transferred from non-cultivating upper caste landlords to enterprising rich farmers often belonging to the middle castes.[12]

The government assured this emergent class of farmers that it would liberally provide subsidised inputs such as water, power, fertilizers, diesel and tractors. The promotion of irrigation, cooperatives, credit schemes, better seed and fertilizer facilities—all part of the Green Revolution—have also benefited these rich peasants. This newly acquired financial resource has had one important consequence. According to Bardhan,[13] in some of the States—such as Punjab, Haryana, Gujarat and Karnataka—where the rich farmer lobbies amongst Jats, Patidars, Reddis and Vokkaligas, for instance, have been strong and have succeeded in obtaining major benefits like support prices, subsidies and low taxes on agriculture, an increasing part of their savings has been going out of the agricultural sector in the form of financial investment. New areas of 'branching out' have included money-lending, trading, transport as well as services. Apart from strengthening their urban political and economic connections, this kind of 'portfolio diversification' has made these families less susceptible to the vagaries of agricultural production. Among such strengthening avenues or paths to diversification is education.

The acquisition of educational qualifications has come to the

[12] See P.C. Joshi, 'Land Reforms in India' in A.R. Desai (Ed.), *Rural Sociology in India*, Popular Prakashan, Bombay, 1969, pp. 444–75.

[13] Pranab Bardhan, *The Political Economy of Development in India*, Oxford University Press, Delhi, 1984, pp. 48 and 64.

fore as the prosperous sections of the dominant castes[14] have engaged in intense competition for greater job opportunities and better educational facilities. They have sought elected posts for themselves at all levels in the village from panchayats to cooperatives. As the importance of educational qualifications, which have become necessary for employment, has been realised, the demand for education has grown. Politicians and caste leaders have patiently catered to caste sensitivities while promising the setting up of schools and colleges to 'better' the lot of the people belonging to their own castes. They have strongly used 'caste associations and caste appeals to rally people behind them for influence in education, employment and other concessions'.[15] However, they have ensured that any such activity entails profits for themselves, and at the same time they have utilised all caste associations and resources to further their own social, political and economic interests.

In the Indian situation, where there have been several processes operating simultaneously, the pattern of class and caste convergence has been unstructured and complex. A rich Lingayat industrialist, for instance, may use caste sentiments to start an all-Lingayat-managed private college for profit motives. Therefore, as Rao has observed, 'the nature of the Indian state cannot be abstractly conceptualised in terms of simple class dominance or rule.' Such dominance cannot be denied, but it is yet 'uncrystallised'.[16] Thus, we do not see any neat class formations; they are always intermeshed with caste and other structures of domination. However, we may find a Vokkaliga leader, who is a rich landowner, taking up the cause of the peasants when it suits him. At another time he may use only caste appeals to secure votes for himself because that suits him more. Consequently, there is no structured pattern of one-dimensional interests predominating at all points of time. The

---

[14] A dominant caste, according to M.N. Srinivas, not only exercises a preponderant influence economically and politically, but is also numerically the strongest in the village or local area. See M.N. Srinivas, *The Dominant Caste and Other Essays*, Oxford University Press, Delhi, 1987, pp. 96–115.

[15] Gail Omvedt (Ed.), *Land, Caste and Politics in Indian States*, op. cit., p. 29.

[16] K. Raghavendra Rao, 'Understanding the Indian State: A Historical Materialist Exercise' in Zoya Hasan, S.N. Jha and Rasheeduddin Khan (Eds.), *The State, Political Processes and Identity: Reflections on Modern India*, Sage Publications, New Delhi, 1989, p. 89.

education process in the form of the capitation fee phenomenon in Karnataka reveals the complexity of such a reality.

It is worth noting, as Ghanshyam Shah has done, that all caste members do not necessarily share common economic interests.[17] 'Different strata of the same caste pursue different, and at times, opposite economic interests.'[18] However, the social bond perpetuates class consciousness and such a situation has worked to the 'advantage of upper caste/class entrepreneurs who can seek the support of and mobilise their poor caste brethren'[19] to suit their own interests. Lacking any political base other than their own caste, the elites rely upon caste-based organisations to win political power. In our context, the setting up of a caste-based capitation fee college, besides being a source of financial gain, secures for a caste leader the electoral support of his caste group. There is evidence to prove that several colleges have funded the election campaigns of candidates belonging to their caste. Thus, there is a clear link between caste, class and education, especially higher education. In order to understand its operation in the case of the capitation fee system, it would be useful to place it in a historical perspective.

The Pre-Independence Phase

Designed to serve colonial interests, the system of education introduced by the British was 'primarily motivated by the political, administrative and economic needs of Britain in India'.[20] Education in nineteenth-century India was accessible mainly to the offsprings of the upper strata of society.[21] Most graduates and matriculates in the three Presidencies of Bengal, Madras and Bombay had urban connections and belonged to families associated with administrative and professional work or the land-owning strata.

[17] Ghanshyam Shah, 'Caste, Class and the State,' *Seminar*, March 1990, pp. 31–35.
[18] Ibid.
[19] Ibid.
[20] A.R. Desai, *Social Background of Indian Nationalism*, 5th edn., Popular Prakashan, Bombay, 1975, p. 140.
[21] See Anil Seal, *The Emergence of Indian Nationalism*, Cambridge University Press, Cambridge, 1968; and Aparna Basu, *The Growth of Education and Political Development in India: 1898–1920*, Oxford University Press, Delhi, 1974.

The convergence between caste and class continued. The educated elite was drawn mainly from the upper castes who had a literate tradition behind them. In Bengal, the Brahmins, the Kayasthas and the Baidyas—the *bhadralok*[22]—had taken the largest share of higher education in Calcutta. In Bombay Presidency, the Chitpavan Brahmins of Maharashtra and the Parsis of the city took the lead,[23] while in Madras the Brahmins were the forerunners.

This elitist, upper-class orientation of the colonial educational policy was also reflected in the simultaneous neglect of education for the masses. Thus, at the time of Independence, only about 16 per cent of the population was literate.[24] Yet another aspect that was neglected during the British rule was technical and professional education. A look at the reasons for this neglect will serve as a background for our examination of the interaction of the capitation fee system and professional education.

Technical and Medical Education Under the British

Since the policy of the British government was not to convert India's natural resources and raw materials for developing a strong, self-reliant industrial base, it did not provide for generating skills in that direction. Thus, technical education under the British 'suffered from want of opportunity to aid scientific research and

[22] There is a considerable body of literature concerning the definition of *bhadralok*. Poromesh Acharya has defined them as a socio-cultural group. According to him, they belong to a 'leisured class' and 'do not participate physically in any major operation of the production process whether in agriculture or in industry'. However, they take to education and white-collared jobs for their sustenance and thereby supplement their income from land. So, they have essentially rural origins while maintaining urban links owing to their jobs. See Poromesh Acharya, 'Development of Modern Language Textbooks and the Social Context in Nineteenth Century Bengal,' *Economic and Political Weekly*, Vol. XXI, No. 17, 26 April 1986, p. 750.

[23] Anil Seal, op. cit., pp. 25–113; Ravinder Kumar, *Western India in the Nineteenth Century: A Study of the Social History of Maharashtra*, Routledge and Kegan Paul, London, 1968, pp. 51–53; and Gail Omvedt, *Cultural Revolt in a Colonial Society: The Non-Brahmin Movement in Western India*, Scientific Socialist Education Trust, Bombay, 1976, pp. 76–78.

[24] A. Mishra, *Educational Finance in India*, Asia Publishing House, Bombay, 1962, p. 540.

higher manipulative skills. It grew mainly as part of general education, concerned more with theory than with practice.'[25]

The need for education in engineering was felt out of the necessity for training overseers for the construction and maintenance of public buildings, roads, canals and ports and for the training of artisans and craftmen for the use of the apparatus that was required for the navy, army and survey departments. The need for the much desired revenue through agriculture created the necessity of irrigation works. Technical personnel were required to design, construct and maintain them. Thus in 1847 the first engineering college was set up at Roorkee for training civil engineers required mainly for the construction of the Upper Ganges Canal.

It was as late as 1917 that the first degree classes in mechanical and electrical engineering were started at the Benaras Hindu University. These courses were later introduced in Sibpur (Calcutta), Poona and Guindy (Madras) in the 1930s. While the average annual cost of educating a pupil in an arts college in 1916–17 was Rs. 151, in a professional college it was Rs. 317.[26] These figures reveal the scant attention paid to professional education. In fact, by the close of the first decade of the century, only 4 per cent of students graduating from Indian universities were engineering students.[27] There were only four recognised engineering colleges with an annual output of 74 engineering graduates in 1916–17.[28] From Table 1.1 we may observe that the total number of engineering colleges rose to five in 1921–22 from four in 1911–12. There was only a marginal increase in the total number of students during this period. Between 1931–32 and 1939–40 there was no addition to the total number of engineering institutions in the country.

There was general dissatisfaction with the efforts of the colonial state in imparting technical education. Elite groups in India expected that the effects of the Industrial Revolution which would see a beginning of industrialisation would be felt in India too. They were

[25] B.B. Mishra, *The Indian Middle Classes: Their Growth in Modern Times*, Oxford University Press, London, 1961, p. 286.

[26] See Aparna Basu, 'Technical Education in India, 1854–1921' in *Essays in the History of Indian Education*, Concept Publishing Company, New Delhi, 1981.

[27] B.B. Mishra, op. cit., p. 294.

[28] *Report of the Industrial Commission 1916–18*, Vol. I, p. 70 cited in A. Basu, *The Growth of Education and Political Development in India: 1898–1920*, Oxford University Press, Delhi, 1974, p. 90.

Table 1.1

State of Engineering Education in India between 1911 and 1940

Year	Engineering colleges	No. of students
1911–12	4	1,187
1916–17	4	1,319
1921–22	5	1,443
1931–32	7	2,171
1939–40	7	2,509

Source: B.B. Mishra, *The Indian Middle Classes: Their Growth in Modern Times*, Oxford University Press, London, 1961, p. 332.

therefore disappointed that their aspirations for acquiring scientific and technical education remained unfulfilled. Hence they made alternative efforts largely outside the ambit of state control. One such effort, the National Education Movement, will be discussed later in the chapter.

India was relatively advanced in medical education and had its own long tradition in the field. The ancient Hindus had made considerable progress in the study of medicine, herbs and physiology.[29] However, the British rulers, instead of catering to mass health services, succeeded in developing science and medicine in a limited way and the indigenous system of medicine was gradually destroyed.[30]

Medical education received little encouragement, and the number of medical graduates was disproportionately small compared to the number of arts and law graduates.[31] As there were only four to five medical colleges, few students could opt for medicine. The Grant Medical College was set up in Bombay in 1845; a medical school established in Madras was given the status of a college in 1851. Gaining admission to such medical colleges was difficult and

[29] See selections from Adam's Report on Indigenous Education in Bengal and Bihar; Survey of Nattare, Thana, where 485 villages had 123 native general practitioners, 205 village doctors, 21 Brahmin smallpox inoculators, 227 women midwives and 722 snake conjurers in Dharampal, *The Beautiful Tree: Indigenous Indian Education in the Eighteenth Century*, Biblia Impex Pvt. Ltd., New Delhi, 1983, p. 43.

[30] Ibid., pp. 53, 56, 78–79.

[31] *Seventh Quinquennial Review of Education in India, 1912–17*, Vol. II, p. III, Table 28.

the fees were exorbitant. Since the number of hospitals was small, government employment was limited and the prospects of private practice were also uncertain. Yet there were more applicants than available seats. For example, in the Calcutta Medical College in 1914–15, there were 702 applicants and 154 admissions; in 1917–18, the corresponding numbers were 830 and 164 respectively.[32] As indicated in Table 1.2, while the medical colleges doubled in number between 1911 and 1917 from four to eight, they were still insufficient to meet the growing demand for medical education. There was no increase in the next five years. Between 1931–32 and 1939–40, only one more college was added to the list. By 1947, there were 24 medical colleges in the country with an enrolment of 8797, a low figure indeed for a population of 400 million.[33]

Table 1.2
State of Medical Education in India between 1911 and 1940

Year	Medicine	
	Colleges	*Students*
1911–12	4	1,396
1916–17	8	2,511
1921–22	8	4,065
1931–32	11	4,201
1939–40	12	5,640

Source: B.B. Mishra, *The Indian Middle Classes: Their Growth in Modern Times*, Oxford University Press, London, 1961, p. 332.

The British failed to develop the economy towards creating a sizeable industrial infrastructure. Owing to lack of industrial growth, educational expansion, particularly in the professions, remained limited. Engineering and medicine accounted for only 2.25 and 4.23 per cent of the enrolments in 1916–17 (Table 1.3) while 88 per cent of the enrolments in the same period were concentrated in general education.

The weaknesses and marginality of technical and medical education were conspicuous in the overall educational programme of British rule in India. It was neither aimed at invigorating the

[32] *Report of the Calcutta University Commission*, 1919, Vol. III, pp. 67–74.
[33] *Education in India*, 1947–48, cited in Aparna Basu, op. cit.

Table 1.3
Arts vs. Professional Colleges, 1916–17

	No. of institutions	No. of pupils
Arts colleges	124	154,952
Engineering colleges	9	1,815
Medical colleges	5	2,279
Law colleges	28	5,476

Source: Progress of Education in India, 1912–17, Vol. II, pp. 98, 157, 158, 159. Cited in Aparna Basu, *Essays in the History of Indian Education*, Concept Publishing Company, New Delhi, 1981, p. 17.

production process by integrating skill generation nor was it oriented towards mass-health programmes.

Nationalist Initiatives

As against the colonial policy, there were educational movements inspired by nationalist ideals in north India. These made an effort to develop an alternative model of education, outside the state orbit and to suit Indian requirements and ethos.[34] What is of interest to note is that such private initiatives largely came from landed, upper castes who were imbued with a nationalist fervour. In Bengal, for instance, the National Education Movement was supported by the urban-based *bhadralok* comprising the intelligentsia, the English-educated sections of the landed gentry, the landed middle class who had entered professions belonging to the Hindu community, and so on.[35] Even the Benaras Hindu University, set up in 1916, derived its support from the resources of the Hindu community—ruling princes, noblemen and leading landed business and industrial interests.[36]

[34] These included Tilak's Deccan Education Society, Sri Aurobindo's Ganganath Vidyalaya at Baroda, the Nationalist Education Movement of Bengal, Tagore's School at Shantiniketan, the Gujarat Vidyapeeth, Kashi Vidyapeeth, the Maharashtra Vidyapeeth and the Bihar Vidyapeeth.

[35] See Poromesh Acharya, op. cit., p. 748, and Haridas Mukherjee and Uma Mukherjee, *The Origins of the National Education Movement: 1905–1910*, Jadavpur University, Calcutta, 1957.

[36] See S.L. Dar and S. Somaskandan, *History of the Benaras Hindu University*, B.H.U. Press, 1966.

This was in contrast to the picture south of the Vindhyas. The social and economic oppression and domination of the upper castes in the South led to the rise of the non-Brahmin movements and the aims and objectives of the middle and lower castes—whether reformist, nationalist or educational—got circumscribed by their respective caste interests.[37] The fact that education could bring in its wake social and material advantage 'triggered', as Krishna Kumar has stated, 'a competition in the caste hierarchy'. In fact, 'the role of education in disturbing traditional social hierarchies was more clearly expressed in the South than in the North.'[38]

The mass upheaval of the middle and lower castes manifested itself in the form of non-Brahmin movements in the South, in Maharashtra, Tamil Nadu and Mysore.[39] In Maharashtra, the non-Brahmins felt that if the Brahmins were not challenged they would strengthen their control over the governmental machinery and enhanced caste oppression would follow with the withdrawal of British rule. Therefore, the non-Brahmins felt that they should ask for more privileges and a fair share in representative institutions to finally get their share of political power. Such arguments were presented to the Kunbis (peasants) through the Satya Shodhak Samaj by Jotiba Phule and his lieutenants like Mukundrao Patil.[40] The Satya Shodhak workers demanded education not only from the government, but also set up schools and hostels, most of which were financed and supported by middle caste associations. 'Wealthy men had to be appealed to for funds and very often it was caste channels that proved most effective in this'.[41]

[37] In the case of Tamil Nadu, for instance, there is an assertion that the state is in the grip of the forces of 'regionalism' or 'cultural nationalism' or of 'primordial sentiment'. For details, see Robert L. Hardgrave, Jr., *The Dravidian Movement*, Popular Prakashan, Bombay, 1965, and Marguerite Ross Barnett, *The Politics of Cultural Nationalism in South India*, Princeton University Press, Princeton, New Jersey, 1976.

[38] Krishna Kumar, 'Colonial Citizen as an Educational Ideal,' *Economic and Political Weekly*, Vol. XXIV, No. 4, 28 January 1989, p. 48.

[39] M.S.A. Rao, 'Education, Stratification and Mobility' in S.C. Shukla and Krishna Kumar (Eds.), *Sociological Perspective in Education: A Reader*, Chanakya Publications, Delhi, 1985, pp. 147–59.

[40] See Ravinder Kumar, *Western India in the Nineteenth Century: A Study of the Social History of Maharastra*, op. cit., pp. 313–14, and Gail Omvedt, *Cultural Revolt in a Colonial Society: The Non-Brahmin Movement in Western India—1873–1930*, op. cit., pp. 160–61.

[41] Gail Omvedt, op. cit., p. 166.

In Madras Presidency also, there were 'spontaneous stirrings' of groups drawn from lower castes against the oppressive dominance of the Brahmins.[42] The Dravidian social reform movement (also known as the self-respect movement) led by E.V. Ramaswami Naicker (Periyar) in 1925 was oriented towards oppressed groups in the caste hierarchy and also towards untouchables, women and youth.[43] Hardgrave's study[44] deals with the stirrings of large masses drawn from the Nadar caste in Tamil Nadu against social oppression. The Nadar Mahajan Sangam, a caste-based association, promoted educational activity, welfare and philanthropic work amongst the Nadars between 1917 and 1921. The pace of this transformation gained momentum with the demand for securing greater government patronage and educational opportunities by the Nadars.[45]

In Mysore State (now Karnataka), as we will see in greater detail in the next chapter, it was the middle castes such as the Lingayats and Vokkaligas who tried to assert their economic strength and aspire for more opportunities in education, employment and politics. The non-Brahmin movement in Mysore also aimed at doing away with Brahmin dominance in education and in the services. Caste associations such as the Mysore Lingayat Educational Fund Association (M.L.E.F.A.) and the Vokkaliga Sangha were formed in the first decade of this century to assert caste solidarity and seek greater political representation.

To realise this objective, it became necessary to promote education. Private initiatives were taken by associations like the Karnataka Lingayat Education Society (K.L.E.S.) which was set up in 1916 with a view to uplifting the ignorant masses and regenerating the 'illiterate and backward brethren by means of education'.[46] Inspired by the example of the Deccan Education Society of Lokmanya Tilak, caste associations set up schools and colleges. Donations came from within the ranks of the Lingayats, from princes like

[42] N. Ram, 'Dravidian Movement in its Pre-Independence Phases,' *Economic and Political Weekly*, Vol. XIV, Nos. 7 and 8, February 1979, p. 379.

[43] See Eugene F. Irshick, *Politics and Social Conflict in South India: The Non-Brahmin Movement and Tamil Separatism 1916–29*, Oxford University Press, Bombay, 1969.

[44] Robert L. Hardgrave, *The Nadars of Tamil Nadu: The Political Culture of a Community in Change*, Oxford University Press, Bombay, 1969.

[45] Ibid.

[46] Karnataka Liberal Education Society, *Diamond Jubilee Souvenir 1916–76*, Belgaum, 1979, pp. 1–2.

Raja Lakhamagouda Sardesai of Wantamuri, Swamis (of *mutts*) like Jagadguru Tentadaraya, prominent landlords and business magnates like G.I. Bagwadi, and even the public.[47]

The aim of the Vokkaliga Sangha, founded in 1906, was to promote the 'social, cultural and educational aspirations' of the agricultural community—the 'ryots of the state'.[48] The Vokkaliga Saarvajanika Hostel had been providing hostel facilities to a large number of students for over 50 years. There were over 8,000 students in the Sangha's various colleges.[49] Those supporting this initiative included rich landlords, businessmen, and even ordinary people from amongst the caste group. These activities were all part of the drive for upward mobility of the middle castes to realise their aims of expanding educational and employment opportunities for themselves. All these initiatives were private.

The idea of caste solidarity and caste development and progress has continued to be echoed by caste-based associations to espouse their cause, although private enterprise in education has undergone major changes, where control over educational resources is seen as one involving material rewards, prestige and power. Under these changed circumstances, setting up and managing professional colleges by caste-based associations has taken on a more 'narrow and partisan meaning'.[50]

The Constitutional Perspective

Here we will examine the reaffirmation of caste and group identities and private initiative in the Constitutional context and how they are related to education. The Indian Constitution has laid down certain egalitarian objectives for achieving social change in India. At the same time it has guaranteed rights to various social groups to pursue their own interests. The stronger social groups have taken undue advantage in exercising these rights. This has led to further tensions in the domain of education.

[47] Ibid., p. 14.
[48] Kempegowda Institute of Medical Sciences, Bangalore, *Prospectus 1985–86*, and Bangalore Institute of Technology, *Prospectus 1986–87*.
[49] Ibid.
[50] S.H. Rudolph and Lloyd I. Rudolph, *Education and Politics in India: Studies in Organization, Society and Polity*, Oxford University Press, Delhi, 1972, p. 20.

Although the Constitution has aimed at eliminating inequalities, it has been 'undetailed in its treatment of the institution of caste and existing group structure in society'.[51] It has emphasised protection of group identities, aimed at protecting the integrity of cultural, religious and linguistic groups,[52] permitted voluntary associations,[53] and conferred the widest freedom of association to individuals.[54] We will see how this freedom has been utilised for narrower aims, especially in the sphere of education, so much so that, over the years, the possibility of using education as an instrument of equality, justice and social change has become debatable.[55]

In modern Indian history, social mobilisation based on caste has been a major phenomenon. It has mostly been in the form of a defence of existing caste status or by creating new opportunities for emerging caste groups. The capitation fee phenomenon has much to do with this process. While the Constitution has proclaimed a commitment to build a society which would eliminate inequalities, the posture of the legal system has been different. 'The law', as Galanter has remarked, 'befriends castes by giving recognition and protection to the new social forms through which caste concerns can be expressed (caste associations, educational societies, political parties, religious sects).'[56] In the Indian political system, community and caste have been utilised as solid blocs of support by political contenders. Several studies have viewed the involvement of castes in politics as a process of mobilisation of different sections of society into organised politics.[57] Though the Indian state is based on universal adult franchise, it has been observed that franchise, in fact, has functioned as a channel for religious and caste groups to

[51] Marc Galanter, *Competing Equalities*, Oxford University Press, Delhi, 1984, p. 350.

[52] Articles 25–30, 347, 350A, 350B of the Constitution.

[53] Articles 19 (1) (C), 25, 26, 30 of the Constitution.

[54] Marc Galanter, op. cit.

[55] See A.H. Halsey, 'Can Education Contribute to Changing Society?' in *Education on the Move*, UNESCO, Paris, 1975, pp. 14–18; also Torsten Husen, 'Economic and Social Reforms Must Precede Pedagogical Changes' in *Education on the Move*, ibid., pp. 74–75. Both these sources have been cited in A.R. Kamat, 'Education and Social Change: A Conceptual Framework' in Amrik Singh and G.D. Sharma (Eds.), *Higher Education in India: The Social Context*, Konark Publishers, New Delhi, 1988, p. 31.

[56] Marc Galanter, op. cit., p. 559.

[57] See, for instance, Rajni Kothari (Ed.), *Caste in Indian Politics*, Orient Longman, New Delhi, 1970.

advance their aspirations in the struggle for political power. Hence caste structures have persisted and even expanded under the impact of political parties and adult franchise.[58] The capitation fee phenomenon, as we will see, has been a reflection of the aspirations of contending caste groups for greater political and economic power. Amongst the prosperous sections of these middle castes particularly, as has been observed earlier, this competition has been intense, and education has been a significant avenue used for upward mobility.

Thus the Indian state, operating within its Constitutional framework, has been faced with certain inherent contradictions in the sphere of education. This has been in consequence of the commitments enshrined in the Constitution to egalitarian objectives on the one hand, and the rights guaranteed to private interests on the other. It is not possible to understand education as a state function without recognising the conflicting demands placed upon it. In the sphere of education also, as in other sectors, the Indian state has permitted the growth of the private sector together with that of the state sector. Private initiative has been allowed in terms of freedom of choice, while state efforts have been directed to meet the constitutional demands for equality and justice. Here we will examine this dichotomy.

The Constitution has conferred wide personal freedom consistent with public good.[59] Through its several legislative measures and legal norms, it has assumed the 'right to income through ownership, viz. profits, rents and interests, as not merely proper and just, but as a guiding principle for inducing development'.[60] Economic individualism, accepted in India's liberal democratic set-up, has also encouraged, 'competition as a legitimate strategy for the betterment of one's fortunes'.[61] The norm of profit in business or trade has not been ruled out.[62] However, in the context of free competition, private ownership and profit motive, the definitions

[58] M.N. Srinivas, *Caste in Modern India and Other Essays*, Asia Publishing House, Bombay, 1962.

[59] See Parts III and IV of the Constitution.

[60] A.R. Deasi, *India's Path of Development*, Popular Prakashan, Bombay, 1984, p. 26.

[61] Krishna Kumar, 'Reproduction or Change? Education and Elites in India', *Economic and Political Weekly*, Vol. XX, No. 30, 27 July 1985, p. 1280.

[62] Article 19 (1) (g) of the Constitution.

of freedom and equality, according to Michael Apple, no longer remain 'democratic', but turn 'commercial'.[63]

The welfare state that was stipulated in this Constitution has reiterated its egalitarian values to gain legitimacy. The state, based as it is on a certain coalition of classes, has sought to legitimise its dominance while still retaining the rhetoric of equality and justice in order to counter the growing tensions of civil society. A concrete example is provided in the Constitution in the form of a clear distinction between Fundamental Rights and non-justiciable Directive Principles of State Policy. The advocates of private property, for instance, have been in a position to advance their claim for the expansion of their prerogatives in all political and social institutions including educational. The right to education is still not a fundamental right for all (though the Supreme Court in the recent 'capitation' case declared it to be so), and the Directive Principles' stipulation to provide universal education has not been implemented. It is this contradiction that we seek to explore. The need for professionals and the growth of private enterprise, including capitation fee colleges, will now be examined in the light of such contradictions.

Expanding Professional Education

The need for qualified and technically skilled manpower was recognised soon after the attainment of Independence. It was realised that the system of education in India had to be geared to meet the requirements of a developing economy. It was also felt that 'only an industrialised economy could provide sufficient resources for the balanced satisfaction of wants of all sections of society'.[64]

The Radhakrishnan Commission was appointed to look into the reconstruction of university education for meeting the scientific, technical and other manpower requirements for the socio-economic development of the country. The Commission noted that 'for a fuller realization of the democratic principles of justice and freedom

---

[63] Michael W. Apple, 'Critical Introduction' in Roger Dale, *The State and Education Policy*, Open University Press, Milton Keynes, 1989, p. 9.

[64] Partha Chatterjee, *Nationalist Thought and the Colonial World*, Zed Books, The U.N. University, Tokyo, 1986, p. 158.

for all, we need growth in science and technology'.[65] It was observed that in the 1940s the yearly output of engineers was extremely small—being one-fortieth of that of the United States and one-thirtieth of that of England. The Commission suggested that the number of engineering schools be increased and new engineering colleges be established in line with the types of engineering service needed in India.

The demand for medical education also increased considerably with an increase in the number of students entering the portals of universities. At the time of Independence there were 15 medical colleges in the country with an admission capacity of 1200.[66] The need for more doctors, health services and hospitals was also realised and numerous projects were initiated. However, the pace of development and the growth of professional cadres did not coincide.

The demand for medical and technical personnel was growing and so was the severity of competition for admission to degree courses in these two fields. The number of engineering and allopathic medical colleges increased rapidly till 1966–67. Subsequently, during the 12-year period 1967–79, the number of engineering colleges increased from 105 to 117 only, that is, one new college per year in the whole country. The number of medical colleges increased from 98 to 117 during the decade 1967–77, that is, two new colleges per year. The growth in numbers that came about after 1979 was largely due to the increase in the number of private unaided colleges in the fields.[67] During the period from 1951–52 to 1961–62, about 14 out of every 100 students in universities were enrolled in engineering and medical courses, but during the period from 1971–72 to 1981–82, only about eight out of every 100 were enrolled.[68] The chances of a student of given merit getting admitted to any of the two courses were just a little better than half of what they used to be two decades ago. Thus, there was a heavy rush for

[65] *Report of the University Education Commission 1948–49*, Vol. I, Publications Division, Government of India, New Delhi, 1951, pp. 46–47.

[66] J.P. Naik, *Equality, Quality and Quantity: The Elusive Triangle*, Allied Publishers, New Delhi, 1975, p. 84.

[67] See V.N. Kothari, 'Private Unaided Engineering and Medical Colleges: Consequences of Misguided Policies,' *Economic and Political Weekly*, Vol. XXI, No. 4, 5 April 1986, pp. 593–96.

[68] Ibid., p. 593.

engineering and medical courses; admissions to these were selective and through merit. In the 1980s India had 22 scientists and engineers and eight technicians per 1000, as against 311 and 456 in the U.S.S.R. and 100 and 50 in the West.[69] For a population of over 700 million, there were 2,68,712 doctors, which is about one doctor for every 2,600 people.[70] No wonder, then, that the demand for engineering and medical degrees has continued.

With the growth of industrialisation, and to meet the consequent increased needs of technical personnel and doctors, the government set up the Indian Institutes of Technology, regional engineering colleges and medical colleges. But these could not fully meet the demand for professional education.

Although the state was making an effort to expand facilities, education as a whole remained a low-priority area vis-à-vis budget allocations. The financial outlays on education were declining. From 7.6 per cent in the First Five-Year Plan, the outlay was reduced to 5 per cent in the Fourth Plan and was down to 2.6 per cent in the Sixth Plan.[71] India has been spending on an average not more than 3 per cent of its GNP on education, of which only 2.9 per cent has been used for technical education.[72] The allocation for education in the Central Budget for 1989–90 worked out to roughly 2.2 per cent. The outlay for professional education was even lower.

From time to time, the Central and State governments proclaimed their commitment to expand professional education. But partly owing to the paucity of funds and partly because of lack of political will, the initiative by the Indian state remained limited in this sphere. However, to meet the rising demand, private enterprise played an important role. In the Indian state's mixed economy

[69] J.D. Sethi, *The Crisis and Collapse of Higher Education in India*, Vikas Publishing House, New Delhi, 1983, pp. 208–209.

[70] Askari H. Zaidi, 'Doctors in Distress,' *The Times of India*, 22 August 1988.

[71] See Government of India, *Five-Year Plan Documents*, The Planning Commission, New Delhi.

[72] In developed Western countries like the U.S.A., Great Britain, France and Japan as also in the erstwhile U.S.S.R., the percentage has ranged from 6 to 8 per cent. In some Asian countries like Malaysia, Jordan and Saudi Arabia, it has been 5.8, 4.4 and 11.1 per cent respectively. See Government of India, *Trends of Expenditure on Education: 1968–69 to 1979*, Ministry of Education and Culture, New Delhi, 1980, p. 40.

structure there was legitimate room for the private sector to operate without disturbing the existing ownership pattern.[73]

Hence private enterprise in education was also no aberration and, as we have seen, it grew and flourished in the spaces available within the Constitution—a Constitution that in effect enshrined the right to property, proclaimed freedom for the pursuit of any trade or business, and also gave the right to minorities to run educational institutions of their choice. Today, it is not only religious and linguistic minorities but several registered community and caste societies and trusts that are running educational institutions in the private sector. In certain states, more predominantly in the South, private enterprise in education has acquired greater prominence. For instance in Karnataka, the landed castes like the Vokkaligas and Lingayats have set up colleges that are led and supported by prosperous sections amongst these groups. They have been utilising new opportunities in their competition with the Brahmins in the pursuit of power.

Private initiative in education was permitted within the Constitutional framework but the rationale behind it then was that it would supplement state effort. The Second Education Commission (1964–66) had maintained that the growing educational needs of a modernising society could only be met by the state and that private enterprise could only have a limited role in the national education system of the future.[74] Till about the mid-seventies the government was committed, rhetoricaly at least, to a policy of socialism by which was meant a large public sector. It 'tended to be critical of moves to expand opportunities for private investment'.[75]

In the 1980s and early 1990s, however, the government's commitment to economic liberalisation and policies to reduce controls, and the market-friendly approach of Narasimha Rao's government has made private enterprise the norm. What has emerged in India, as Desai has remarked, has been planned economic production 'under a system of indicative capitalistic planning' which was a

[73] Anupam Sen, *The State, Industrialisation and Class Formations in India*, Routledge and Kegan Paul, London, 1982, pp. 101–02.

[74] Government of India, *Report of the Education Commission: 1964–66*, Ministry of Education, 1966, pp. 464–87.

[75] Myron Weiner, *The Indian Paradox: Essays in Indian Politics*, Sage Publications, New Delhi, 1989, p. 284.

mixture of public and private enterprise, but which has essentially operated 'according to the postulates of capitalist market economy'.[76] Professional skills have been sought to be evolved to serve this specific development. The New Education Policy (1986) underlined the need for restructuring the education system to meet the challenges of emerging areas of science and technology and modernisation.[77]

It was also pointed out that universalisation and vocationalisation of education together with the expansion of technical and medical education necessitated raising of funds of sizeable proportions. This involved encouraging private entrepreneurs to contribute to educational development.[78] The National Policy on Education also stated that resources could be raised by mobilising donations and 'by raising fees at the higher levels of education'.[79] In 1991 the Human Resource Development Minister did not announce any radical departure from the National Education Policy of 1986 in this matter and admitted that the state alone could 'not take on the entire burden of education'.[80] Thus, a conscious role was assigned to privatisation in the educational sphere.

In the pre-Independence period, national initiatives moulded education to suit Indian needs. Even after Independence there have been some non-state and voluntary initiatives. Such efforts can be creative, purposive and consistent with the egalitarian objectives of the Constitution. However, such initiatives have been few and their influence has not permeated. What has become dominant has been the spread of commercial initiatives by interest groups, especially by middle caste elites and entrepreneurs reflecting the caste–class convergence in the domain of education. A large number of private professional colleges have sprung up in various states in India founded with community or caste support. As we will see in the case of Karnataka, the main objectives behind the setting up of these institutions were initially to promote

[76] A.R. Desai, *India's Path of Development*, Popular Prakashan, Bombay, 1984, p. 49.

[77] Subhash C. Kashyap (Ed.) *National Policy Studies*, Tata McGraw-Hill Pub. Co. Ltd., New Delhi, 1990.

[78] Government of India, *Challenge of Education: A Policy Perspective*, Ministry of Education, New Delhi, 1985, pp. 85–89.

[79] Government of India, *National Policy on Education*, Ministry of Human Resource Development, New Delhi, 1986, p. 28.

[80] *The Times of India*, New Delhi, July 7, 1991.

the interests of caste members, and enhance their political power and social position. However, over a period of time, these objectives have undergone a change in complexion, and have acquired an entrepreneurial character. Profit seems to have become a major motivator. As Tilak has observed, 'education, the "non-profit sector" has been turned into a high profit-making sector not only in terms of social and political power, but also in terms of financial returns.'[81]

The managements of these private colleges charge a sizeable amount of capitation fee for admission and now provide access to education primarily on the basis of the economic status of guardians. There has come into existence a class of well-to-do people consisting of small and big industrialists, business executives, bureaucrats, politicians, traders, businessmen, professionals, and of course, the rural gentry, who can afford and are prepared to pay large donations. It seems that the ruling elite has decided that the domain of higher education would continue to be an 'almost exclusive preserve of the upper and middle classes who would make use of it mainly to perpetuate and strengthen their privileges and status'.[82]

Thus, it has not just been paucity of government funding and Constitutional contradictions, but also pressure from the dominant groups, which has led the state to allow private interests to enter the field and shape professional education to fulfil their own needs and aims. It is in this context that we have observed the dynamics of caste, class and politics in the Indian educational setting. The State of Karnataka provides a good example of the interplay of these forces, and we will examine these in detail in the next few chapters.

---

[81] Jandhyala, B.G. Tilak, 'The Privatisation of Higher Education,' *Prospectus*, Vol. XXI, No. 2, 1991, p. 236.

[82] J.P. Naik, *The Education Commission and After*, Allied Publishers, New Delhi, 1982, p. 160.

2

SOCIETY, POLITY AND EDUCATION IN KARNATAKA

There has been a steady growth of private financing in professional education in post-Independence India. Karnataka has been foremost among the states where private enterprise in higher education has flourished. In this chapter we will draw a linkage between society, economy, politics and education in the State. We will also show how the two dominant social groups—the Lingayats and the Vokkaligas—and other social groups have extended their economic and political influence into the educational sphere.

It is not difficult to see why a community or group would want to exercise its influence in education. Control of education offers rich dividends in terms of caste support, political power and economic gains. 'Village level leaders cultivate Ministers for privileges and for a variety of favours, and the Ministers in turn need the help of village leaders during elections. Many if not most Ministers at the State level are also leaders of their castes, and thus, of their regions also.'[1] A village leader setting up an educational institution in the local area earns social prestige, caste support, and a vote bank.

[1] M.N. Srinivas, *Caste in Modern India and Other Essays*, Asia Publishing House, Bombay, 1962, p. 6.

In Karnataka, a large number of private professional institutions have been managed by various Lingayat and Vokkaliga organisations. Seeing the success of the dominant caste in this sphere, other communities in Karnataka have followed suit, although higher education has essentially catered to the needs of the dominant social groups. The manner in which private professional education has been in operation in Karnataka provides several interesting dimensions which will be discussed in subsequent chapters. Here we will focus on the State's society, economy and polity, without which it is not possible to understand the developments in the sphere of education.

The Social Situation

Before we begin our analysis, it is necessary to clarify and define the term 'dominant caste' to which we will be making frequent references. According to M.N. Srinivas, dominance is based on ownership of land, numerical strength, education and ritual status.[2] Amongst the Hindus, the two dominant majority castes in Karnataka have been the Vokkaligas and the Lingayats. Although the Vokkaligas were numerically stronger before the reorganisation of the States in 1956, it was the Lingayats, being ritually higher and better educated, who took the lead in State politics. However, now these groups have become 'locally numerically preponderant and own the bulk of the arable land'.[3] Their substantial landholdings, according to James Manor, gave them sufficient wealth to engage

[2] M.N. Srinivas, *India: Social Structure*, Hindustan Publishing House, Delhi, 1980. S.C. Dube in his study on the Shamirpet village in Andhra Pradesh has stated that the Reddi caste is the dominant section of the group of agricultural castes in the area. The Reddis are the largest landowners there. See S.C. Dube, *Indian Village*, Routledge and Kegan Paul, London, 1955. Beteille in another study has observed that amongst the Other Backward Classes, who occupy a low position in the *varna* hierarchy and have lacked traditions of literacy, there are castes who occupy a dominant position in the economy and political systems of the villages. Often they are 'small landowners; when they are also numerically preponderant, their control over a village, a group of villages or even a district may be decisive'. See Andre Beteille, *Castes: Old and New*, Asia Publishing House, New Delhi, 1969, p. 111.

[3] M.N. Srinivas, *India: Social Structure*, op. cit., p. 19.

in money-lending and in 'small-scale agricultural entrepreneur-ship'.[4] Thus, they acquired important positions in traditional village councils and held powerful hereditary village headships since the early years of the nineteenth century. When they wanted urban advancement in the early part of this century, they found that in urban centres it was the Brahmins who were dominant in every sphere. As we will see later, anti-Brahmin feelings grew particularly stronger in the urban areas of Mysore.

The term 'Vokkaliga' or 'Okkaliga' is derived from the Kannada word *Okku* which means 'to thresh'. In this sense, Vokkaliga means 'cultivator'. Most of the peasants found in the Mysore region are Kannada-speaking. Before 1900, the Vokkaligas consisted of a number of distinct castes of cultivators not structurally linked to one another. To begin with, this large category was without much social content, but according to Hettne, slowly and in response to the development of 'political arenas like the Representative Assembly and Legislative Council the Vokkaliga category became a handy base for mobilisation'.[5] Today, the Vokkaligas can be found engaged in other occupations besides agriculture. There are several Vokkaliga castes such as the Hallikars, Halus, Marasus and Gangadikaras, and normally each caste is endogamous. But, for political purposes, the term 'Vokkaliga' also includes the Kannada-speaking Kunchatigas, and the Telegu-speaking Bunts and Reddis. They constituted, in the 1980s, 10.81 per cent of the total population of Karnataka.[6] They have not been a homogenous group; some of them have been Shaivites, while others Vaishna-vites.[7] Brahmins have also been invited to officiate as priests by the Vokkaligas.[8] Vokkaliga headmen, elders and landowners have also received respect from poorer Brahmin neighbours in the villages. However, in terms of caste or ritual status, they have not made any claims to parity with Brahmins. The Vokkaligas also

    [4] James Manor, *Political Change in an Indian State: Mysore 1917–55*, Manohar Book Service, New Delhi, 1977, p. 30.

    [5] Bjorn Hettne, *The Political Economy of Indirect Rule: Mysore 1881–1947*, Ambika Publications, New Delhi, 1978, p. 143.

    [6] Government of Karnataka, *Report of the Karnataka Third Backward Classes Commission*, Vols. I and II, Bangalore, 1990, p. 45.

    [7] Shaivites are the followers of the god Shiva; Vaishnavites believe in the god Vishnu.

    [8] See Government of Karnataka, *Karnataka State Gazetteer, Part I*, 1982, pp. 482–83.

have had their *mutts* (monasteries) headed by *swamijis* (head priests).

The Lingayats have also been a land-based caste that developed as a religious sect from the Veer Shaivya cult of the twelfth century. As a protestant faith, being opposed to the ritualism of Vedic religion, it drew adherents from a number of castes.[9] Basava, the founder of Veer Shaivism, a Saiva Brahmin by birth, repudiated Brahminical rituals, and reinterpreted the hierarchical ordering of occupations into high and low status ones.[10] The Lingayats, or Veer Shaivyas as they are also referred to, adhere to vegetarianism and wear the *linga* which is symbolic of Shiva. They claim equality with Brahmins and have their own *gurus* or priests known as Jangamas. They were originally agriculturalists and later took up other occupations, including trade and commerce. Some of the main sections are the Jangamas, Banajigas (traditional traders), and Sadars (traditionally agriculturists).[11] There are also other sections of Lingayats engaged in different occupations. According to the *Report of the Third Backward Classes Commission (1990)*, they constitute 15.39 per cent of the total population of Karnataka, and predominate culturally, socially, economically and politically in the northern and western regions where Veer Shaivism was successful. The *mutts*, headed by members of the Jangama order, have been the principal local power centres in areas where the Lingayats have been dominant. The inner cohesion, more pronounced among the Lingayats than among the Vokkaligas, has been explained by Manor[12] as the influence of the powerful *mutts* and the high respect for the *guru* amongst the Lingayats, which has made the *swamijis* of the *mutts* very powerful.

In Karnataka, despite their numerical weakness, the Brahmins enjoyed an important position in education and State service. By the mid-nineteenth century, they had also begun to migrate from villages to towns and cities in their search for education and

[9] Ibid., p. 475.
[10] C. Parvathamma, 'Religion and Social Change: A Study of Tradition and Change in Virasaivism' in M.N. Srinivas et al. (Eds.), *Dimensions of Social Change in India*, Allied Publishers, 1977, pp. 243–52. For more on Virasaivism, also see C. Parvathamma, *Sociological Essays on Virasaivism*, Popular Prakashan, Bombay, 1972.
[11] *Karnataka State Gazetteer*, op. cit., pp. 475–76.
[12] See James Manor, *Political Change in an Indian State*, op. cit., p. 38.

employment.[13] While migrating, they sold their land and privileges to the Lingayats and Vokkaligas, and this in turn, led to a decline in their economic power in the rural areas. They constituted 3.46 per cent of the total population and were therefore not very important as political allies. Protective discrimination in Karnataka had also curtailed their opportunities to some extent.

The Kshatriya and Vaisya groups among the Hindus have had little numerical strength. The Kshatriyas constituted 0.40 per cent of the population and the Vaisyas 0.70 per cent. The Kshatriyas were the traditional warriors. The 1901 census included the Arasus, Rajputs, Coorgis, Kshatriyas and even the Sikh migrants from the North under the Kshatriya group. The Vaisyas were traditionally traders and are also called 'Komatis' or 'Komatigas'. Chetty or Chettiyar, the trading class of South India is a related group.[14] However, the scheduled castes comprising 16.72 per cent and the Muslims forming 11.67 per cent of the population have been the other important social groups.[15] Though the scheduled castes have been numerically significant because of their low ritual status and exploited economic position, they have required special support for representation in political administrative bodies. The Other Backward Classes (O.B.C.) category in Karnataka consists of the other remaining Hindu castes, communities and scheduled tribes—Kurubas, Bedas, Idigas, Kumbaras and Bestas like shepherds, toddy tappers, potters, carpenters, barbers and washermen. They have been weak socially and economically, and have not wielded any significant numerical strength to be able to exercise political power. Later, and more so since the early 1970s, this group of castes has been making efforts to fight the dominance of the upper castes.

The above profile, which has focused on different castes, groups and communities in Karnataka, is significant for our study. In the process of seeking economic opportunities and political gains, different social groups have asserted their caste, ethnic and other identities in addition to meeting their class objectives. Since education has led to such gains and has also helped them realise their

[13] See M.N. Srinivas, 'Sanskritisation and Westernisation' in *Caste in Modern India and Other Essays*, op. cit., p. 51.

[14] See Government of Karnataka, *Report of the Second Backward Classes Commission*, Bangalore, Vol. III, 1986, pp. 28–30.

[15] Population percentages from Government of Karnataka, *Report of the Karnataka Third Backward Classes Commission*, Vol. I, 1990.

respective interests, various castes, particularly the landed dominant castes, have sought to enhance their status through the means of education.

It is in this context that education can be seen to reflect the various socio-economic and political processes operating in the State. The following discussions on Karnataka's economy and polity will therefore be useful in examining the way private interests and pressure groups in Karnataka's society have been trying to advance their cause through the channel of private education.

Karnataka's Economy

Karnataka has essentially been an agricultural state, and nearly two-thirds of its population (4,40,88,597 estimated in 1990)[16] has depended on agriculture for its livelihood. Of the 10.18 million workers, 4.10 million have been cultivators and 2.70 million agricultural labourers constituting 67.7 per cent of the total workers.[17] In 1983–84, agriculture accounted for 3092.50 crore of the State's domestic product (68.4 per cent).[18]

The State's lack of adequate irrigation facilities has been a handicap for its agricultural production. In 1985–86, as per the *Annual Season and Crop Report*, only 16.47 per cent of the net area sown was under irrigation.[19] Hence although Karnataka has been predominantly an agricultural State, the area under irrigation has been low and much of the land dry. As much as 800,000 hectares of land of the total of 19,050,000 hectares of land in the region in 1988–89 were barren and uncultivable.[20] Thus, as in many other regions of India, we find disparity in the character of the agricultural economy in Karnataka.

However, considerable progress has been made in the agricultural

[16] Ibid., p. 48.
[17] K. Puttaswamaiah, *Economic Development of Karnataka: A Treatise in Continuity and Change*, Vol. I, Oxford and IBH Publishing Company, New Delhi, 1980, p. 107.
[18] Government of Karnataka, *Karnataka's Economy in Figures*, Directorate of Economics and Statistics, Bangalore, 1987, p. 10.
[19] Ibid., p. 24.
[20] Government of Karnataka, *Karnataka at a Glance 1989–90*, Directorate of Economics and Statistics, Bangalore, 1990, pp. 17–18.

sector through several measures, such as propagation of high-yielding varieties, increased input of fertilisers, and soil conservation. This has largely benefited the rich peasants of the middle castes who have taken advantage of the Green Revolution.

With land being the prime rural asset, inequality in distribution of land has also been of considerable significance, notwithstanding the implementation of the Land Reforms Programme. The number of marginal and small farmers and landless labourers has been high. Poor cultivators holding up to 4 hectares of land numbered 41,20,000 (84 per cent) covering 56,34,000 hectares of land, while those holding large landholdings (above 10 hectares) were only 153 in number (just a little over 3 per cent) covering a total area of 23,64,000 hectares (nearly 20 per cent of the total cultivable area) (see Table 2.1).

Table 2.1
Number of Agricultural Landholdings and Area, 1985–86

Type	Number ('000s)	Area ('000 ha)
Marginal (below 1 ha)	1792	866
Small (1–2 ha)	1293	1899
Semi-medium (2–4 ha)	1035	2879
Medium (4–10 ha)	646	3881
Large (more than 10 ha)	153	2364
TOTAL	4919	11,879

Source: Adapted from Government of Karnataka, *Karnataka at a Glance*, op. cit., pp. 22–24.

The number of marginal, small and semi-medium landholdings (4 hectares and below) rose from about 26,72,000 in 1976–77 and 31,23,000 in 1980–81[21] to 41,20,000 in 1985–86. Since the dominant landed castes were the Vokkaligas and the Lingayats, the bulk of the arable land was held by them. While some small and marginal farmers belonged to both these castes as well as other non-Brahmin backward castes like Kurubas, Nayakas, Yadavas and Bedars, agricultural labourers came mainly from either these backward castes or the scheduled castes.[22]

Venkataraman et al. in their study have observed that though

[21] Government of Karnataka, *Karnataka's Economy in Figures*, op. cit., p.15.
[22] See G. Thimmaiah and Abdul Aziz, *Political Economy of Land Reforms*, Ashish Publishing House, New Delhi, 1987, p. 16.

the development expenditure on agriculture, irrigation and power increased over time, the pace of rural development did not match the overall development efforts. 'A common aspect of asset distribution among rural households is its highly iniquitous and skewed distribution . . . .'[23] Among cultivators, as has been observed in the study, the top 39 per cent of the households owned 80 per cent of the assets in 1971–72. About 58 per cent of the rural population were below the poverty line in 1983, i.e. the rural poor had less than Rs. 130 per capita per month to spend. The proportion of labourers and farm workers who were below the poverty line was nearly 79 per cent. The poorest 30 per cent of the State's population shared less than 16 per cent of the aggregate consumption expenditure.[24]

The living standards of a large majority of people, the overall rate of growth of the State and the development of agro-based industries are all related to the performance of the agricultural sector and its increase in yield.

Land reforms introduced in Karnataka since Independence have not been able to change the power structure on land, and it has been the rich landed interests, mainly amongst the dominant landed castes, who have largely stood to gain from the policies of the State government.[25]

In princely Mysore, all the land legally belonged to the monarch, and private ownership of land was not a common feature of the Indian agrarian structure. However, much of the land was *Inam* land—these were lands granted by the government for the personal benefit of individuals or to religious or charitable institutions in recognition of services rendered to the ruler or the government or to the village community. *Inam* lands were held free of assessments in some cases, and in other cases, were subject to *jodi*, i.e., payment of a nominal rent. *Inam* lands were further subleased to cultivators either on payment of rent or on payment of a part of

[23] L.S. Venkataraman, M. Prahladachar and R.S. Deshpande, *Dynamics of Rural Transformation in Karnataka: 1956–76*, Institute for Social and Economic Change, Bangalore, 1985.

[24] Government of Karnataka, *Draft Seventh Five-Year Plan 1985–90*, Planning Department, Bangalore, Table 2.68, pp. 37, 5.

[25] See Narendra Pani, *Reforms to Pre-empt Change: Land Legislation in Karnataka*, Concept Publishing Company, New Delhi, 1983. Also see Atul Kohli, *The State and Poverty in India: The Politics of Reform*, Cambridge University Press, 1987.

the produce. Personal *inams* were more numerous, and these grants were made primarily to Brahmins for their livelihood. Even religious and charitable *inams* were vested with, or at least controlled by, the dominant minority Brahmin community.[26]

As was stated earlier, from the mid-nineteenth century onwards, the Brahmins began migrating from the villages to towns and cities for securing education and employment, and they sold their rural landholdings to finance their migrations. This naturally resulted in weakening their numerical strength and economic power between 1900 and 1935 in 'rural political arenas'.[27] Since lands belonging to Brahmins were largely sold to Lingayats and Vokkaligas, this further added to their power in rural areas. These two groups had been already engaged in agricultural entrepreneurship and money-lending.

When the Brahmins migrated to towns and cities they entrenched themselves in well-paid urban literate occupations including the administrative service. As Manor has pointed out, 'Lingayats, Vokkaligas and other rural non-Brahmins were much slower to leave the land to enter the race for urban advancement.'[28] When they began to move in small numbers to towns (in the first two decades of this century), they found Brahmin preponderance in urban areas exasperating. The anti-Brahmin sentiment gained momentum among the newly urbanised Vokkaligas and Lingayats and manifested itself in the form of a non-Brahmin movement, which we will discuss later in this chapter.

At the time of Independence, the State of Mysore inherited a bureaucracy that was controlled by the Brahmins. They were also, in many cases, the absentee-landlords holding land in villages. Their *inam* and non-*inam* lands were cultivated by tenants who belonged to the peasant castes, like the Vokkaligas and Lingayats, or the landless castes, such as the backward minority communities and Harijans. The tenants and the landless who were numerically large formed the vote banks for the Congress Party in power. This situation suited the non-Brahmin landed groups, the Lingayats and Vokkaligas, who exercised control over the State government. The *inamdars*, who were Brahmins, did not possess much numerical strength or political power. They were being opposed by the other

[26] See G. Thimmaiah and A. Aziz, op. cit., pp. 32–34.
[27] See James Manor, op. cit., pp. 28–34.
[28] Ibid., p. 32.

landowning communities. The State leadership, which hailed mainly from the non-Brahmin landed castes, undertook to abolish *inam* lands. The political leaders wished to help the tenants who belonged to their own communities, and as a consequence, gain votes for themselves and also reduce the economic power of the Brahmins. But the Brahmin *inamdars* who controlled the State bureaucracy resorted to delaying tactics to stall the process of *inam* abolition. These tactics were intended to gain time to enable the *inamdars* to sell the land to the highest bidders (to fetch a good price) instead of allowing the State government to acquire them at unattractive prices. The political leaders seemed disinterested in the methods of abolition, and as Thimmaiah and Aziz have stated, they were more interested in granting ownership rights on land to tenants who belonged largely to their own communities.[29] Thus, the competition of the aspirant groups with the entrenched upper caste group continued while the State leadership, keeping in mind its larger political gains vis-à-vis land reforms, acted accordingly.

Land reforms during 1956–71 also helped the landed interest groups. The Lingayats, who were spread out in different parts of the Deccan plateau, were included in the new Mysore area after the reorganisation of the State in 1956. This further strengthened the hold of the dominant castes on Karnataka's economy and polity. They owned the bulk of the land in Karnataka. Also, as has been indicated in several studies,[30] at different levels of decision making, like the legislature and the Parliament, the landed castes were able to make their representatives promote their interests (see Tables 2.2 and 2.3).

As we can see from Table 2.2, which shows the caste composition of the State Legislature from 1952 to 1972, the Lingayats and Vokkaligas, the traditional landowners in the State, held a majority in the legislature. Table 2.3 reveals that the dominant castes were amongst those households who owned larger landholdings (above 10 acres).

Through the provisions of the 1961 Act, which was put into

[29] G. Thimmaiah and A. Aziz, op. cit., p. 54.

[30] Ibid., Amal Ray and Jayalakshmi Kumpatla, 'Zilla Parishad Presidents in Karnataka: Their Social Background and Implications for Development,' *Economic and Political Weekly* Vol. XXII, Nos. 49 and 43, 7–24 October 1987, pp. 1825–30. See also Government of Karnataka, *Reports of the First, Second and Third Backward Classes Commissions,* Bangalore, 1975, 1986 and 1990.

Table 2.2

Composition of the Karnataka Legislative Assembly by Caste: 1952–72 Elections

Caste/community	1952		1957		1962		1967		1972	
	No.	Percentage	No.	Percentage	No.	Percentage	No.	Percentage	No.	Percentage
Brahmin	14	11.0	9	6.3	8	6.0	8	5.8	11	6.2
Lingayat	45	35.4	47	33.1	45	34.0	49	35.5	43	24.2
Vokkaliga	33	26.0	35	24.7	35	26.5	36	26.1	52	29.2
Other Hindus	12	9.5	22	15.5	20	15.2	17	12.3	37	20.8
Scheduled castes	20	15.7	22	15.5	21	15.9	24	17.4	23	12.9
Scheduled tribes	—	—	2	1.4	1	0.8	—	—	2	1.1
Christian	—	—	1	0.7	—	—	1	0.7	5	2.8
Jain	2	1.6	3	2.1	1	0.8	1	0.7	1	0.6
Muslim	1	0.8	1	0.7	1	0.8	2	1.5	4	2.2
TOTAL	127	100.0	142	100.0	132	100.0	138	100.0	178	100.0

Source: Government of Karnataka, *Karnataka Backward Classes Commission Report*, Vol. IV, Bangalore, 1975, pp. 822–23.

Table 2.3
Distribution of Households by Caste and Size of Operational Holdings: 1961

Caste/tribe/community	Size of holding (acres)					Total households	No. of households in each caste as percentage of total households
	Less than 1.00	1.00–2.50	2.50–5.00	5.00–10.00	10.00		
Vokkaliga	9 (1.18)	87 (11.43)	178 (23.39)	244 (32.06)	243 (31.93)	761 (100)	15.18
Lingayat	10 (0.79)	87 (6.89)	176 (13.94)	263 (20.82)	727 (57.56)	1,263 (100)	25.19
Kuruba	8 (1.49)	72 (13.43)	145 (27.05)	161 (30.04)	150 (27.99)	536 (100)	10.69
Scheduled castes	41 (7.26)	201 (35.64)	184 (32.64)	102 (13.08)	36 (6.38)	564 (100)	11.25
Scheduled tribes	—	1 (16.67)	4 (66.67)	—	1 (16.67)	6 (100)	0.12
Brahmin	19 (6.79)	25 (8.93)	40 (14.29)	63 (22.50)	133 (47.50)	280 (100)	5.59
Other Hindus	82 (8.20)	209 (20.90)	251 (25.10)	247 (24.70)	211 (21.10)	1,000 (100)	19.95
Muslim	50 (9.16)	105 (19.23)	121 (22.16)	119 (21.79)	151 (27.66)	546 (100)	10.89
Christian	4	7	8	9	2	30	0.60
Jain	—	4	3	10	10	27	0.54
TOTAL	223	798	1,110	1,218	1,664	5,013	100.00

Source: G. Thimmaiah and A. Aziz, op. cit., pp. 62–63.

effect only in 1965, the landed interests stood to gain—they were successful in procuring for themselves a liberal ceiling on landholdings. For coffee, tea, rubber, pepper and cardamom plantations, there was no ceiling. The State government did not seem interested in any stiff land-ceiling laws because it drew its strength and support from these cultivating landlord castes.

The events following 1971 brought into focus different interest groups in the political scenario. Devraj Urs' government, backed by the non-dominant backward communities which did not have extensive landed interests, came into power. The government now wished to serve the interests of other groups besides those of the Lingayats and Vokkaligas. In 1974, an amendment to the Land Reforms Act of 1961 was introduced. The Act lowered land ceilings to 10 standard acres, aimed at abolition of tenancy, and gave emphasis to the formation of land tribunals to decide on claims of tenants on the land they cultivated.[31] It was hoped that through the success of ceiling laws, some surplus land would be distributed amongst the landless labourers. However, there was only a negligible surplus available and so the problem of landlessness could not be effectively tackled. The rural base of the landowning communities did not change.[32] In his study, Narendra Pani has argued that in Karnataka the land reforms in the 1970s did not hurt the interests of the dominant classes—the reforms were from 'above' and so the control of the existing dominant class was further strengthened. He has observed that 'the same set of landlords who controlled a feudal system now controlled a more capitalist one.'[33]

Thus, despite land reforms in rural areas, the leading castes continued to dominate economically. Thimmaiah's study[34] has revealed that the annual per capita income of 41.74 per cent of the Vokkaligas and Lingayats was over Rs. 3,000 in 1974–75, while it was at this level for only 17 per cent of the other dominant Hindu castes, and 11.73 per cent of the scheduled castes and scheduled tribes.

Land reforms could not solve the problem of landlessness. Even

[31] For provisions and details of the 1974 Act, see M.A.S. Rajan, *The Land Reform Law in Karnataka*, Government of Karnataka, Bangalore, 1979.
[32] See Amal Ray and Jayalakshmi Kumpatla, op. cit.
[33] Narendra Pani, op. cit.
[34] See G. Thimmaiah and A. Aziz, op. cit., Table 3.7, p. 22. Also see, G. Thimmaiah and A. Aziz, 'The Political Economy of Land Reforms in Karnataka,' *Asian Survey*, Vol. XXIII, No. 7, July 1983, pp. 810–29.

after four years of these reforms less than 8 per cent of the legal surplus land (less than 45,000 acres) was redistributed.[35] This was the level of success achieved, although according to the government's own estimates, there should have been about half a million acres of surplus land in the State. As a result, the bulk of the rural poor continued to be landless labourers and marginal peasants.

Even though Karnataka has been primarily an agricultural State, the emergence of new social forces, growing urbanisation and industrial growth also had their impact on society in the form of greater demand for education. After Independence a number of industries were set up in the region. In fact, even prior to Independence, the stage had been set for this kind of development due to the policies pursued by the Dewans of the former Mysore State. Sir Visvesvaraya felt that besides education productive works and industries would be the main avenues for the progress of the country. The production of steel, cement, paper and chemicals reached its peak around 1940.[36] The expansion of industry during the Second World War and in the post-war period created an increasing demand for technicians of all grades, which was met by expanding the existing technical institutions and opening new occupational institutions. By 1955–56, the number of industrial and vocational schools had risen to 15.[37]

Karnataka has rich mineral resources like copper, manganese and iron ore. Forest products like sandalwood have been among its other natural resources. Central and State governments have set up industries, including the manufacture of machine tools, aircraft, telephones, watches, electronic and engineering goods as well as silk fabrics, sandalwood products, and iron and steel products. Since 1956, four important industrial projects have been located in Bangalore—Indian Telephone Industries, Hindustan Aeronautics, Hindustan Machine Tools and Bharat Electronics.

Between 1956–57 and 1974–75, the share of the industrial sector increased by 8 per cent.[38] The contribution of the industrial sector

[35] Figures have been taken from *Reforms Progress in the State up to the End of November 1980*, Revenue Department, Government of Karnataka, Bangalore, 1980.

[36] Bjorn Hettne, op. cit., pp. 266–315.

[37] Government of Karnataka, *Karnataka State Gazetteer*, op. cit., pp. 643–44.

[38] See K. Krishnamurthy and Paramjit Wahan, 'Industrial Development,' in V.K.R.V. Rao (Ed.), *Planning in Perspective: Policy Choices in Planning for Karnataka: 1973–74 to 1988–89*, Allied Publishers, New Delhi, 1978, pp. 95–113.

to the State income was about 21 per cent in 1974–75 at 1956–57 prices. The rate of increased industrial output in Karnataka between 1960 and 1974 was almost one-and-a-half times that of the industrial output of the country. The Commerce Research Bureau, on the basis of the data from the Annual Survey of Industries for 1960 and 1970, pointed out that while the per capita income generated in large-scale manufacturing in the country was Rs. 20 and Rs. 53 respectively for 1960 and 1970, the corresponding figures for Karnataka were Rs. 11 and Rs. 58. Starting from a much lower base, Karnataka was able to get ahead of the country within 10 years,[39] although it still remained behind in terms of its share of finished goods turned out by large industries. Industrial establishments in Karnataka expanded between 1979 and 1984 as Table 2.4 indicates. (See Table 2.5 for selected economic indicators.)

Table 2.4
Industrial Establishments, 1979–84

Year	Registered under Factories Act, 2m (i), 2m (ii) & Section 85	Small-scale units
1979–80	9,942	24,893
1980–81	11,175	27,669
1981–82	10,379	31,065
1982–83	10,710	37,161
1983–84	11,073	44,739

Source: 1. Office of the Chief Inspector of Factories & Boilers, Government of Karnataka, Bangalore.
2. Department of Industries & Commerce, Government of Karnataka, Bangalore. Cited in Government of Karnataka, *Statistical Abstract 1983–84*, p. 200.

The industrial sector showed a respectable growth and industrial incomes increased by an average of 6.0 per cent during the five years ending 1982–83 compared to an annual average of just 3.3 per cent during the previous five year period.[40] In the Seventh Plan

[39] See V.K.R.V. Rao, N.A. Sharma and K. Krishnamurthy, 'Macro Perspective,' in V.K.R.V. Rao (Ed.), op. cit., pp. 1–14.
[40] Government of Karnataka, *Draft Seventh Five-Year Plan 1985–90*, op. cit., p. 18.

period the annual average growth rate was 6.6 per cent compared to 3.6 per cent of the Sixth Plan period.[41]

Meanwhile industrialisation in agriculture started in the 1930s. One example of the agriculture–industry link was the sugar complex in Mandya. To bear the cost of construction and maintenance of a dam across the Cauvery river, it became necessary to introduce the cultivation of sugarcane. Besides the irrigated land which was provided by the government, a factory for the manufacture of chemical manures was started. Hettne has stated that 'the new crop was the raw material for the sugar factory established with state-aid. From the by-product (molasses) alcohol was produced in a distillery unit in Mandya,' and later the company started making confectionery of various kinds.[42]

After Independence, with land reforms and the Green Revolution, industrialisation in agriculture in the 1960s gained further impetus. Subsidised modern inputs of improved high-yielding seeds, fertilisers, pesticides, improved irrigation facilities like mechanised pumps, installation of tube-wells and the use of farm machinery to enhance farm efficiency—all gave a boost to industrialisation in agriculture. However, it was the bigger landlords who benefited from all these innovations. Modern techniques involved investment and small farmers could afford only old techniques. In Raichur, for instance, as Nair[43] has pointed out, small farmers were used to growing their crops with only rain water which was free, while they had to pay for the canal water once they agreed to take it, irrespective of whether they used it or not. Frankel's study has also recognised that 'a capital intensive agricultural strategy' tended to 'increase disparities with tenants and small farmers sharing less than larger farmers in the gains from the application of the new technology.'[44] In studies conducted by Epstein to assess the impact of irrigation in two villages in Mandya district, it has been observed that the wealthy farmers became richer and their savings were invested in profitable ventures to enhance their wealth, while the middle and

---

[41] See Government of Karnataka, *Economic Survey 1990–91*, Planning Department, Bangalore, p. 3.

[42] Bjorn Hettne, op. cit., pp. 299–300.

[43] See Kusum Nair, *Blossoms in the Dust*, Gerald Duckworth and Company Limited, London, 1961, pp. 46–51.

[44] Francine R. Frankel, *India's Green Revolution: Economic Gains and Political Costs*, Princeton University Press, New Jersey, 1971, pp. 3–11.

Table 2.5

Selected Economic Indicators, Karnataka, 1980–81 and 1985–86 to 1990–91

Indicators	Units	1980–81	1985–86	1986–87	1987–88	1988–89	1989–90	1990–91
1. Net state domestic product								
(a) At current prices	Rs. crore	5,866	10,510	12,124	13,870	16,447(PR)	18,012(Q)	19,614@
(b) At (1980–81) constant prices	Rs. crore	5,866	7,076	7,741	8,139	9,000(PR)	9,323(Q)	9,479@
2. Per capita state income								
(a) At current prices	Rupees	1,596	2,564	2,900	3,254	3,787(PR)	4,075(Q)	4,368@
(b) At (1980–81) constant prices	Rupees	1,596	1,727	1,852	1,909	2,072(PR)	2,109(Q)	2,111@
3. Foodgrains production	Lakh tonnes	62.02	57.89	73.38	62.80	67.32	71.23(P)	63.67@
4. Production of cotton	Lakh bales of 170 kgs each.	5.97	5.08	4.50	5.54	9.19	9.21(P)	6.68@
5. Sugarcane production	Lakh tonnes	121.27	141.11	143.73	178.75	186.82	211.58(P)	171.57@
6. Oilseeds production	Lakh tonnes	6.50	9.81	12.54	14.94	13.70	13.89(P)	14.09@
7. Irrigation potential created (Cum)	Lakh hectares	22.36	26.96	28.00	28.66	29.66	29.78(P)	30.55@
8. Installed capacity of power generation	M.W.	1,470	2,530	2,530	2,530	2,530	2,645	2,972@
9. Price indices*								
(a) Wholesale price index of agricultural commodities in Karnataka	Number (1952–53 = 100)	545	821	813	958	1,065	1,110	1,228**

(b) Consumer price index for working class in Karnataka (average of 10 centres)	(1960=100)	433	674	721	786	883	934	990**
(c) Consumer index for agricultural labourers in Karnataka	(1960–61=100)	374	550	551	596	714	757	787**

Source: Government of Karnataka, *Economic Survey 1990–91*, Planning Department, Bangalore, p. 12.

@—Anticipated; *—Annual Average; **—Up to December 1989; PR—Partially Revised Estimates; P—Provisional; Q—Quick Estimates.

poor farmers found things more difficult.[45] The rich landowners, the majority of whom came from the dominant castes, were able to wield not only economic power and political control, but also tried to gain a foothold in all important spheres. The landowners, whose incomes continued to rise following the effects of the Green Revolution, started investing their savings in urban real estate— cinema theatres, urban buildings, shopping complexes—and industry. Some significant studies have shown that there was a drain of surplus from agriculture in Karnataka and the landlords were turning entrepreneurial by investing the surplus outside agriculture.[46] For instance, the number of Lingayats and Vokkaligas controlling cooperative sugar factories and textile and spinning mills in Karnataka during 1984–85 was 39.82 per cent and 19.25 per cent respectively.[47]

This industrial development led to an increased need for technical manpower and gave a fillip to institutions imparting professional and technical training. From then on the tempo of growth was maintained. The landowners were quick to avail of the opportunity, and invested some of their agricultural surplus into professional education, borne out by the number of engineering and medical colleges that were floated in the State by the Lingayat and Vokkaliga educational societies.

Not much official data has been available regarding the social composition of the industrial working class in Karnataka. However, Holmstrom's study on factory workers in Bangalore[48] has indicated that the Brahmins were strongly represented in managerial and skilled jobs. Of 104 respondents, 16 were Brahmins. The

[45] T.S. Epstein, *Economic Development and Social Change in South India*, Manchester University Press, Manchester, 1962 and *South India: Yesterday, Today and Tomorrow*, Macmillan, London, 1973.

[46] For Karnataka, see Narendra Pani, op. cit., and G. Thimmaiah and A. Aziz, op. cit. For a macro-level comment on the situation, see Pranab Bardhan, *The Political Economy of Development in India*, Oxford University Press, New Delhi, 1984 and G. Haragopal, 'Dimensions of State Politics: A Political Economy Perspective,' paper presented at the I.C.S.S.R. Seminar on '*India Since Independence*,' New Delhi, 26–30 December 1988.

[47] Government of Karnataka, *Report of the Second Backward Classes Commission*, Bangalore, 1986, op. cit., Vol. III, Annexure 8–13, p. 82.

[48] See Mark Holmstrom, *South Indian Factory Workers: Their Life and Their World*, Cambridge University Press, London, 1976, pp. 30–34.

study has also indicated that the Lingayats and Vokkaligas did not form a very large percentage of the workforce in factories. Of the total of 104 workers in his study, only five were Lingayats. They were 'sons of owner or tenant farmers, craftsmen, shopkeepers, petty officials or owners of small business.'[49] Hence, they were not really suffering from poverty or unemployment and, except in menial jobs, were found in most jobs in factories. The 'menial and unskilled workers', especially cleaners and watchmen, were Harijans. The Vokkaligas and the Lingayats, as it appears, were shaping themselves after the Brahmins and had a similar attitude towards menial jobs. And as Srinivas has pointed out, 'as a caste rises in hierarchy, its ways become more Sanskritized.'[50] The non-Brahminical castes adopt not only Brahminical rituals but also Brahminical institutions and values.

Urbanisation has led to the migration of the upper and middle castes to cities and towns. As we have seen, the Brahmins were the early migrants who acquired professional jobs because of their education. In 1918, of the total number of 370 gazetted posts, the Brahmins held 64.86 per cent of the posts as well as 69.64 per cent of the non-gazetted posts.[51]

The situation changed gradually and their dominance was reduced to nearly half by 1947. The Vokkaligas and Lingayats, who were emerging as beneficiaries of agricultural development, then began migrating to the urban areas, competing for jobs with the Brahmins and aspiring for an elite status. In 1957, the Brahmins were still able to retain 35.72 per cent of the gazetted and 27.65 per cent of the non-gazetted jobs.[52] Hence, a triangular competition ensued. For the middle castes, one way to acquire avenues for employment was through education. Other social groups responded to the process and began asserting their claims for opportunities in education and employment as well. Thus, it was this competitive situation which gave rise to entrepreneurship in education in Karnataka.

[49] Ibid.
[50] M.N. Srinivas, *Caste in Modern India*, op. cit., p. 46.
[51] Government of Karnataka, *Report of the Second Backward Classes Commission*, Vol. I, Bangalore, 1986, p. 18.
[52] Ibid.

Polity and Education in Karnataka

Pre-Independence Developments

In the earlier sections we have seen how the dominant landed castes were exerting their influence in the State. Here, we will examine how education has been used as a channel of social mobility through which social, political and economic dominance has been sought to be maintained. We will do this by first examining the development of education in Old Mysore[53] in the context of the non-Brahmin movement to bring into focus the rise of the Lingayats and the Vokkaligas in the educational sphere.

The traditional dominant groups like the Brahmins were quick to avail of the new educational opportunities provided by the princely administration. Realising that the fruits of education were being reaped by Brahmins, the emerging social forces also set up autonomous associations leading to a major social movement in Mysore, the non-Brahmin movement, which gathered momentum gradually. The British responded by offering a larger share of jobs and educational opportunities to social groups other than the Brahmins who faced stiff competition from the Lingayats and Vokkaligas. These two groups doubled their strength in employment and in the Legislative Assembly within 20 years. Thus, the policy of the Mysore State in introducing a British type of education—the autonomous caste associations of the Lingayats and Vokkaligas, the non-Brahmin movement, and the British response to it—all reinforced one another in bringing about substantial gains for the emerging social groups.

It was towards the end of the eighteenth century when Old Mysore came under the suzerainty of the British. The State had been annexed by the British who, instead of bringing it under their direct rule, installed the descendants of the Old Mysore royal family—the Wadiyars—on the throne. The British Resident kept a sharp vigil on the happenings in the State, while the Rajas exercised a certain amount of power under the supervision of the British.

[53] Old Mysore refers to the bulk of the present Karnataka State as it existed prior to the reorganisation of the Indian States in 1956. It was called Mysore till 1972 and was named Karnataka in that year.

While disclaiming any desire to interfere with the freedom of the Maharaja of Mysore in the internal administration of his State, the Governor General-in-Council retained the power of exercising intervention 'by virtue of the general supremacy and paramount authority vested in him'.[54]

The colonial system of education was introduced in Mysore in 1833 when the then ruler of Mysore established a free English school in Mysore city under the advice of the British Resident, Major General Frazer.[55] The immediate aim of the educational policy of the British was similar to their objectives elsewhere in India—to obtain loyal and economical functionaries for the middle and lower echelons of administration and to impart Western education to the natives to win them over as their friends and well-wishers.[56]

Systematic activity in the field of education began in Mysore with Wood's despatch of 1854. Devereux, the Judicial Commissioner of Mysore, drew up a scheme of education for Mysore. There was to be a department of education under the direct control of the Commissioner and there was to be a Director of Public Instruction with a supporting staff.[57]

In Mysore, among the Hindus, Western education became first accessible to persons from the upper *varnas* like the Brahmins, Kshatriyas and Vaisyas. They all hailed from an urban background and had a tradition of literacy and education, and therefore, were quick to exploit the opportunities for employment and upward mobility offered by the new system of education. The Brahmins took over the white-collared jobs in the bureaucracy, which were vested with authority and power. They were to constitute the core of the 'modern elite' that took charge of the administrative system which the British developed during the late nineteenth century.[58] The new system of education and the opportunities it offered thus strengthened and reinforced the superior position of the Brahmins. Their dominance in education continued unchallenged till about the 1920s.

[54] Treaty of Mysore, 1913, *Mysore State Papers*, Vol. I, p. 55.

[55] Government of Karnataka, *Karnataka State Gazetteer*, op. cit., p. 529.

[56] S.C. Shukla, 'Educational Development in British India: 1854-1904,' Ph.D. Thesis, Faculty of Education, University of Delhi, 1959.

[57] Government of Karnataka, *Karnataka State Gazetteer*, op. cit., p. 529.

[58] M.N. Srinivas, *Caste in Modern India and Other Essays*, op. cit., p. 68.

As stated in Table 2.6, 78.87 per cent of those receiving education in 1916 were Brahmins, while only 4.01 per cent of the Lingayats and another 4.56 per cent of other high caste Hindus had this opportunity. In the early years of this century, the non-Brahmin castes, particularly the dominant peasant castes of the Lingayats and Vokkaligas, began to realise the importance of the opportunities offered by Western education of which the Brahmins took full advantage. Till then, their progress in Western education was slow mainly due to their rural background where facilities for it were negligible. The lack of a tradition of education and literacy among the Vokkaligas and Lingayats might also have been a source of a certain indifference evinced by them to formal learning.

Table 2.6
Social Composition of Students Receiving College Education in 1916

Caste and other categories	Students	
	Number	Per cent
Europeans and Eurasians	10	1.38
Indian Christians	20	2.76
Mohammedans	21	2.90
Brahmins	571	78.87
Kshatriyas	25	3.45
Vaishyas	10	1.38
Lingayats	29	4.01
Other high caste Hindus (including Vokkaligas)	33	4.56
Jains	3	0.41
Parsis	1	0.14
Others	1	0.14
TOTAL	724	100.00

Source: *Review of the Progress of Education in Mysore State: 1911–16*, Bangalore, 1918, p. 27. Cited in Chitra Sivàkumar, op. cit., p. 15.

In the post-1915 period, there was a significant rise in the educational aspirations of the Lingayats and Vokkaligas and also to a certain degree of the lower non-Brahmin and untouchable castes. The non-Brahmin movement played a crucial role here.

Efforts of Lingayats and Vokkaligas Towards Their Advancement

In the early years of this century, even before the non-Brahmin movement, some Lingayats and Vokkaligas, who had been able to secure jobs in the civil service, joined a few landlords to form associations.[59] Autonomous organisations arose in the form of two associations, the Mysore Lingayat Education Fund Association (M.L.E.F.A.) and the Okkaligara Sangha, founded in Bangalore in 1905 and 1906 respectively. Both these associations pledged to work for the educational advancement and general betterment of the two communities all over the State. They desired to achieve this by raising funds for scholarships and student hostels and by asking the government for concessions in the form of scholarships and appointments to the civil service.

Initially, both the Association and the Sangha had difficulty in raising funds. The foundation stone of the Okkaligara hostel was laid in 1909, but due to insufficient funds, the building could not be completed till 1923 when an appeal for government funds was made.[60] The M.L.E.F.A. leaders could not operate on a large scale due to inadequate support from wealthy Lingayats until 1919 when a large Lingayat hostel was set up in Bangalore. Later, funds came from merchants, a *swamiji*, and in the form of a grant from the government. However, the non-Brahmin movement in the 1920s provided a cause and gave strength of these associations to hold together.

From the 1920s onwards, these associations did a great deal to create an educated elite bearing strong identification with their respective communities. Both the Sangha and the M.L.E.F.A. were engaged in petitioning the authorities for better opportunities for the youth. All their efforts were a manifestation of the growing consciousness of each category as a distinct group, each seeking its own identity.

[59] See James Manor, 'The Evolution of Political Arenas and Units of Social Organizations: The Lingayats and Vokkaligas of Princely Mysore,' in M.N. Srinivas et al. (Eds.), *Dimensions of Social Change in India*, Allied Publishers, New Delhi, 1977, pp. 170–87.

[60] *Proceedings of the Mysore Representative Assembly* (hereafter P.M.R.A.), Oct. 1923, p. 96.

The Lingayats and Vokkaligas also contested elections to the Assembly. In 1920, 10 Vokkaligas, and in 1921, 25 were sent from general constituencies to the Mysore State Assembly.[61] They gradually secured a majority while the Brahmins lost their earlier predominance. Between 1926 and 1930, all district boards were permitted to elect presidents, and by 1930, seven of the eight boards had non-Brahmin presidents. Of these three were Vokkaligas and four Lingayats.[62]

The Non-Brahmin Movement

In 1917, a small circle of Lingayat and Vokkaliga leaders joined together with a few members of other communities to form an 'all non-Brahmin' group. C.R. Reddy, an educationist, initiated the non-Brahmin movement in Mysore. The Praja Mithra Mandali, the first non-Brahmin movement in Mysore, was founded at the same time as the Justice Party in Madras—in the first decade of the century.[63] The non-Brahmins petitioned the government for an end to the Brahmin domination of the civil services, and prepared a list of demands: special privileges in the fields of education; administration and politics; special privileges in the form of reservation of seats and jobs in educational institutions; special scholarships and free studentships; reservation of seats in the Representative Assembly and in other political bodies; and reservation of jobs in the administration. The movement claimed to represent the interests of the powerful dominant peasant castes as well as those of the untouchables.

The Brahmins who comprised just 3.9 per cent of the population[64] occupied 54.23 per cent of the government jobs. The Lingayats who formed 13.3 per cent of the population secured only 5.99 per cent of the posts while the Vokkaligas who comprised 23.6 per cent of the population held 4 per cent of the jobs (Table 2.7).

[61] Official papers connected with the Constitutional Development in Mysore (1929), Bangalore, pp. 85–86.
[62] See Lelah Dushkin, 'The Non-Brahmin Movement in Princely Mysore,' Unpublished Ph.D. dissertation, University of Pennsylvania, 1974, pp. 85-86.
[63] See Bjorn Hettne, op. cit., p. 144.
[64] Population figures have been taken from Census of India, 1911, Vol. XXIII, Mysore, Part II tables, Bangalore, 1922, pp. 106, 115–16.

Table 2.7
Numerical Strength of Members of Various Castes and Other Groups Appointed to Various Government Posts in Mysore State during 1921–24

Caste or other group	Appointees	
	Number	Per cent
Brahmins	570	54.23
Kshatriyas	13	1.24
Vokkaligas	42	4.00
Lingayats	63	5.99
Mudaliars	18	1.71
Other caste Hindus	197	18.74
Depressed classes	13	1.24
Muslims	89	8.47
Indian Christians	46	4.38
TOTAL	1,051	100.00

Source: *Report of P.M.R.A.*, Dasara Session, October 1924, Bangalore, 1925, p. 337, cited in Chitra Sivakumar, op. cit., p. 18.

Thus, obviously, there was a lurking fear among the dominant peasant castes that the Brahmins with their strength in education and bureaucracy could wield power even after Independence. The movement offered to them an opportunity to deal a severe blow to the so far unchallenged supremacy of the Brahmins and to assure for their future a firm political base.

These new political developments seem to have been responsible for the changes in the educational policy of the government. It is in this context that Bjorn Hettne has commented that the non-Brahmin movement was encouraged by the British as a part of the 'divide and rule' strategy. The Brahmins had reaped the fruits of Western education and occupied an elite status in the administrative system developed by the British. But the danger of being too dependent upon the Brahmins was realised by the colonial power by the late nineteenth century. The risk was all the more because the Brahmins also provided leaders for the Congress movement which challenged the colonial regime. 'The obvious solution was the spread of government patronage to other social groups, some of which did not hesitate to take advantage of the new opportunity.'[65] Hence, while the British were trying to find alternative social

[65] Bjorn Hettne, op. cit., p. 142.

groups for patronage, the Lingayats and Vokkaligas were trying to find new opportunities to strengthen their socio-economic position.

The government appointed a committee in August 1918 to suggest measures for improving the representation of backward communities in government service. This was the Miller Committee. Among the specific issues that the Committee was asked to address were provision of special facilities to encourage the backward communities to take to higher and professional education and special measures to increase the representation of the backward communities in public service. The government order stated that there was a 'large preponderance of the Brahmin community in the public service' and other communities should also be 'adequately represented therein'.[66]

Knowledge of English was the only criterion by which 'forward' castes were distinguished from 'backward' castes by the committee. It defined as 'backward' all those communities which had less than 5 per cent of literates in English. This left only the Brahmins, Anglo-Indians and Europeans in the 'forward' category. The Miller Committee recommended that within seven years the non-Brahmin strength in the higher services must be raised to half and in the lower services to two-thirds; the setting up of more educational institutions and special schools; and an increase in the number of scholarships and hostels for them. The committee also suggested exemption from competitive examinations for backward class candidates, their induction into any service by nomination and an increase in their age limit for jobs from 25 to 28 years. The government accepted the Miller Report. In May 1921, it constituted the Central Recruitment Board and reserved 75 per cent of the vacancies for the backward classes.[67] As a result of this, the position in the recruitment changed a little for the better as Table 2.8 reveals.

The government's acceptance of almost all the suggestions of the Miller Committee provided proof of the influence the dominant peasant caste leaders exercised over the government. The government, on its part, was looking for powerful allies for support during the turbulence of the movement for Independence. In

---

[66] *Report of the Miller Committee*, quoted in Government of Karnataka, *Report of the Second Backward Classes Commission*, Vol. I, op. cit., p. 15.

[67] Government of Karnataka, *Report of the Second Backward Classes Commission*, Vol. I, op. cit., p. 17.

Table 2.8
Pattern of Recruitment of Brahmins/Non-Brahmins in Public Services, 1918–27

Service or Department	Year	Brahmins	Non-Brahmins
Amildars*	1918	56	22
Amildars	1927	59	17
Deputy Commissioners	1927	8	—
Public Works Department	1924	62	3
Education Department	1926	81	14
Judicial Department	1927	45	13

Source: Government of Karnataka, *Report of the Second Backward Classes Commission*, Vol. I, op. cit., p. 17.

* Amildars were revenue collectors at the taluk level. See James Manor, *Political Change in an Indian State*, op. cit.

Mysore, during this period, the freedom struggle was led by the Western-educated Brahmins who were also powerful within the Congress. But after the success of the non-Brahmin movement and after securing power for themselves, the Lingayat and Vokkaliga leaders aligned themselves with the Congress and joined the freedom struggle. Among the important Congress leaders were C.R. Reddy, K.C. Reddy and Veeranna Gowda (Vokkaligas), and T. Siddalingaya and Manjappa (Lingayats).[68]

An awareness of the crucial significance of Western education for social mobility had been created among the non-Brahmin castes, especially the Lingayats and Vokkaligas, by the non-Brahmin movement. This movement and the incentives given by the government paved the way for progress in education amongst the dominant peasant castes and other non-Brahmin castes, although the Brahmins still continued to hold sway in higher education. While the Lingayats formed only 4 per cent of the total strength of students in colleges in 1916, by 1924–25, they constituted 6.8 per cent of those who appeared for different university examinations, and by the 1940s their representation in higher education increased to 8.1 per cent.[69] The Vokkaligas had almost negligible representation in 1916; in 1924–25, they constituted 3.6 per cent of those

[68] See Hettne, op. cit., pp. 179–206.
[69] *Annual Report of the University of Mysore (1924–25)*, Mysore, 1925, Appendix C (ix), pp. 50–53; and *Annual Report of the University of Mysore (1943–44)*, Mysore, 1944, Appendix I, pp. 25–27. The table for 1916 has been cited earlier.

appearing for various university examinations and their representation in higher education rose to 5.8 per cent in the 1940s.[70]

This rate of educational progress amongst the Lingayats and
Vokkaligas can perhaps be understood in terms of their economic
and political power at the State level. Besides, prosperous landowning members from these castes had started funding hostels and
scholarships from their personal earnings to promote education
among members of their respective castes.

The lower non-Brahmin castes and the scheduled castes did not
gain much in terms of educational advancement. While the stigma
of untouchability hindered the progress of the scheduled castes,
the lower non-Brahmin castes lacked economic and political resources and strength to make much headway. The government, on
its part, was following a pragmatic policy, keeping in tune with the
newly emergent political forces and interest groups, and appeasing
these sections.

We have seen above how the post-1915 period witnessed a
growth in the educational aspirations of the Lingayats and Vokkaligas. We have also seen how the colonial power adopted the
strategy of balancing sectional interests. The way to benefit from
the flow of education and jobs being provided by the government
was to organise an association and make petitions. The Lingayats
and Vokkaligas did this much to their advantage. The government
responded, keeping in mind its tactical gains. Education and job
concessions extended to the dominant castes as a result of the non-
Brahmin movement naturally whetted their aspirations. To what
extent they were successful in this direction has to be seen in the
context of the post-Independence developments in Karnataka.

Post-Independence Developments

Universal adult franchise was introduced in India after Independence. The new government was now dependent on the electorate
to remain in power. The dominant peasant castes in Karnataka
used their numerical strength and the power they had acquired to
further strengthen their position and extend their influence.

[70] See Chitra Sivakumar, op. cit., p. 36.

The State's political history can be divided into two distinct phases: before and after the State's reorganisation in 1956. In the pre-1956 phase, the State consisted only of Old Mysore, roughly the southern half of the present-day State (see frontispiece). The Chief Ministers between 1947 to 1956 were all Vokkaligas. The first Chief Minister was K.C. Reddy (1947–1952) followed by K. Hanumanthaiah and then Kadidal Manjappa. The Lingayats took over after 1956. Between 1956 and 1972, when the State boundaries were redrawn and the Lingayats outnumbered the Vokkaligas, every Chief Minister was a Lingayat. S. Nijalingappa was followed by B.D. Jatti and then Veerendra Patil. Hence between 1947 and 1972, the spoils which became available to those in control of State power largely went to the Lingayats and Vokkaligas, thus strengthening their dominant position at the local level.

During the period 1947–72, these two landed groups dominated the Congress Party. Since the Congress was the ruling party in Karnataka, the Vokkaligas and Lingayats controlled the State-level politics as well. They used their influence at the village level to ensure victory for the Congress Party in elections. The members of these two groups later took control of the State Legislature and important ministries.

We can see from Table 2.9 that the Lingayats and Vokkaligas dominated the Assembly between 1952 and 1967. Scholarships in colleges and jobs in public service tended to go to members of these two groups. In order to build and sustain a broad support for themselves, the then Chief Ministers, S. Nijalingappa, B.D. Jatti and Veerendra Patil, followed a policy of placating the dominant landed castes. Substantial government aid was granted to both the Lingayats and Vokkaligas in the form of subsidies on agricultural inputs and condoning of government loans which were not repaid.[71]

The Vokkaligas and Lingayats also benefited from the constitutional provisions for privileges for backward communities. The Government of India appointed the First Backward Classes

[71] James Manor, 'Caste, Class, Dominance and Politics in a Cohesive Society,' in Francine R. Frankel and M.S.A. Rao (Eds.), *Dominance and State Power in Modern India: Decline of a Social Order*, Vol. I, Oxford University Press, New Delhi, 1989, pp. 322–61. Also see James Manor, 'Structural Changes in Karnataka Politics,' *Economic and Political Weekly*, Vol. XII, No. 44, 29 October 1977, pp. 1865–69; and James Manor, *Political Change in an Indian State: Mysore 1917–55*, op. cit.

Table 2.9

Representation of Selected Castes and Groups of Castes in Karnataka Legislative Assembly between 1952 and 1967

	1952	1957	1962	1967
Lingayats	18	73	69	70
Vokkaligas	42	46	57	47
Brahmins	6	18	12	18
Marathas	—	9	8	9
Scheduled castes and scheduled tribes	19	29	29	29
Muslims	—	9	7	8
Christians	—	2	1	3
Other backward classes	12	16	17	18
TOTAL	97	202	200	202

Source: S. Bheemappa, 'Analysis of Elections,' *The Times of India*, Bangalore, 25 April 1987.

Commission in 1953 under Article 340 of the Constitution to identify the socially and educationally backward classes of citizens and to make recommendations for their improvement. Though the Commission failed to find proper criteria to identify backward classes, it recommended reservations for them in technical institutions and in government service. The Government of India asked the State governments to use their discretion and choose their own criteria for defining backwardness. Accordingly, in Mysore, a backward classes committee, the Nagan Gowda Committee, was appointed in January 1960 to determine which sections of people should be treated as 'socially and educationally' backward and 'who should secure preference as may be determined by government, in respect of admissions, to technical institutions and appointment to government service',[72] In its report some 399 castes were recommended as 'backward' and 'more backward'. The reservations recommended for 'backward' and 'more backward' castes in technical institutions were 50 per cent, while for government posts they were 45 per cent. Together with the reservations already existing for scheduled castes and tribes, the total reservations came to 67 per cent and 63 per cent (government posts) respectively.[73] The

[72] Government of Mysore, *The Nagan Gowda Committee Report*, February 1960, p. 3.
[73] Government of Karnataka, *Report of the Second Backward Classes Commission*, Vol. I, op. cit., p. 26.

Nagan Gowda Committee treated the whole of the Lingayat community as 'forward' as their representation in the services and their education level were above the State average. The Lingayats vehemently resented their exclusion from the backward classes list. The government had to finally yield to the pressure of the Lingayats and, in subsequent orders, thought it prudent to include them in the list.[74]

In the period between the late 1940s and early 1970s, a large number of Vokkaligas and Lingayats were recruited into the State's administrative service and also other sections of the State bureaucracy as a means of enhancing the influence of these social groups over state politics. The percentage of posts in Karnataka services held by different communities (not less than 2 per cent of the population) at different levels in March 1972 is given in Table 2.10. We can see that although the Brahmins were doing reasonably well in Karnataka services in proportion to their numerical strength, the Lingayats and Vokkaligas also gained conspicuously. The Lingayats with a population of 14.64 per cent, held 17.92 per cent of Class I and II posts, 19.98 per cent of Class III posts and 7.41 per cent of Class IV posts. The Vokkaligas, comprising 11.82 per cent population in Karnataka, held 11.71 per cent Class I and II posts, 9.61 per cent of Class III posts and 13.13 per cent of Class IV posts.[75]

With their economic and political dominance, it was natural for these castes to exert pressure for greater educational opportunities for those belonging to their caste to add to their power and extend their influence, and to gain for themselves, what Lelah Dushkin has called, 'elite benefits'.[76] These according to her were: 'Class I and II administrative government posts, admission to the universities and especially medical and engineering colleges, seats in Parliament and the State legislatures, and nominations to high office.'[77]

[74] V.K. Nataraj, 'Backward Classes and Minorities in Karnataka Politics,' in Ramashray Roy and Richard Sisson (Eds.). *Diversity and Dominance in Indian Politics: Division Deprivation and the Congress*, Vol. II, Sage Publications, New Delhi, 1990, pp. 170–186.

[75] Government of Karnataka, *Report of the First Backward Classes Commission*, 1975, Vol. I, p. 75.

[76] According to Lelah Dushkin, 'elite benefits' are largely of concern to a small elite within a category and they involve things that the elites in society at large want for themselves and their own offspring.

[77] Lelah Dushkin, 'Backward Class Benefits and Social Class in India 1920–70,' *Economic and Political Weekly*, Vol. XIV, No. 14, 7 April 1979, p. 662.

Table 2.10
Percentage of Posts Held by Different Communities in March 1972

Community	Per cent of population	Class I & II posts	Class III posts	Class IV posts
Beda	5.06	1.15	1.70	2.27
Brahmin	4.23	30.10	17.81	4.41
Christian	2.09	2.78	4.09	3.80
Gaugakula	2.38	0.73	1.22	2.77
Idiga	2.25	1.14	1.25	1.70
Kuruba	6.77	1.67	2.65	4.83
Lingayat	14.64	17.92	19.98	7.41
Mahratta	3.45	1.01	3.23	4.26
Muslim	10.63	5.85	10.65	12.96
Scheduled castes	13.14	4.58	8.46	20.84
Vishwakarma	2.30	1.12	1.96	1.12
Vokkaliga	11.82	11.71	9.61	13.13
TOTAL OF ABOVE COMMUNITIES	78.76	79.79	82.61	79.50
KARNATAKA TOTAL	30,008,050	7,396	190,619	43,483

Source: Government of Karnataka, *The Second Backward Classes Commission Report*, Vol. I, op. cit., p. 18. Population percentage as given in 1975.

In this context, the Nagan Gowda Committee had bestowed some privileges on the other backward castes. However, as also pointed out by Justice K.S. Hegde in *Viswanath* vs. *State of Mysore*, the scheme set out in the Government Order of 1963 and based on income-cum-occupation did not really help the backward classes amongst the Hindus like the Kurubas and Bedas, while the Brahmins, Lingayats and Vokkaligas gained. It was observed that of the 936 seats filled in the engineering colleges of the State, 307, which was about one-third of the seats, belonged to the Brahmin community which constituted 4.28 per cent of the population. Lingayats, who constituted 15.57 per cent of the population, obtained 35 seats in the backward class pool while the Vokkaligas constituting 12.98 per cent of the population obtained 35 seats. In addition, the Lingayats obtained 111 seats and the Vokkaligas 32 seats in the merit pool.[78]

[78] All India Reports 1964, Mysore 132. *Viswanath* vs. *State of Mysore*, cited in Government of Karnataka, *Second Backward Classes Commission Report*, 1986, Vol. I, op. cit., p. 66.

Thus, wanting to gain greater political and social leverage and to build a professional cadre of their own caste brethren, the landed castes gradually extended their influence into the educational sphere. However, there was a fresh intervention in this situation during the tenure of Devraj Urs.

The Devraj Urs Phase

As a leader favoured by the Central leadership, Devraj Urs, with the help of Indira Gandhi's support, won the elections to the State Assembly in 1972.[79] The influence of the Vokkaligas and Lingayats continued in the 1970s under Urs. However, there was one difference. He was the first Chief Minister who sought the support of the other backward castes—an amorphous group consisting of the non-Brahmin Hindu castes other than the Lingayats and Vokkaligas—and kept the dominant groups reasonably satisfied. While his predecessors represented the interests of the Lingayats and Vokkaligas, Urs brought about a new formation without disaffecting the two dominant groups. He wooed the rest of the backward castes, the scheduled castes and the scheduled tribes.

Before Devraj Urs's tenure, these other backward castes, though covered by the reservations policy as per the Nagan Gowda Committee, had never been the main beneficiaries. Their representation in the State Legislative Assembly was 8–9 per cent in the 1957, 1962 and 1967 elections.[80] These castes, which included the potters (Kumbars), washermen (Agasas), fishermen (Bedas), barbers (Nayundas), toddy tappers (Idigas), and shepherds (Kurubas), were economically weak and hence dependent on the dominant castes who retained power all the time. While they tried hard to fight the dominance of the upper castes, they did not achieve any measure of success. 'With the plums of office changing hands from the Brahmins to the Vokkaligas and then to the Lingayats, power

[79] For more details, see M.N. Srinivas and N. Panini, 'Politics and Society in Karnataka,' *Economic and Political Weekly*, Vol. XIX, No. 2, January 1984, pp. 69–75; Atul Kohli, *The State and Poverty in India: The Politics of Reform*, Cambridge University Press, Cambridge, 1987; and V.K. Nataraj, op. cit.

[80] S. Bheemappa, 'Analysis of Elections,' *The Times of India*, Bangalore, 25 April 1987.

was transferred horizontally from one section of the upper crust to another, leaving the other non-Brahmin castes untouched.'[81] It was only under Urs that they were able to put up a semblance of opposition to the dominance of the Lingayats and Vokkaligas. They became more eloquent in expressing their dissatisfaction, especially as regards their getting an unequal share of the reservations.

The anti-dominant-caste feeling was getting accentuated in the State, and Urs realized that his own 'bid for power had to find a base quite different from the old one which had sustained his predecessors in office'.[82] Thus, Urs was regarded by some scholars like James Manor as a 'pragmatic progressive' who was credited with having 'changed the structure of politics in Karnataka' through his programmes and policies for the backward castes.[83] However, Urs's local strategy was merely consistent with the larger populist politics of Indira Gandhi who was also emphatically declaring her commitment to the welfare of the minorities, the scheduled castes, and the scheduled tribes. He initiated several schemes for the poor (like housing schemes, pensions schemes, debt relief acts) and for furthering the interests of groups other than the Vokkaligas and Lingayats, and also made an attempt at land reforms. According to Srinivas and Panini, the Land Reforms Amendment of 1974 enabled tenants to become owners of the land they were cultivating. 'This generally happened where the owners were not locally resident. However, where the tenants were cultivating land owned by members of the powerful dominant castes, the latter were usually able to evict the tenants and *resume cultivating the land* themselves.'[84] The 1974 Amendment for lowering land ceiling was aimed at abolishing tenancies, but this did not help much because the surplus accruing from land ceiling was not sufficient for redistribution. According to Atul Kohli, land reforms were only a part of the 'overall populist thrust'.[85] In fact, as has been pointed out by Ray

[81] H. Kusumakar, 'The Name Tag Tells All in the South', *The Times of India*, New Delhi, 1 September 1985.

[82] Lalita Nataraj and V.K. Nataraj, 'Limits of Populism: Devaraj Urs and Karnataka Politics,' *Economic and Political Weekly*, 11 September 1982, pp. 1503–06.

[83] James Manor, 'Pragmatic Progressive in Regional Politics: The Case of Devraj Urs,' *Economic and Political Weekly*, Annual No. 1980, pp. 201–13.

[84] See M.N. Srinivas and M.N. Panini, 'Politics and Society in Karnataka,' op. cit., p. 71.

[85] Atul Kohli, op. cit., pp. 165–66.

and Kumpatla, Urs could not change the rural power base from the landowning communities to the rural poor.[86] Only less than 45,000 acres or less than 9 per cent of the estimated five lakh acres of the surplus land was redistributed.

To champion the cause of the groups which had been primarily dominated by the Lingayats and Vokkaligas and in response to the demands for a review of reservations, Devraj Urs appointed the First Backward Classes Commission under the Chairmanship of L.G. Havanur. The backward groups—communities, castes and tribes who accounted for 44.52 per cent of the total population of the State—were granted a reservation of 16 per cent, 10 per cent and six per cent respectively. The Lingayats were not treated as backward, but the Vokkaligas continued to be the beneficiaries of protective discrimination. While placating the backward communities, Urs was cautious with the two dominant groups and did not shut them out completely to avoid a backlash.

The Lingayats lost through Urs's policy of preferment in education and government employment, but as Manor has remarked, they are a large category 'divided into various *jatis* and occupational groups which are often in conflict with one another'.[87] The conflict between the Sadar (or the cultivators) and the Banajigas (or the merchants and traders) has often been bitter. Before the arrival of Urs, the Jangama (priestly group) and Banajigas, who were both traditionally urban and literate groups, had done better than the cultivating groups in education and government employment.[88] Urs took advantage of the estrangement between the urban Banajigas and the Jangamas and the cultivating Lingayats with their numerical and economic strength.[89] He granted some benefits to some Sadar Lingayats and secured their support for his government. This, in a way, was a measure of success for Urs, for he was able to take political advantage of the tension among the sub-castes.

However, power relations based on land remained unchanged; the Lingayats and Vokkaligas continued to hold the bulk of arable

[86] Amal Ray and Jayalakshmi Kumpatla, 'Zila Parishad Presidents in Karnataka: Their Social Background and Implications for Development,' *Economic and Political Weekly*, Vol. XXII, October 1987, pp. 1825–30.

[87] James Manor, 'Pragmatic Progressive in Regional Politics: The Case of Devraj Urs,' op. cit., p. 205.

[88] Ibid.

[89] Ibid.

land—the Lingayats held 38,549 acres of dry, irrigated and garden land, while the Vokkaligas held 17,150 acres.[90]

Politically speaking, their representation in the Legislative Assembly suffered a marginal setback due to some improvement in the representation of the Other Backward Castes between 1972 and 1978. Even then, the Lingayats won 58 and the Vokkaligas 47 of the 212 seats in 1972, while in 1978, they won 53 and 47 of the 225 seats respectively.[91]

The bulk of the jobs in the State services were held by these two dominant groups. In 1972, the percentage of Class I, II and III employees in Karnataka's State services was 19.90 per cent for the Lingayats and 9.69 per cent for the Vokkaligas. With the exception of the Brahmins who held 18.30 per cent of the jobs, the other communities and castes were rather poorly represented.[92]

During Urs's tenure, the Brahmin representation in education and services continued to be high. In medical colleges, they enjoyed 21.53 per cent representation. The Lingayats and Vokkaligas also continued to have a sufficiently high percentage of representation. In medical colleges, for instance, they together secured 16.47 per cent of the seats between 1977 and 1983.[93] It was realised by these castes that education, particularly professional education, would bring its own rewards. Skill and knowledge would accentuate the process of social mobility, add to their political and economic strength, and open greater avenues of employment for their people. No wonder then that the competition for a 'backward' status amongst these dominant castes continued. At the same time, the other backward groups were also coming up through the avenues provided by Urs. In medical colleges, the total representation of the Kumbars, Besthas and Idigas, for instance, rose to 12.26 per cent between 1977 and 1983.[94] There was a jump in their political representation from 18/212 in 1967 to 36/212 in 1972 and 45/225 in 1978 in the Karnataka Legislative Assembly.[95] Urs, while extending

[90] Government of Karnataka, *The Havanur Report*, Bangalore, 1975, Vol. IV, Socio-Economic Survey Compilation, Table 15, pp. 489 and 494.

[91] S. Bheemappa, op. cit.

[92] Government of Karnataka, *The Havanur Report*, op. cit., pp. 265–68.

[93] Government of Karnataka, *Report of the Second Karnataka Backward Classes Commission*, Vol. I, op. cit., pp. 174–75.

[94] Ibid.

[95] See S. Bheemappa, op. cit.

some benefits to the other backward groups, did not abandon traditional blocs of political support. Competitiveness amongst the prevailing groups for social mobilisation and political leverage was reinforced, providing an opportunity for private enterprise in education to grow. Urs's tenure alone saw the rise of 11 capitation fee colleges.[96]

Situation in the 1980s

The alliance between Urs and Mrs. Gandhi came to an end in June 1979. Urs had to resign in 1980 when his party could not secure even a single seat in the mid-term elections to Parliament.

Urs's successor, Gundu Rao, was no champion of the cause of backward classes. He altered Urs's strategy. Whereas Urs had wooed the backward castes, with Gundu Rao a changed situation emerged and the signs of dominant caste resurgence became visible.[97] Since the Lingayats had been protesting against the reservations policy and other issues, Gundu Rao stated that a commission would be appointed to review afresh the issue of beneficiaries and reservations. He also agreed to give consideration to their appeals for greater State patronage.

The Janata government which came to power was headed by Ramakrishna Hegde as the Chief Minister. It was anticipated that as a Brahmin, Hegde would not have any independent social base for power and so there would be greater likelihood of his balancing the interests of different social forces, specially the powerful groups on land. So, when he formed his team of 24 Ministers, it consisted of four Vokkaligas, five Lingayats, two Muslims, and one each from the other backward castes.[98] Later, in 1987, 16 out of the 35 positions in Hegde's Cabinet were shared by the Vokkaligas and Lingayats.[99]

[96] See Government of Karnataka, *White Paper on Professional Colleges and Institutions*, Department of Education and Youth Services, Bangalore, March 1983, pp. 25 and 44.

[97] James Manor, 'Blurring the Lines Between Parties and Social Bases: Gundu Rao and the Emergence of a Janata Government in Karnataka,' *Economic and Political Weekly*, Vol. XIX, No. 37, 15 September 1984, pp. 1623–32.

[98] *Indian Express*, Bangalore, 17 February 1983.

[99] Amal Ray and Jayalakshmi Kumpatla, op. cit., p. 1829.

Some programmes of the Janata government were also aimed at helping the landowning interests. These included subsidies on insecticides and pesticides, concessions on taxes, and help in developing agro-based industries.

The Janata government appointed the Second Backward Classes Commission in Karnataka under the Chairmanship of T. Venkataswami. In its report the other backward castes were divided into A and B groups with benefits of reservations of 14 and 13 per cent respectively. Vokkaligas and Lingayats were both excluded from the list of backward classes. There was considerable opposition to the report, particularly from the Vokkaligas. In the wake of the agitation by the Vokkaliga Sangha, the State government rejected the report in October 1986.

The agitation also brought to light the rivalry between the two dominant communities, each declaring that the other was not a socially and educationally backward class and each keen to be included in that category. This conflict of interests was not unnatural. The two communities claimed that they were still not capable of competing on equal terms with the upper castes, particularly the Brahmins.

After the government's rejection of the Report, an ad-hoc list of other backward classes was prepared. It was to be in operation till such time as a new commission could review the issue of reservations. Under the Janata government's order, the beneficiary castes included both the Vokkaligas and Lingayats, thus negating the earlier exclusion of the Lingayats by the Havanur Commission. By bringing the Vokkaligas and Lingayats into the backward list, Hegde bowed to the pressure of the dominant communities, who constituted about 37 per cent of the State's population, and would now have access to 25 per cent reservation (half the total reservations for backward classes) for educational opportunities and 27 per cent of the government jobs.[100]

When the government designed the system of democratic decentralization and constituted the Zilla Parishads in the new Panchayat system of Karnataka, 10 of the 18 Zilla Parishad Presidentships went to the Lingayats and Vokkaligas. With adult franchise the upper crust of these castes stood for elections, approached

[100] Janaki Nair, 'Fighting for Backwardness: Venkataswamy Commission Report and After,' *Economic and Political Weekly*, Vol. XXI, No. 42, 18 October 1986 pp. 1837–38.

electorates, and cultivated constituencies. This enabled them to occupy strategic positions in the political life at the village level, through the Taluk and district levels to the State level. The Report of the Karnataka Second Backward Classes Commission further underlined this fact.

In 1983, the Lingayats and Vokkaligas dominated the rural leadership as chairmen and vice-chairmen and members of the village Panchayats. The Lingayats, with a population of 16.92 per cent (as per the 1984 survey), occupied 30.17 per cent of the seats of chairmen and vice-chairmen and 21.72 per cent of the seats as members. The Vokkaligas constituting 11.68 per cent of the population had 23.82 per cent of the seats of chairmen and vice-chairmen and 17.40 per cent of the seats as members.[101]

Again, in the 175 Taluk Development Boards in 1983, the Lingayats secured 25.72 per cent of the seats and the Vokkaligas 23.18 per cent. The scheduled castes won 17.17 per cent of the seats, while the other castes and communities won between 5.75 per cent and 1.13 per cent.[102] Between 1978 and 1985, the Lingayats and Vokkaligas were heavily represented in the State and national level elected bodies. The Lingayats secured 26.02 per cent of the seats of M.L.A., M.L.C. and M.P. and the Vokkaligas got 20.30 per cent.[103] In 1983, the Lingayats secured 65 seats (in a total of 222 seats) and the Vokkaligas 54 in the Legislative Assembly. In 1985 they secured 64 and 52 seats each (in a total of 224).[104]

A segment of these communities also tried to enhance their ability to influence public policy-making by occupying a number of key positions in the civil services and para-civil services (advisory bodies) in Karnataka. Between 1977 and 1984, the percentage of Lingayat Class I officers in the administrative services was 14.15 per cent and Vokkaliga officers 19.19 per cent. These two communities were more highly represented than the other backward groups, but Brahmins continued to be predominant and entrenched with 13.13 per cent representation.

After Hegde, the Lingayat leader S.R. Bommai's assumption of the Chief Minister's office in 1988 signalled a reversion to a political

---

[101] Government of Karnataka, *Report of the Second Backward Classes Commission*, Vol. I, op. cit., pp. 162–63 and Annexure 8.6, Vol. III, pp. 58–59.

[102] Ibid., Vol. II, p. 166.

[103] Ibid., Vol. III, Annexure 8.11, p. 71.

[104] S. Bheemappa, op. cit.

and administrative machinery filled with representatives of the Lingayat community.[105] The Lingayats were again favoured by the Congress high command when the latter, sifting through the available party leaders before the 1989 elections, picked up Veerendra Patil. A possible motive for this action was the weaning away of their votes to the Congress. The pro-Lingayat approach was continued by the Patil government.[106] The Third Backward Classes Commission Report appointed under the chairmanship of Justice O. Chinappa Reddy also revealed that in terms of numbers, in the castewise distribution of employees working in the Karnataka State Civil Services (groups A, B, C and D) in 1988, the Lingayats were at the top occupying 61,655 (16.68 per cent) posts; the Brahmins obtained 44,649 (12 per cent) of the posts while the Vokkaligas secured 42,655 (13 per cent) of the posts.[107]

The numerically preponderant Lingayats and Vokkaligas dominated the political scene as well. According to the Chinappa Reddy Report, for their combined population of about 26 per cent, they had a representation of about 46 per cent in the Legislative Assembly, 54 per cent each in the Parliament and the Legislative Council, and 51 per cent in the Zilla Parishads. About 63 per cent of the Zilla Parishad Presidents also came from these communities. This political dominance is, in fact, a reflection of the economic dominance of the two groups. Justice Chinappa Reddy's random survey of 523 villages in Karnataka revealed that for a population of about 18 per cent in these villages, the Lingayats controlled as much as 27 per cent of the land held by all the communities together, while for a population of about 13 per cent, the Vokkaligas controlled as much as 28 per cent.[108]

The Third Backward Classes Commission's broad recommendations seemed different in going beyond the caste and community criteria and declaring as backward several occupational groups that were economically weak. They were put in a category that was to have the benefit of one-tenth of the reservations in admission to educational institutions and government service. But political

[105] 'Caste and Power Game in Karnataka,' *Economic and Political Weekly*, Vol. XXV, Nos. 42 and 43, October 1990, pp. 2359–60.

[106] Ibid.

[107] See Government of Karnataka, *Report of the Third Backward Classes Commission*, 1990, Vol. I, pp. 112–17, Vol. II, pp. 200–02.

[108] Ibid., Vol. I, pp. 49–51.

groups who had a vested interest in reservations were said to be agitated over the Commission's action in keeping 32 caste groups out of the backward list including the numerically strong and politically powerful Lingayats and Vokkaligas. The reaction of Veerendra Patil's government was to refer the report to the cabinet sub-committee, thus putting off an immediate decision. No action has been taken on the report since 1990. Chief Minister Bangarappa stated that the Cabinet sub-committee constituted in June 1990 and reconstituted twice in November 1990 and August 1991 had met only twice for discussion.[109]

For gaining a foothold in the political and social spheres in the post-Independence period in Karnataka, there was an intensification of 'caste philanthropy' in educational activities by rich individuals and organisations belonging to the two dominant castes. This, as we have seen, led to the formation and activisation of caste and community associations which went back to the promise of assistance given to members listed as 'backward' in the Miller Committee Report. According to Dushkin,[110] the formation of such associations was directly related to the constitutional reforms of 1923 in Mysore, and since Independence, to the appointment of commissions for backward classes—both at the central and State levels.

Despite the Vokkaligas and Lingayats being treated as 'backward', they were still in competition with the entrenched Brahmin positions in education and employment. Thus, they were keen to further their own interests by strengthening caste solidarity, and providing educational services for members of one's caste. This covered a wide range of possibilities. The more affluent sections among these castes were able to exploit the caste factor to their advantage. The rich caste leaders whipped up prejudices against other castes and generated false hopes among their caste brethren that their economic, political and educational situation could be improved if they supported their caste leaders in securing posts in services or in setting up educational institutions to serve their interests.

Thus, schools and colleges charging capitation fees, including professional colleges, were set up for the benefit of caste groups. In the professional sphere, particularly in the fields of engineering

[109] See The Statesman, New Delhi, 11 June 1990; also Deccan Herald, Bangalore, 3 September 1991 and P. Radhakrishnan, op. cit.

[110] Lelah Dushkin, 'Caste Associations in Bangalore,' Economic and Political Weekly, Vol. XV, No. 37, 13 September 1980, pp. 1551–57.

and medicine, a network of educational institutions sprang up to create their own intelligentsia and gain more opportunities for better employment.

As we have observed earlier, the Lingayats and Vokkaligas had stood to gain in education since the days of the Miller Committee Report. But till then, the Brahmins had been the entrenched elites in education. In 1924–25, there was not a single Lingayat or Vokkaliga student who appeared for an engineering degree or M.B.B.S. examination.[111] Of a total of 212 students who appeared for the engineering degree examination in that year, 106 were Brahmins and 16 of the 19 students who appeared for the Part I M.B.B.S. examination were also Brahmins. Later, the Vokkaligas and Lingayats, who had been aspiring for an elite status, improved their position considerably. As was seen earlier, between the years 1977 and 1983, the Vokkaligas secured 9.37 per cent of the seats in medical colleges while the Lingayats got 7.10 per cent. The Brahmins remained at the top having secured 21.53 per cent (see Table 2.11).

In engineering colleges also, a survey undertaken in 1984–85

Table 2.11
Position of the Lingayats and Vokkaligas in Medical Colleges, 1977–83

Religion/Caste	Percentage of seats secured to the total in medical colleges from 1977 to 1983	Percentage of the population as per 1984 survey
Brahmin	21.53	3.81
Scheduled Castes	12.32	15.86
Vokkaligas	9.37	11.63
Muslims	7.14	10.97
Lingayats/Veershaivyas	7.10	16.92
Scheduled tribes	2.00	2.82
Others*	40.56	38.00

Source: Government of Karnataka, *Report of the Second Backward Classes Commission*, Vol. I, op. cit., pp. 174–75.

    * Others include Idiga, Bunt, Balija, Vaisya, Kuruba, Bestha, Golla, Vishvakarma, Jain, Devanga, Maratha, Nayar, and Christian.

    [111] Chitra Sivakumar, op. cit.

showed that the Brahmins had secured 20.09 per cent of the seats, while the Lingayats were second on the list with 14.91 per cent, and the Vokkaligas came after them with 13.45 per cent (see Table 2.12). The scheduled castes secured 6.96 per cent of the seats while none of the other backward castes got more than 2.14 per cent.

Table 2.12
Position of the Lingayats and Vokkaligas in Comparison to Brahmins in Engineering Colleges in the State during 1984–85

Caste	No. of students admitted to engineering colleges				
	Government	Aided	Private	Total	Total percentage
Brahmins	170	524	492	1,186	20.09
Lingayats	19	367	494	880	14.91
Vokkaligas	43	270	480	793	13.45

Source: Government of Karnataka, *Report of the Second Backward Class Commission*, Vol. III, op. cit., Annexure 8.21, pp. 100–1.

The Chinappa Reddy Commission also pointed out that the Brahmins, who ranked only next to the Lingayats and Vokkaligas in the power structure, were represented heavily in employment and higher education up to the extent of 19.5 per cent and 21.5 per cent respectively. In 1988, the Vokkaligas secured 11.63 per cent of the seats in professional colleges and postgraduate institutes while the Lingayats secured 15.68 per cent. Thus, as in the traditional society the Brahmins have been 'still esconsed at the summit of the social hierarchy'[112] and various social groups have been competing for similar social and educational advancement. Tables 2.13 and 2.14 show the castewise distribution of students in medical and engineering colleges during 1988–89 and 1977–89. Other communities and castes who had a lower representation in such institutions were also taking the cue from the dominant groups and were wanting to set up their own colleges for acquiring greater economic and political status. The Agasas, for instance, had 0.28 per cent representation in medical colleges, Bedas 0.72 per cent, Besthas 1.75 per cent and Kurubas 0.55 per cent. In engineering

[112] P. Radhakrishnan, 'Karnataka Backward Classes,' *Economic and Political Weekly*, Vol. XXV No. 32, 11 August 1990, p. 1753.

Table 2.13

Caste-wise Distribution of Brahmin, Lingayat and Vokkaliga Students
Admitted to Medical Colleges in Karnataka during 1988–89

Caste	Seats obtained*	Percentage
Brahmin	157	17.92
Lingayat	112	12.79
Vokkaliga	100	11.42

Source: Government of Karnataka, *Report of the Third Backward Classes Commission*, Vol. I, 1990, pp. 92–94.
* Total number of seats filled were 876.

Table 2.14

Admission of Brahmin, Lingayat and Vokkaliga Students to
Engineering Colleges between 1977 and 1989

Caste	Percentage
Brahmin	24.37
Lingayat	12.06
Vokkaliga	11.07

Source: Government of Karnataka, *Report of the Third Backward Classes Commission*, Vol. I, 1990, pp. 72–76.

colleges as well their numbers were insignificant; these being 0.26 per cent, 1.75 per cent, 0.85 per cent and 0.31 per cent respectively.[113]

In the 1980s and early 1990s, a multiple competition again ensued between different social groups. The Vokkaligas and Lingayats had been contending for dominance with the Brahmins in education and jobs. Urs' strategy was to put the Lingayats and Vokkaligas in opposition to the other backward groups as well. This triangular competition (between the dominant castes, Brahmins and the other backward classes) which started in the 1970s, got sharper and became a multiple-level competition in the 1980s, as other social forces like the scheduled castes and the Muslims entered the fray, and began setting up their own colleges. Thus, numerous capitation fee colleges mushroomed in the State of

[113] Government of Karnataka, *Report of the Karnataka Third Backward Classes Commission*, Vol. I, op. cit., pp. 68–76.

Karnataka. The capitation fee phenomenon as it emerged was a manifestation of the linkage between caste, class, politics and education in the State.

Urbanisation, industrialisation, modernisation of agriculture (the Green Revolution as it was called) and the emergence of middle castes as dominant groups had all given rise to an increase of employment opportunities. Competition for availing such opportunities became intense. The rise of these trends has also to be viewed in the context of the competitive party politics becoming sharper. Any ruling political party in Karnataka would not wish to lose support of the dominant groups as also of groups acquiring new significance and power like the scheduled castes, the other backward castes and the Muslims. Hence, the parties in power did little to prevent private professional colleges being set up by castes and communities who were utilising education as a channel of mobility and dominance.

Investing in a professional institution was also proving to be a good source of profit, and hence, this sphere attracted private entrepreneurs as well. The capitation fee system as it emerged and evolved in Karnataka, the various interests it served and the government's attitude towards it will be taken up in the subsequent chapters.

3

EVOLUTION OF THE CAPITATION
FEE PHENOMENON IN KARNATAKA

Emergence of the Phenomenon

We have seen in the previous chapter that the major support to
professional education in Karnataka in the form of capitation fee
institutions came from the dominant castes, the Vokkaligas and
Lingayats. However, interestingly, the first institution that chose
to function outside the government sector was established by the
Brahmin community, namely the Kasturba Medical College in
Manipal set up in 1953 by Dr. T.M.A. Pai. This was ostensibly a
private initiative to provide greater opportunities for higher education but, as we will see later, it unfolded a new channel through
which certain socio-economic interests consciously began to operate
in the domain of education.

After the Kasturba Medical College was established, many more
private unaided medical and engineering colleges were established
in Karnataka. In 1988, when this study was conducted, Karnataka
had a total of 49 engineering colleges, which was nearly 20 per cent
of all such colleges in India.[1] Of the total of 49 such colleges, there

---

[1] The number of engineering colleges had swelled to 51 in 1991. Two more
private unaided colleges have come up since 1988 (information gathered from the
Directorate of Technical Education, Government of Karnataka, Bangalore).

were five government and university colleges, 11 private aided colleges and 33 private unaided colleges. We can see from Table 3.1 that since 1970, while there has been practically no growth in the number of colleges in the government sector and a marginal increase in the private aided sector, the private unaided sector has shown a significant increase, especially after 1979. There has been an apparent demand for technical education in Karnataka even when there have not been sufficient outlets for employment. Much of the demand seems to have been motivated by the hope that acquisition of technical skills will one day fetch employment. But, in fact, after 1983 there has been a growing trend of unemployment amongst engineering graduates in Karnataka.

Table 3.1
Growth in the Number of Engineering Colleges in Karnataka

Year	Government colleges and universities	Private aided	Private unaided
1956–57	3	3	1
1970–71	4	8	4
1978–79	4	8	4
1982–83	4	8	27
1987–91*	5	11	35

Source: Government of Karnataka, *White Paper on Professional Colleges and Institutions*, Department of Education and Youth Services and Department of Health and Family Welfare, Bangalore, March 1983, p. 1.
 * The figures for 1987–91 have been added on the basis of information provided by the Directorate of Technical Education, Government of Karnataka, Bangalore.

Of the 18 medical colleges in Karnataka in 1988, the four government colleges were located in Bangalore, Mysore, Hubli and Bellary. From amongst the 14 private medical colleges, only St. John's Medical College, Bangalore, did not charge capitation fees from its students. The remaining 13 colleges were all private and unaided (see Table 3.2). In 1991, the total number of medical colleges in the State rose to 19 and the number of such private institutions increased to 15 from 14 in 1988.

In 1984, out of the 13 medical colleges in Karnataka, five were located in Bangalore city. There were then already about 70,000 doctors in the State and of them about 8,000 doctors were unemployed. The World Health Organization, after considering

Table 3.2
Growth in the Number of Medical Colleges in Karnataka

	Number of medical colleges		
Year	Government colleges and universities	Private aided	Private unaided
1956–57	2	—	1
1970–71	4	—	5
1978–79	4	—	6
1982–83	4	—	8
1987–91*	4	—	15

Source: Government of Karnataka, *White Paper on Professional Colleges and Institutions*, op. cit., p. 1.
    * The figures for 1987–91 have been added on the basis of information provided by the Directorate of Medical Education, Government of Karnataka, Bangalore.

relevant statistics, was of the view that there should be one medical college for every 50 lakh of population.[2] The population of Karnataka then being about 371.36 lakh,[3] seven medical colleges were more than sufficient but the number had increased from 13 in 1984 to 19 in 1991.

The Kasturba Medical College was also the first medical college in the country to charge capitation fees from its students. Since then, the practice of charging this fee has grown phenomenally, not only in Karnataka's professional colleges, but elsewhere in the country. Maharashtra has a large number of private medical and engineering colleges. In fact, in 1988 the engineering institutions in Maharashtra numbered 55. This number rose to 62 in 1991, a figure higher than in Karnataka. The sheer number of the institutions is staggering considering the vast resources which have to be raised by the private enterprises concerned. In 1983, the Ninth Joint Conference of the Central Council of Health and Family Welfare passed a resolution, which was supported by the Maharashtra government, stating that 'no new medical colleges should

    [2] *Indian Law Reports*, 1985, Karnataka, pp. 1204. Figures provided in this paragraph quoted by Justice J. Rama Jois in the case *Indian Medical Association* vs. *State of Karnataka*.
    [3] Government of Karnataka, *Karnataka's Economy in Figures, 1985–86*, Directorate of Economics and Statistics, Bangalore, 1987 p. 2.

be allowed to be opened in any State or Union Territory without the approval of that State or Union Territory Government, the Medical Council of India and the Government of India'. A few months later, in 1984, the Maharashtra Government sanctioned some private capitation fee based medical colleges at Loni, Ahmadnagar, Karad, Satara and Amravati. Backed by powerful political figures, a number of applications were made in 1989. The government sanctioned more private colleges and allowed them the use of its hospitals.[4] If one takes the case of medical education in India, officially there were about 20,000, and unofficially, about 50,000 unemployed or semi-employed junior doctors in India.[5] This meant that there was a large number[6] of well-trained and well-educated young doctors who could be put into the health-care delivery system. While this has not been done, the number of colleges charging capitation fees has increased. The number of private medical institutions in the State has risen to 15 in 1992.

This phenomenon has spread to Kerala and Tamil Nadu as well. Three private engineering colleges were started in Kerala in Palghat, Kottamangalam and Quilon in late 1985. The Kerala government in 1991 was also actively considering a proposal to allow the private sector to open medical colleges in the State. Though a late-starter, Tamil Nadu has not lagged behind and has allowed as many as 24 private engineering colleges to be set up almost in one go. It has used the term 'self-financing' for these institutions, to connote that technically they were independent of any state grant-in-aid and also, possibly, so as not to be involved in the controversy about capitation fees. The correct position, however, was that all these colleges did collect and were dependent on capitation fees in one form or another.

Following closely on the heels of Karnataka, several private capitation fee colleges were established in Andhra Pradesh during the tenure of Chief Minister J. Vengal Rao who, in 1977, allowed the setting up of an engineering college at Vijaywada. Dr. Chenna Reddy's tenure also saw the rise of privately managed technical

[4] *Frontier*, 11 August 1984, Vol. 16, No. 51, pp. 11–12. Also see, Sandhya Srinivasan, 'Capitation Colleges: Teaching Shops?' *The Illustrated Weekly of India*, 29 August–4 September 1992, pp. 12–13.

[5] Ibid.

[6] 18,499 in 1984 as quoted in the Parliament in 1984 by Mrs. Mohsina Kidwai, the then Minister of State for Health. See *The Times of India*, 24 September 1984.

institutions and the trend soon spread. By 1986, there were 14 private engineering colleges in the State. The ostensible reason given by the government for allowing these colleges was the increasing societal demand for educational opportunities and the inability of the State government to meet this demand. Also, a large number of students from Andhra Pradesh were given admission to colleges in Karnataka; as a result, there was a large outflow of money from the State. The Telugu Desam party, after it assumed power in the State in 1983 decided to 'nationalise' the institutions and prohibit the charging of capitation fees. Perhaps 'nationalise' is not an appropriate term, for according to the Act passed by the State Legislature in January 1983, all the institutions concerned continued as private enterprises, but were precluded from charging any capitation fee. Admissions were made from a common pool of applicants who had qualified on the basis of a State-wise admission test. However, after the students had been selected for government colleges as per their position on the merit list, the remaining students who had qualified could opt to enter any private college of their choice. While the government did not allow the charging of capitation fees, in actual practice, the transaction was between the college and the candidate concerned, and large amounts were taken for granting admission. The State government did not assume any financial responsibility for the institutions. For the recurring expenditure, the colleges were required to depend on tuition fees which had become very high over the years.

Amidst public protests—including a State-wide *bandh*, student agitations and condemnation of the collection of capitation fees in the State Legislative Assembly—the Janardhan Reddy government went ahead to sanction more medical colleges in the private sector. Although the Andhra Pradesh High Court struck down the State government's order permitting such institutions and Reddy had to eventually resign as a result of public outcry,[7] the fact of the matter is that capitation fee colleges have grown at a rapid rate and have spread to many States in the country, mainly in Karnataka, Maharashtra, Tamil Nadu, and Andhra Pradesh. The cause of this emergence and the dynamics of their growth may have had some specificity in each State. However, there is evidence to show that

---

[7] *Indian Express*, New Delhi, 25, 26, and 27 August 1992 and 19 and 21 September 1992.

their emergence was initially related to the pursuit of the middle castes towards social mobility. Later, several socio-economic groups entered the field. It is in this context that we will examine more closely its evolution in Karnataka, which has been the trend-setter in this regard.

The Karnataka Picture

In the previous chapter we have observed how the two dominant landowning groups tried to establish their hold over the educational sphere through the economic and political power they wielded. These groups were able to establish private professional colleges to supposedly serve their caste interests. Other communities like the Muslims and scheduled castes followed suit and tried to further their own group interests. Seeing the profitability of such educational ventures, private entrepreneurs also entered this field. In the light of our analysis of the socio-economic process and the political developments in Karnataka, we will take up the specific issues which gave rise to the capitation fee phenomenon.

Caste, Class and Development

We have seen how the caste factor and the competition between the Brahmins and the other backward castes, which include the dominant landed groups, have played an important role in the setting up of capitation fee based private colleges. The two major contending castes, the Vokkaligas and Lingayats, who were the beneficiaries of the reservation policy and the development of the interests of rich peasants, invested in education, and set up a large number of private professional colleges. The Lingayats were the trend-setters in this regard, especially in North Karnataka where the Karnataka Lingayat Education Society (K.L.E.S.) was involved in educational activities. Later, the K.L.E.S. was renamed the Karnataka Liberal Education Society. This change came about in the wake of a bill in the 1960s which discouraged caste hostels and stated that no government grants would be given to them because

they served as 'nurseries for caste-based ideologies'.[*] The other
backward groups, besides the Lingayats and Vokkaligas, also
established some colleges. The Brahmins, who had been sidelined
by rich peasant development and the reservation policy of the
State, wished to retain their hold on education. The scheduled
castes who had benefited from protective discrimination also set
up some professional institutions. The Muslims as well started
some capitation fee based colleges as 'minority' institutions through
their trusts like the Al-Ameen.

In fact, the pressure exerted on the State government by these
groups was the principal factor that enabled these colleges to
obtain sanctions for their establishment. Although most colleges
were managed by single caste trusts, caste factors were generally
set aside by colleges in granting admissions, and bidders paying the
highest capitation fee were preferred. This paradox needs to be
explained. It is true that caste leaders in the management catered
to their caste clientele for personal gains, social recognition and
political power. In setting up a caste-based college, they were able
to get the support of the majority of those belonging to their caste
on the pretext that the educational interests of their caste would be
adequately served and their community further strengthened. But
even amongst the boys and girls of their own caste, preferences for
admission were on the basis of the student's capacity to purchase a
seat. Various concessions that may have been granted in certain
cases were more of an exception, not the rule. Moreover, on an
average, as we will see later in this study, only about 20 to 30 per
cent of the seats went to students belonging to the caste managing
the college. The bulk of admissions were from amongst the non-
caste students who could afford to give large donations. So, the
benefits of this kind of system have not really percolated to the
vast majority of the poor caste members who may have initially
supported the idea of a college for 'their own community'. Whether
it has been a Vokkaliga- or Lingayat-run college, a large number
of seats have gone to non-Vokkaligas and non-Lingayats as well as
to other non-Karnataka students.

The emergence of the capitation fee phenomenon in Karnataka
may also be traced to the large-scale reservation of seats made by
the former Mysore State in government institutions for backward

[*] Personal interview with Professor M.N. Srinivas, 14 November 1987.

communities and scheduled castes and scheduled tribes.[9] This led to the diminishing of educational opportunities for a large section of students who did not belong to those communities, mainly the Brahmins, and inevitably the response to the situation came in the form of two private enterprise colleges started by the Pais (Brahmins), totally independent of government aid and charging capitation fees for their operations.[10]

As mentioned earlier, the Kasturba Medical College at Manipal was the first private experiment in higher professional education in Karnataka. Seeing the paucity of medical education then available in India, Dr. T. Madhava Anantha Pai, the founder of the college, felt that the government alone could not be depended upon to provide adequate educational facilities, and therefore, the people had to also come forward to bear the cost of education. The need for better medical facilities was deeply felt, but motivation for the Kasturba Medical College also arose from a feeling of indignation over the denial of medical education to able Brahmin applicants in Madras because of anti-Brahmin considerations.[11] The Mysore Medical College alone could not cater to the needs of the Mysoreans who had to go to Madras to study medicine. The non-Brahmin movement in Madras was directed against the Brahmins who had been running the government and largely monopolising education. The first State elections had brought the non-Brahmins to power in Madras. There was some justice in reserving a large number of college seats and government positions for those who were qualified and belonged to the scheduled castes and tribes who had for long been submerged. But when this principle began to be applied to exclude those of high castes from virtually all opportunities under the State's control, the future looked bleak to the young Brahmins who wished to enter the professions. Many went into business while others entered government service through competitive examinations. But there were still some who wanted to acquire professional education. The Kasturba Medical College was, in a way, a manifestation of this desire as well.

[9] *Miller Committee Report*. See details in Chapter 2.

[10] Personal interviews with Dr. Ramdas Pai and Mr. Ramesh Pai, Manipal, November 1987.

[11] See Selden Menefee, *The Pais of Manipal*, Asia Publishing House, 1st edn., 1967; The Academy of General Education, 2nd edn., 1984.

The scheduled castes and other weaker sections also tried to avail of the new opportunities that came in the wake of reservations, but few managed to gain the advantage of higher education or even professional education. However, in Karnataka, professional colleges like the Ambedkar Medical College and the Ambedkar Institute of Technology run by scheduled caste trusts were set up. Here, although there were a certain number of seats reserved for scheduled caste students, a large number of admissions were also from amongst the non-scheduled castes. In fact, seats were open to anyone willing to pay the capitation fee, which put 'more premium on money power',[12] and it was not as though scheduled caste students alone stood to benefit from this system in colleges run by their own social groups. Besides these castes and community colleges, some private engineering and medical institutions managed by private entrepreneurs were also established.

Besides caste, another important social factor that has given impetus to the capitation fee system is related to the values of the people as manifested in the system of dowry. Dowry may be seen as part of the larger commercialisation process in society. The son of an engineer or a doctor fetches a good deal of dowry and it is considered a matter of great pride and prestige if the parents of a daughter can find a professionally qualified son-in-law. In fact, many are prepared to pay the entire amount of the training fee inclusive of the capitation amount to get a doctor or an engineer for a son-in-law—a professional degree is a certified credential, a passport to a comfortable settlement of their daughter's life. This is a fact peculiar not only to Karnataka; colleges in the State have been catering not only to the local population, but have acquired an almost all-India character catering to young aspirants from practically all parts of the country. Dowry may be sought in terms of capitation fee or even as a compensation for the fee. Thus, it has become a channel for integrating the economic process with the social process.

Apart from the key role played by the non-Brahmin movement and the resulting political alignments in Karnataka in promoting professional education, other factors such as the State of Mysore coming under the spell of industrialisation and thereby contributing to the need for technical colleges, were also responsible.

[12] See Lelah Dushkin, 'Backward Class Benefits and Social Class in India: 1920–70,' *Economic and Political Weekly*, 7 April 1979, pp. 661–67.

The economic policies pursued by the Dewans of the Old Mysore State, including Visvesvaraya, had created an environment for technical, scientific and industrial growth. There thus arose a need for technical manpower. At the same time there was also lack of adequate facilities for medical education in the State, and till 1953, there existed only one medical college, the Mysore Medical College, in Karnataka. Seeing this need, as we have seen earlier, engineering and medical institutions were set up not only by the dominant castes, but also by minority communities, and later by private entrepreneurs.

It was during Sir Visvesvaraya's tenure as Dewan of the princely Mysore State (1912–1918) that the concept of industrialisation gained importance. This period has been aptly described by Bjorn Hettne as a 'fascinating experiment in economic development' in Mysore State.[13] With the advent of World War I, there emerged a need for technological innovations because imported technology could no longer be relied upon. This in turn encouraged a spirit of self-reliance. Visvesvaraya thus gave emphasis to education, industrialisation and rural modernisation and felt that the State should perform an important role in all spheres. He also coined the phrase 'industrialise or perish'.[14] In 1928, in defence of his economic policy, he stated that 'the country must progress. Productive works and industries are the main avenues at present next to education for the advancement of the country.'[15] According to Visvesvaraya, education was to occupy the key role in the development process. The speech he delivered in 1912 at the Central College in Mysore is worth quoting:

The reason why, roughly speaking, the earning power of an average Englishman is more than twenty times that of an average Indian is the former's acquired capital, skill and working capacity. In the U.K. about 95 per cent of the population can read and write, in America, in Canada, in Belgium and in Japan, 80 to 90 per cent or more. In only one Mysore village out of five is there a school. Only one boy out of four grows up educated and only

[13] Bjorn Hettne, *The Political Economy of Indirect Rule: Mysore 1881–1947*, Ambika Publications, New Delhi, 1978.

[14] Ibid., p. 258.

[15] V. Sitaramaiah, *M. Visvesvarya*, New Delhi, 1971, p. 144, cited in Hettne, ibid., p. 258.

one girl out of eighteen. The causes of our low standard of living are obvious. The nearer we approach England and other foreign countries in respect of the proportion of educated people in the country the greater will be our earning capacity and material progress.[16]

Visvesvaraya was also the main driving force behind the foundation of Mysore University which was established in 1916. Prior to this, most Mysoreans attended Madras University for higher education.

Besides Mysore University, the other economically relevant institutions which were established by Visvesvaraya as an important part of his development strategy were the Department of Industries and Trade (1913), the Mysore Bank (1913), and the Mysore Chamber of Commerce (1916). Through these institutions, efforts were made in the period after 1910 to create an institutional framework necessary for indigenous industrialisation, which was the ultimate goal.

Visvesvaraya was replaced by Kantharaj Urs who, owing to poor health, could not take charge until June 1919. In the meantime, Albion Banerjee became the officiating Dewan, and ultimately replacing Kantharaj Urs in 1922, remained in office till 1926. Banerjee, who had also been one of Visvesvaraya's main critics, followed the 'classical liberal go-slow strategy'.[17] He emphasised private enterprise, small-scale light industries, and simple technology in contrast to Visvesvaraya's emphasis on government involvement, large-scale heavy industry, and advanced technology.

Mirza Ismail (1926–1941) replaced Banerji in 1926. Ismail, who represented the 'mixed economy' approach, was always careful to cooperate with private enterprise. The state was not to play the role of an enterprising pioneer any more, but instead private entrepreneurs were to be supported and encouraged by the government. The state and private capital were to make a joint effort to promote industrialisation. In a lecture in 1934, he said: 'We in Mysore have always been alive to the economic functions of government and we have endeavoured . . . to aid and encourage the growth and starting of new enterprises by private capitalists.'[18]

[16] Ibid., p. 124.
[17] Hettne, op. cit., p. 282.
[18] Dewan's address, *Proceedings of the Mysore Representative Assembly* (P.M.R.A.) October 1935, p. 2.

In some industrial enterprises like the expansion of the Iron Works at Bhadravati, which were initiated by the government, private capital was invited to cooperate. So, although the main initiative lay with the government, private entrepreneurs were encouraged in a number of ways. The basic idea was that the state in due time should withdraw from the economic field and leave it open for private capital. One important goal was economic self-reliance, and therefore, a large number of industries were started. At the same time, people in Mysore were exhorted to buy only Mysorean goods. The Mysore Paper Mills were started in 1936. In 1937, a small ammonium sulphate plant was established outside Mysore city at Belagula. It was India's first private fertilizer plant. The production of steel, cement and paper reached a peak around 1940 (Table 3.3). When the War broke out, whatever productive capacity Mysore had was well utilised. All indigenous industries expanded, to the extent that they were not dependent on imported inputs.[19] As a direct result of the War, production of ammunition increased considerably, and the Hindustan Aircraft industry was started. The silk industry also benefited from the manufacture of parachute cloth and silk sewing thread for War purposes.[20]

By the late 1930s and early 1940s, the Congress movement in the country had gained momentum and had also spread to Mysore State. Mirza Ismail resigned in 1941 and the Quit India Movement

Table 3.3
Production of Selected Industries (tons), 1935–41

Year	Steel*	Cement	Chemicals+	Paper
1935–36	371	—	—	—
1936–37	9,524	—	—	—
1937–38	18,493	—	—	—
1938–39	23,639	16,617	—	1,364
1939–40	26,796	24,298	1,811	3,733
1940–41	30,298	23,543	8,525	4,090

Source: *Statistical Abstract of Mysore*, 1951, p. 141 and supplement, p. 102, cited in Hettne, op. cit., p. 294.

* Bars and angles

+ Sulphuric acid and ammonium sulphate

See *Reports of the Department of Industries and Commerce* (R.D.I.C.), Mysore, 1939–40.

[20] R.D.I.C. Mysore, 1940–41.

took place in 1942. Owing to this political upsurge, there was little impetus to industrialisation, and industrial production stagnated during the period 1942–47. Also, no industrial expansion took place during the War.[21]

However, a favourable climate for industrialisation, scientific and technical progress, and private enterprise had been created in Mysore State prior to Independence. The demand for trained personnel grew because developing industries like gold, textiles, sandalwood, silk, steel and iron works needed technical manpower. The State government, after Independence, did not have adequate funds to support educational institutions which could train the required number of professionals. Thus, for several years, Karnataka had only one government engineering college, the B.D.T. College at Davangere, and one university college, the Visvesvaraya College of Engineering, Bangalore. A regional engineering college at Suratkhal was added later. Therefore, where state efforts were inadequate, private enterprise entered to fill the gaps in the sphere of professional education.

In the case of engineering and technical education, some private experiments were made in the form of B.M.S. College Bangalore (1946) and the National Institute of Engineering, Mysore (1950), but these were converted into grants-in-aid colleges in a period of five to 10 years. The first private engineering institution was set up by the Pais of Manipal in the form of the Manipal Institute of Technology (1957).

In the latter half of 1950, the central government, in order to supplement the efforts of the States, decided to invite private enterprise to set up technical institutions. On the recommendations of the All India Council for Technical Education (A.I.C.T.E.), the central government laid down some principles vis-à-vis private enterprise, the more important of which are given below.

The institutions established by private enterprise would be subject to financial, administrative and academic discipline to ensure that they did not lead to chaos. Also the private agencies and the state governments concerned would provide 50 per cent of the maintenance expenditure for the initial five years in mutually agreed proportions. The State governments and private agencies would bear the entire maintenance expenditure after five years.

[21] See Hettne, op. cit., p. 293.

What was most important was the fact that the institutions thus established would not charge any capitation or donation fee from students. Admissions would be made strictly on merit, subject to such reservations as would be laid down by the state government concerned. Each proposal for the setting up of a technical institution was to be examined by the A.I.C.T.E. which spelled out the number of students for each course, the courses of study in each college, the standards of instructional facilities to be provided, financial estimates, administration and management, and other aspects. The establishment of the institution was to be approved by the central government on the basis of the report of an expert committee.

As a result of this policy, private enterprise played a responsible role in building up the system of technical education in India. During the Second, Third and Fourth Plan periods, 35 engineering colleges were set up by private agencies.[22]

Thus, the pace had been set for privatisation in professional education, and this trend of private enterprise in technical education received government support. As this system developed, many groups, including dominant castes, minority communities and private entrepreneurs, began to venture whole hog into the field of education using it as a business enterprise with the profit motive in mind. The system then developed its own peculiar features. This kind of enterprise being totally private received no government aid or assistance, and developed in Karnataka not only in the sphere of technical education, which has already been discussed, but also in the sphere of medical education.

The rapid pace of industrialisation and the consequent modernisation also led to lucrative opportunities for medical personnel. As mentioned earlier, in Old Mysore there was only one medical college, the Mysore Medical College established in 1924, and most Mysoreans had to go to Madras for medical education. When various groups and private entrepreneurs set up engineering colleges in Karnataka, their attention was also drawn towards the setting up of medical colleges. When the Kasturba Medical College was established in Manipal in 1953, there seemed an apparent need for medical education in Karnataka. Besides the solitary government

[22] L.S. Chandrakant, *Private Enterprise in Engineering Education*, Indian Institute of Management, Bangalore, 1986.

medical college in Mysore, the other government colleges came up only after the Kasturba Medical College was set up. The Bangalore Medical College was established in 1954, the Karnataka Medical College at Hubli in 1959 and the medical college at Bellary came up in 1961. As of 1992 the total number of State medical colleges established in Karnataka since 1961 was four, while many more private colleges were in the process of being set up. The private initiative has to be seen in its socio-economic context where the emerging castes and classes have been aspiring for greater prestige and power for themselves. At the same time, this inititative has been developing as an entrepreneurship, and no entrepreneurship functions without profit. An examination of this kind of enterprise follows.

An Enterprise

It is a known fact that engineering and medical education are heavily subsidised in government and government-aided institutions. For instance, in the case of engineering courses at the Indian Institutes of Technology, as pointed out in Chandrakant's study, the per capita expenditure at the first degree level in 1986 was over Rs. 50,000 per year.[23] This did not include the huge capital investment on buildings and equipment. The annual tuition fee collected from each student was only Rs. 250. The capital expenditure on an engineering college conducting first degree courses in engineering and technology was about Rs. 8–10 crore, and the recurring expenditure was between Rs. 80 lakh and Rs. 1 crore for providing full-scale instructional and infrastructural facilities and staff according to the standards prescribed by the A.I.C.T.E.[24] The Union Minister of State for Human Resources Development of the National Front Government also stated in 1990 that setting up a properly equipped engineering college meant an outlay of Rs.10 crore, and a recurring expenditure of Rs.12,000 per annum per student.[25]

[23] Ibid.
[24] Information provided by the Director, Technical Education, Government of Karnataka, 1988.
[25] See *Indian Express*, New Delhi, 6 August 1990.

When these cost factors are carefully considered vis-à-vis the increasing rate of qualified students seeking admission to engineering colleges, it would seem extremely difficult for any government, central or State, to set up more and more colleges to meet the growing demand and to provide the necessary resources.

The important issue in this case is: How does a private enterprise generate and manage such financial resources involved in setting up and running an engineering college? It is obvious that unless it has the backing of a big endowment or some other source of funds, the enterprise will have to raise all the money from the students seeking admission. In operational terms, the process would have to be somewhat like the one described in the following paragraphs.

An engineering college would take about five years to establish itself with all the required infrastructural facilities, and an initial outlay of Rs. 10 crore with an additional sum for recurring expenditure. It is evident that not many private groups would be willing to invest such a large amount of money at one go. If they were to rely on getting this from capitation fees and tuition fees from students during this period, it would mean that, assuming 250 admissions, they would need to collect about Rs. 80,000 per student, and Rs. 10,000 per student per year to take care of the recurring expenditure. It is difficult to imagine a college that has not yet been established to attract students with such a high level of capitation and tuition fees. Therefore, in actual practice, different colleges adopt varying strategies to overcome the initial hurdle. And in this regard, medical colleges are not very different. By and large, the institutions extend the time span of development to as many as eight to ten years. They also save on providing infrastructural facilities like laboratory and workshop equipment, hostels for students, and housing facilities for the staff in order to minimise the capital cost. The admission intake is also raised to much more than that prescribed by the government. All this is evident from the fact that the capitation fee in many engineering colleges varies from Rs. 50,000 to 1 lakh, and in medical colleges, between Rs. 2 to 5 lakhs.

Similar methods are adopted to bring down the recurring expenditure, so that they are able to sustain themselves through the annual tuition fees ranging from Rs. 5,000 to Rs. 7,000. These would include economising on materials and stores pertaining to students' practical work and student amenities and a lower teacher–student ratio.

Thus, the colleges concerned find sufficient ways to gather adequate profits for themselves, and this is where providing for professional education has become a flourishing big business. The profitability aspect is one major factor that explains the phenomenal growth of capitation fee institutions in Karnataka.

While it was not possible to obtain documented evidence regarding the amount of profits that are collected by these private colleges,[26] sufficient proof was provided by the students and the faculty members through the questionnaires and personal interviews conducted during the course of this study. Damle in his study on the growth of education in Dakshina Kannada has observed that private enterprise has shifted its interest towards the expansion of technical education in this region and the 'profit motive seems to be operative in such a shift in emphasis'. [27] Some debates in the Karnataka Legislative Assembly have also taken place around complaints from time to time that capitation fees or donations were being collected in excess of the limits imposed by the State government.[28] In the case of the Gulbarga Medical College, it was stated by Mr. D.B. Kalmankar in the House in July 1972 that 88 M.L.A.s had categorically observed 'that over and above capitation fee they are taking illegal gratifications and the Chairman has amassed huge wealth by such methods . . . .' Although Mr. H. Siddaveerappa, the then Minister of Health, said that all moneys received by the society towards the management of the college 'including capitation fee, benevolences, donations or in any other form through the *golka*[29] installed for the purpose, etc. should be properly receipted and accounted for'.[30] It was a fact verified by

[26] The balance sheets procured from one such insitution, for instance, did not indicate the amount collected through capitation fees, although the management had been collecting them. Hence, a comparative study of investments and profits was difficult. Some colleges were being supported by religious *mutts*, but *mutt* accounts were not open to public scrutiny.

[27] C.B. Damle, 'Growth of Education in Karnataka: A Case Study,' *Bhartiya Samajik Chintan*, Vol. XII, No. 1–2, March–June 1989, pp. 28–52. This paper was also presented at the XII Indian Social Science Congress, 14–17 July 1987, Mysore.

[28] *Karnataka Legislative Assembly Debates*, 11 July 1972, p. 106. This debate pertains to the collection of capitation fees by the medical college at Gulbarga run by the Hyderabad Karnataka Education Society, pp. 105–10.

[29] A collection box where money is collected as donation

[30] *Karnataka Legislative Assembly Debates*, op. cit., p. 108.

several students that capitation fee payments were cash transactions and receipts were not always issued for the full amount taken by the college management or authorities. It was in this context, that Mr.B. Subbaiah Shetty stated in the House that in practice 'the receipts are passed in the name of the Societies which run the Institutions and the moneys are taken to the accounts of the Societies, which are not subject to audit by the Department of Public Instruction.'[31] The capitation fee fixed by the State government was generally based on the estimate of the income and expenditure statements furnished by the private colleges. The government examined the financial gap in each case and stipulated the capitation fee amount to meet this gap.

In this context, the Belgaum Medical College figures were discussed in the Assembly Debates on 24 June 1977, when Mr. P.N. Bangi called the attention of the Minister of Health to the irregularities and malpractices in private medical colleges in the State. One of the conditions for granting of permission to start private medical colleges was that all capitation fees or donations should be received only through crossed cheques and properly accounted for to 'prevent acceptance of hush money'.[32] However, at the Belgaum Medical College, it was found from the report of the enquiry officers appointed by the government that the Dean of the college denied having collected capitation fee of more than Rs. 35,000 (fixed by the government), while the students and their parents wrote to the government that 'the Dean himself assured a seat if they gave Rs. 40,000 over and above the Rs. 35,000 already given and that no receipt would be given as per the decision of the Society.'[33] The authorities also refused to reveal full facts about advance reservations and selection of students they had made prior to the date fixed by the government. It was also reported by the enquiry officers that the K.L.E. Society maintained a *golka* to collect hush money and had admittedly 'collected lakhs in the name of donation. This has no legal sanction . . . . The names of donors and the amount donated are not recorded and accounted

---

[31] Calling attention to exploitation by private educational institutions in Bangalore and Mysore, *Karnataka Legislative Assembly Debates*, 17 June 1978, p. 363.

[32] Statement by Mr. H.M. Channabasappa, Minister of Health, *Karnataka Legislative Assembly Debates*, 24 June 1977, p. 257.

[33] Ibid.

for.' This 'dubious act' of the Society 'offends the provisions of the Societies Registration Act and also contravenes the essential condition of granting permission to start the Medical College . . . .'[34]

The Enquiry Officer gave a statement of the date on which the *golka* was cleared and the amount cleared from January to May 1977, and the period when the majority of candidates were interviewed for selection. The timings of the interviews for reservation of seats and the amounts of moneys collected in the *golka* were revealing enough. They were as follows:[35]

Date of opening and clearing money collected in the *golka*	Moneys cleared from the *golka* (Rs.)
15.1.1977	50,000
2.3.1977	3,50,000
9.3.1977	2,93,000
12.3.1977	1,95,000
17.3.1977	2,12,000
31.3.1977	50,000
15.4.1977	1,25,000
25.4.1977	25,000
27.5.1977	20,631
Total	13,20,631

It was seen that it was during the period of selections that a sum of about Rs. 13.21 lakh was recovered from the *golka*. The enquiry report stated:

In the absence of proper accounts showing the name of the donor, amount received and receipts given, the transactions lead to grave suspicion and lack of honesty of purpose . . . . It would be very difficult to believe that such huge sums of money would be put into the *golkas* by people in such short periods for the mere love of education in the country.

Summing up, the Enquiry Officer observed that all was not well with the working of the Society and the medical college.[36]

[34] All quotes from the *Karnataka Legislative Assembly Debates*, 24 June 1977, p. 260.

[35] Ibid., p. 262.

[36] Ibid., p. 263.

There thus seems adequate evidence to prove that behind the altruistic claims of private managements in running educational institutions, there were clear entrepreneurial profit motives.

For an entrepreneur seeking immediate returns, an entry into the sphere of education is certainly not inspired by philanthropic zeal alone. In spite of other equally or more lucrative industries he may be running, he may still venture into the educational 'business'. Any other enterprise would involve greater risk, raising of loans, some entrepreneurial skills, and know-how. However, to start a private college in Karnataka, a few people can get together, form a Society, get the required licence, hire a building, and on the basis of caste or community, get permission and recognition for the college. In fact, education thus becomes a safe 'no-risk, assured-return' venture. A college expands from receipts and also yields profits.

In the sphere of higher education, the rich who have been to public schools have shown a desire to continue their elitist education and have been willing to pay more for it. Private bodies financing such institutions have also seen them as investments or profit propositions, and therefore, have granted admissions to those students who have had the capacity to purchase seats. There have been several colleges run by entrepreneurs. Also, the composition of the management in the institutions studied show that 30 per cent of the board members were either industrialists or businessmen.

Even though there have been some efforts on the part of the State government to regulate the 'commercialisation' of education through this kind of private enterprise, the system has continued to grow because of the tacit support it has received from the government. Ministers have even stated that these colleges were an asset to the State because they earned foreign exchange by giving admission to foreign students and non-resident Indians and earned revenue by attracting students from other states of India.

Agrarian Interests

In the last chapter we explained how state policies helped the rise and consolidation of rich peasants as a powerful force in rural areas. Their leadership made use of its political and economic power and prestige to gain control over education. Empirical evidence on the management process, which we will present in Chapter 5, has shown that the capitation fee system in Karnataka has been largely controlled by an elite segment of the two dominant landed groups—the Vokkaligas and the Lingayats. The two groups have tried to exercise control in the educational sphere in order to influence public policy-making and to strengthen their dominance and hold in Karnataka society.

The growth of the capitation fee system being linked with the cause of economic development presents a paradox. On the one hand, while the system has been an outcome of the development in the State, limited possibilities of further investments in agriculture has led to the growth of this enterprise. Rich peasants have begun looking for other avenues of investment for more profits. One of the reasons for this has been that only 20 per cent of Karnataka's total cropped area has enjoyed irrigation facilities. With as much as 80 per cent comprising dry land, the success of the State's agricultural operations has relied heavily on favourable monsoons. For instance, after four years of continuous scarcity of rainfall, including 1985–86, when the drought was the worst recorded in the previous three decades, the monsoon again failed in 1987. By July 1987, due to deficit rains, sowing had been completed in only 43.78 lakh hectares as against the total normal *kharif* area of 69.95 lakh hectares.[37] Under such circumstances, where fortunes of agriculturalists get tied to the vagaries of monsoon, the richer sections of the peasantry have looked for alternative channels of investment, and the sphere of higher education has thus become a new avenue for surplus investment.

Amongst those dominant castes who were managing private colleges were several rich peasants and landowners who were also sending their wards to such institutions. They were thus investing in the growth of this kind of education to create a skill structure for the industry, to have an expanded professional cadre of their own caste members, and perhaps more importantly, to also reproduce capital and make profit. Therefore, some of the initial investment required for starting such colleges came from a part of the agrarian surplus generated in the countryside. The fact that the largest number of capitation fee institutions were managed by societies

[37] Government of Karnataka, 'Scarcity Conditions in Karnataka,' Memorandum presented to the Government of India by the Government of Karnataka, Bangalore, August 1987.

and trusts representing landed groups further corroborates this. The data collected on the management board members, as we will examine in Chapter 5, also reveals that 20 per cent of them were rich agriculturalists or landlords.

Political Dimensions

The capitation fee phenomenon with its social, economic and educational ramifications has its political dimension as well. We have seen how in a parliamentary democracy the demand for such institutions stems from various interest groups. Therefore, as a matter of course, every State government has had to observe this development sympathetically. Whenever the government has yielded to pressures from one caste or community group, it has found it difficult to ward off pressures from other groups.

As we have seen, amongst the private groups influencing higher professional education in Karnataka the powerful rural leadership has come principally from the dominant castes representing the rich peasantry. This group, owing to its overwhelming numerical strength in electoral politics, has emerged as a strong political force bidding successfully for a share in political, economic and social power at all levels. It has thus also played an important role in deciding the educational policies and their implementation in the State.

The expansion of higher education has also served a political purpose for the emergent rural leadership. A new university, a medical or an engineering college, a polytechnic, or an agricultural college in the *mofussil* areas, are all simultaneously a manifestation of, and an addition to, the regional political influence, besides bringing educational facilities nearer home to members of their constituencies. In this game, institutions of higher professional education have been established in Karnataka without adequate planning or preparation. As a result, several engineering and medical colleges, with extremely inadequate or even no workshop and hospital facilities, but charging high capitation fees, were set up in Karnataka. The capitation fee system thus became an avenue for gaining dividends in terms of political control and power. And as the Rudolphs have remarked, 'both directly as a political resource for party cadres, supporters and patronage, and indirectly as an instrument of partisan prestige, benefaction and influence, private colleges have played an important role in local politics.'[38]

In Chapter 5, through empirical evidence we will show how several local members of the Legislative Assembly having links with the State government have been involved in the management of such colleges. About 20 per cent of the management board members in the colleges studied were politicians. Many amongst them were also rich landowners, industrialists or businessmen. This has revealed the rural rich–business–politics nexus operating in the domain of education. Local members of the Legislative Assembly, when they start a college, ostensibly argue that their aim is to serve the people of the area. But just as caste- and community-based colleges do not necessarily cater only to students belonging to their caste, area-based colleges also do not necessarily cater to the needs of the students in a particular area. In one legislative assembly debate in July 1978, a Lingayat member, Mr. M.S.R. Bommai, argued that when the people of a particular area came forward with funds and lands to help set up a private college, they should be helped. He stated that, in fact, for starting the medical college at Gulbarga, Rs. 50 lakh was collected, and similarly, for setting up the medical college at Belgaum, donations were collected with the ultimate object of helping that area. According to him: 'Government may consider giving whatever help is possible for the people of that area. Ten per cent may be suggested to the societies. If the society people allot those seats to persons who are outside the State, the very purpose for which the society were started is forgotten.'[39] To this, the then Chief Minister, Mr. Devraj Urs had replied that the societies were free to allot their seats the way they wanted and there was little that the government could do by way of giving seats to the people of the area. From this it becomes clear that any political leader in order to capture votes in his area may announce the opening of a new medical or engineering college and may even succeed in getting one established. But such colleges keep their seats open to all who have the capacity to pay on a 'first-come-first-served' basis. They are not really interested

---

[38] S.H. Rudolph and L.I. Rudolph, *Education and Politics in India: Studies in Organisation, Society and Polity*, Oxford University Press, Delhi, 1972, p. 23.

[39] See *Legislative Assembly Debates*, Karnataka, 13 July 1978, Vidhan Soudha, Bangalore, pp. 337–41.

in serving the needs of that district or area, and definitely not those of the poorer sections who are unable to afford professional education for their sons and daughters, but who nevertheless would have voted for the area leader. One purpose of sanctioning private colleges by a government in power has been to garner votes from various communities and regions by granting colleges to them. In June 1985, six ruling party M.L.A.s from the Kolar district demanded the establishment of either a medical college or an engineering college in the area on the plea that 'except this district all others in the State have engineering colleges' and that 'all along Kolar district had been exploited in many respects, but till today no benefit worth mentioning had been provided.'[40]

Noting that Kolar district had returned two CPM candidates and all Janata nominees in the Assembly elections, the Janata M.L.A.s said that the people had hoped that the political favour shown to the ruling party would be reciprocated. They felt that since most of the other districts in the State had either medical or technical colleges while Kolar district did not have any, there was all the more reason to establish professional colleges in the region. By October 1985, the Karnataka government had sanctioned a capitation fee private medical college in Kolar. In 1987, Kolar had two private engineering colleges and also the unaided private Sri Devraj Urs Medical College.[41] The promoters of these new colleges have often been local caste leaders who are able to mobilise votes for the ruling party. 'An educational entrepreneur prefers to found his own educational institution in an area where he has political ambitions,' and also because in his own institutions he can 'develop a general body, managing committee and teaching staff that is overwhelmingly loyal to him'.[42]

Functioning as the system of capitation fee does within a parliamentary democracy, it has also been noticed that whenever there has been a public outcry against the system, the same government that had supported the process sympathetically has tried to regulate it. Hence, sometimes the government has declared that it would ban the system as the Janata government did when it came to power in Karnataka. At other times, it has initiated ways to

[40] *Deccan Herald*, 19 June 1985.

[41] Information collected from the Directorate of Technical Education, Government of Karnataka, Bangalore, November 1987.

[42] S.H. Rudolph and L.I. Rudolph, op. cit., p. 104.

regulate it. When the former Karnataka Chief Minister, Rama-krishna Hegde, could not succeed in abolishing the system of capitation fee, he tried to regulate the fee structure, and even began defending the system by stating that such colleges would 'cater to the needs of other States'.[43] He added that they would give a boost to the export of talent and technical and professional skills of Karnataka,[44] and that even if black money was used in setting up such colleges, it was a means of unearthing black money.[45]

The colleges continued to increase in number though the State government was reminded time and again that engineering and medical professions had been 'commercialised' and that doctors and engineers had become, as an M.L.A. put it, 'mercenaries of this dirty system'.[46] A majority of such medical colleges were not even recognised by the Medical Council of India, although ministers continued to give assurances that the State government would do 'everything necessary to safeguard the prescribed standard and secure recognition'.[47]

The State government which took the lead in allowing private entrepreneurs to set up capitation fee colleges, in fact, 'responded to the insistent demands of influential urban middle-class and rural notable constituents for more colleges . . . .'[48] The Rudolphs have further added that educational entrepreneurs and 'sect and caste benefactors' thus took advantage of the situation. While 'motives of profit, influence and political power' conspired to accelerate the establishment of these colleges, parents who were keen that their children should have more secure incomes and a better social status which they hoped the degrees would provide 'fuelled the demand for seats'.

We thus find that the State process and the capitation fee system have intermingled with many contradictory characteristics. On the one hand, there have been the ostensible intentions of political leaders promoting equality in education, and on the other, have

[43] *Indian Express*, Bangalore, 26 June 1985.
[44] *The Hindu*, Madras, 30 October 1986.
[45] *The Times of India*, Bangalore, 9 October 1985.
[46] *Karnataka Legislative Assembly Debates*, 30 July 1981, p. 402.
[47] Assurance given by Mr. H. Siddaveerappa, Minister of Health, *Karnataka Legislative Assembly Debates*, 12 August 1974, p. 38.
[48] S.H. Rudolph and L.I. Rudolph, *In Pursuit of Lakshmi: The Political Economy of the Indian State*, Orient Longman, Hyderabad, 1987, p. 296.

been the pragmatic needs of getting support from the more dominant castes and other groups so as not to negate their own interests. Political leaders have publicly criticised the phenomenon of capitation fee, while at the same time have lent their tacit support to it. We find that such colleges have continued to function as instruments of vote mobilisation and patronage, and groups and societies like the *mutts* running these colleges have contributed to elections.[49]

To sum up, we have seen that a combination of economic, political and social forces have led to the rise of the capitation fee phenomenon. The system emerged as an assertion of caste and community rights, and gradually acquired an entrepreneurial character. Its emergence may be explained as partly a reaction to reservations and partly to beat the inadequacy of the state system vis-à-vis professional education. It has also provided an avenue for surplus generated by rich peasants. Steadily, this 'business' has become linked with not only countryside surplus but also industrial capital, and several private entrepreneurs have entered the field. The phenomenon has unravelled the new role of caste as an instrument of power; it has become a dynamic channel through which caste politics, particularly that of the dominant landed castes, gets manifested. In the next chapter we will analyse the State government's policies towards higher education and its interaction with private professional colleges.

[49] Information provided by the District Commissioners of Tumkur and Chikmagalur, July 1988.

4

POLICY TOWARDS PRIVATE COLLEGES

In the previous chapter we have discussed the reasons for the phenomenal growth of private professional education in Karnataka since its inception in the 1950s. In this chapter we will examine the policy of the Karnataka government vis-à-vis such colleges which has resulted in their continued growth.

In this context the questions that need to be examined are: How has the State government allowed such an expansion of private colleges? To what extent has it been able to maintain control over them? Also, in what way are the universities whose responsibility it is to maintain the desired academic standards accountable for the performance of the colleges affiliated to them?

These questions imply a whole range of issues, such as policy perspectives in respect of engineering and medical personnel, and planning for the education system; having a well-structured procedure for approving private enterprise to start a professional institution; monitoring and evaluating the progress of institutions in respect of buildings, equipment, faculty and other institutional facilities; and maintaining educational standards. The questions raised also involve aspects like accountability of the institution for satisfactory performance; identification of the weaknesses of the colleges; and forms of control and coordination exercised by the State government and affiliating universities. At the same time, we have to consider the socio-economic factors, discussed in the last chapter, that have led to the emergence of the capitation fee phenomenon and their impact on policy formulation and the strategies of different political parties.

A significant issue for this analysis is the level of interaction between the government and the private colleges. It would therefore be useful to go into some details regarding the role of the state and the university at the level of: registering an educational trust or a society, granting affiliation to these colleges, fixing the intake of students, appointing teachers, laying down courses, and conducting examinations.

Weak Government Control and Poor University Supervision

While registering an educational institution, the authority has to give due regard to the 'need for providing educational facilities to the people in the locality or for the type of education intended to be provided by the institutions', and also ensure that 'there is adequate financial provision for continued and efficient maintenance of the institution prescribed by the competent authority'.[1] For granting recognition to an institution, a scrutiny has to be carried out which consists of an examination of the standing or status of the entrepreneurs in education,[2] their resources in respect of land, buildings, furniture, equipment and staff, and financial backing for establishing and running an engineering college, location of the institution, courses to be conducted, and the number of admissions to be made. After such a scrutiny, the proposal has to be approved by the State government, and only thereafter, does the university concerned step in to decide whether or not affiliation should be given. A Local Inspection Committee has to be appointed by the university. University bodies like the Academic Council and the Syndicate or the Senate have to go through the Committee's report, and it has to be with the approval of these bodies that a college can be granted affiliation to a university. The university is

[1] Government of Karnataka, *Report of the Joint Select Committee on the Karnataka Education Bill, 1983*, Karnataka Legislature, Bangalore, p. 42.

[2] Ibid., p. 47.

required to lay down the syllabus and curriculum and also conduct the examinations.[3]

In actual practice however, a great deal seemed to be lacking in these otherwise impressive procedures. Neither the State government nor any university in Karnataka had laid down any specific norms vis-à-vis the instructional and other facilities required for private professional colleges and the manner of phasing out these facilities over a four to five year period for building up the institution to adequate standards.[4] What an Inspection Committee would inspect before a college becomes operational was also not clear. Moreover, since private enterprise had to depend on capitation fees and other kinds of donations for both capital and recurring expenditure, any examination of their financial strength even before the institutions had actually started functioning became meaningless.

With the approval of the institutions, the State government ceased to have any further responsibility for them. The Directorates of Technical and Medical Education in Karnataka have exercised almost negligible control over the private unaided engineering and medical colleges, except for filling the government quota of seats.[5] In fact, these two full-fledged independent departments have only been responsible for selection of students for admission to government colleges (and in the case of engineering institutions, also to government-aided colleges) and their inspection. Even the inspection has been limited only to the extent of ensuring that the government grants were not misutilised.[6]

The Directorates have given maintenance grants, building grants and equipment grants to aided and government colleges. However, they have not had the authority or responsibility to administer all technical and medical institutions which were recognised by the

[3] Information provided in personal interviews with Dr. Nanjundappa, Vice-Chancellor, Bangalore University, Bangalore, November 1987, and Dr. Shankar Narayan, former Vice-Chancellor, Bangalore University, November 1987.

[4] L.S. Chandrakant, *Private Enterprise in Engineering Education*, Indian Institute of Management, Bangalore, 1986, pp. 41–42.

[5] Personal interview with the Director, Medical Education, and the Joint Director, Technical Education, Government of Karnataka, Bangalore, June 1986 and November 1987.

[6] *Deccan Herald*, Bangalore, 11 February 1983.

government, irrespective of whether they did or did not receive grants.[7] The total intake in government institutions has been much lower as compared to that in private colleges. In 1982–83 there was a 9 per cent intake in government engineering colleges in Karnataka, 28 per cent in aided colleges, and a major share of 63 per cent was in private unaided colleges.[8] The trend in medical colleges has been almost similar where the major intake was in private colleges.

The unaided private colleges have made full use of the government machinery and university infrastructure for running their colleges and have not been accountable to the Directorates in any way.[9] In the case of both government and private professional colleges, it has been the university which has prescribed and prepared the syllabi and scheme of studies, conducted the examinations and finally awarded the degrees to their students. The very fact that even private colleges sought affiliation to the university has made it incumbent on them to respect the University Act and Statute. Again, the fact that they claimed recognition by the State government has made them subject to scrutiny by the government. While it has been the responsibility of the Directorates of Technical and Medical Education to inspect these colleges and ensure that they had the necessary infrastructure, these bodies in actual practice have not concerned themselves with how the private colleges were managed or whether they provided adequate instructional and infrastructural facilities.

Although the Karnataka Educational Bill (1983) stated that all money collected or granted or allotted to the local authority by or under this Act should be 'expended for educational purposes'[10] by the college management, in practice, no account has been taken by the government of how much capitation fee, tuition fee and other levies were collected from the students, and how all that money

---

[7] Information given in a personal interview with the Director, Medical Education, and the Joint Director, Technical Education, Government of Karnataka, Bangalore.

[8] See Government of Karnataka, *White Paper on Professional Colleges and Institutions*, Department of Education and Youth Services and Department of Health and Family Welfare, March 1983, pp. 2–3.

[9] Vatsala Vedantam, 'Directorate Sans Direction', *Deccan Herald*, Bangalore, 14 February 1983.

[10] Government of Karnataka, *The Karnataka Educational Bill, 1983*, Karnataka Legislative Assembly, Bangalore, 7th Assembly, Third Session, Chapter VII, p. 39.

was utilised or accounted for. The government also has not concerned itself with the maintenance of adequate educational standards, and in fact, has passed on this onus to the universities to
which the colleges are affiliated. In the case of medical colleges,
some government nominees have been members of the college
governing council. Some routine inspections by State officials also
took place periodically because government hospitals were attached
to these colleges. However, in cases where State officials were sent
for the appointment of teachers or for the review of the budget,
strictly speaking, 'there was no quarrel between them and the
private management.'[11]

We have so far discussed the administrative lapses owing to non-
adherence to various norms. However, administrative decisions
based on various pressures have also led to a violation of norms.
For all private medical and engineering colleges, affiliation to a
university was granted on a year-to-year basis till the colleges were
made permanent. Each year an inspection committee was sent by
the university to the colleges to report on the infrastructural and
instructional facilities provided by the institutions and whether
affiliation to the university should be extended.[12] This gave significant control and authority to the university over private colleges.
But in practice, this has become a ritual, as was observed in the
course of this study. For even where the state of affairs in a college
left much to be desired in terms of basic facilities (the computer
departments in some colleges had no computers, the laboratories
and libraries were inadequately equipped), the colleges had been
granted affiliation by the university. And it was unusual to come
across a case where the university had withdrawn affiliation.

The Acts of some universities, like the Bangalore University,
provide for two university representatives in the managing committee or governing council of private institutions, the aim being to
ensure that the management of the affairs of the colleges is satis-
factorily conducted. In medical colleges there have been two government nominees in the governing council—Deputy Secretary,
Department of Health, and Director, Medical Education. But
they have not been able to perform effectively and important

[11] Personal interview with the Honorary Secretary, J.J. Medical College, Davangere, June 1986.
[12] Interview with the Vice-Chancellor Bangalore University, November 1987.

decisions have in fact been taken by the promoters of the institutions.[13]

In the prevalent set-up, the universities in Karnataka have also seemed unequal to the task of supervising the manner in which private institutions have been functioning. Their authority and autonomy have been so circumscribed that they have hardly been able to do anything without the approval of the State government.

Let us examine this aspect in the context of the Karnataka State Universities Act, 1976 (also known as the Common Universities Act). One of the main aims of the Act was to replace the acts of different universities (Mysore, Bangalore and Karnataka) by one single unified legislation that would introduce a common system of governance and administration in all the concerned universities. However, an important effect of the Act was to curtail the powers of the highest policy-making and executive authorities in the universities, particularly of the Senate and the Syndicate. It also resulted in changing their composition so as to reduce the weightage given to academic elements drawn from within, thereby diminishing the role of the Vice-Chancellor as the de-facto executive head, and vesting far greater powers in the Chancellor. In this way university administration was centralised to an exceptional degree, thus widening the scope for intervention by the State government, particularly the ruling party in matters relating to the management of universities. The Act also gave powers to the State government to scrutinise all decisions taken by the universities. Every statute, ordinance and regulation had not only to receive the assent of the Chancellor, but had also to be submitted to him through the State government.[14] The lack of autonomy of universities has not been restricted to Karnataka alone. It has been an all-India trend. However, one of the main reasons for poor university supervision has been this lack of autonomy. In the process, the students, according to Sumit Sarkar, have been the worst sufferers, 'with diverse and declining teaching standards, higher fee',[15] and the like.

[13] Personal interview with the Deputy Secretary, Department of Health, Government of Karnataka, Bangalore, June 1986.

[14] See *Universities in Karnataka, Report of the Review Commission*, (Chairman: K.N. Raj), Bangalore, 1980, pp. 20–22.

[15] See Sumit Sarkar, 'Autonomy for Whom?,' *Social Scientist*, Vol. 17, Nos. 9–10, September–October 1989, pp. 27–33. Also see Manoranjan Mohanty, 'University and the State,' *P.U.C.L. Bulletin*, Vol. 2, No. 2, February 1982, pp. 8–10.

The Act of 1976 granted authority to the State government to grant affiliation to colleges, and the university had a negligible role to play in this regard. This power has been used by the State government to sanction an affiliation even when there has been opposition on sound academic grounds from the university concerned. For instance, in 1979–80, nine private engineering colleges were allowed to be established in one year.[16] Very often this has happened because the ruling party has wanted to patronise and strengthen its support base. Thus we see a political process in operation behind such decisions. Affiliation of colleges should actually be an academic matter, and as was stressed by the Education Commission more than two decades ago, it should be granted only by the universities, though in consultation with the State government since such an affiliation could lead to financial liabilities for the government. But, as we have stated earlier, with the 1976 Act, the State government was able to tighten its hold over universities in Karnataka. They became merely recommendatory bodies, which also implied that the State government was not bound by a university recommendation.

In fact, the universities in Karnataka have not formulated any specific policy for engineering and medical colleges to guide or direct their responsibilities in these spheres.[17] Engineering and medical science have been regarded as only two of the many disciplines within the university system and have received only as much attention as any other discipline in the university. The large number of colleges affiliated to the universities in the State have made it almost impossible for a university to study individually the institutions attached to it.[18] Besides, the universities, being mainly examination-oriented organisations for the award of degrees, have hardly been in a position, expertise- and experience-wise, to provide advice, guidance or assistance to engineering and medical colleges in institution building and development. In the event, the colleges have been left to fend for themselves.[19]

Thus, the reasons are clear why the universities have not been able to exercise effective control over the working of private

[16] *Universities in Karnataka, Report of Review Commission*, op. cit., p. 23.
[17] Personal interview with Dr. Shankar Narayan, former Vice-Chancellor, Bangalore University, Manipal, November 1987.
[18] Ibid.
[19] See. L.S. Chandrakant, op. cit., p. 47.

colleges. While this is a reflection of administrative failure, it also reveals how the parties in power have been able to cleverly manipulate the education process in order to maintain and strengthen their support base.

Growth of Private Colleges: Government Legislation and the Fee Structure

We will now to go into some details regarding the kind of policies and legislation the Karnataka government has been formulating vis-à-vis private colleges. The State government's efforts to check the growth of these colleges have been half-hearted. While the legislations of various governments in the State only aimed at regulating the amount of capitation fee to be collected, the number of institutions based on this system steadily increased. In the pre-Devraj Urs period, specially in the 1960s, 10 private colleges were set up. Four of these medical colleges gradually developed and acquired a good reputation. They also came to be recognised by the Medical Council of India. These were: Kasturba Medical College, Manipal (1953), J.J.M. Medical College, Davangere (1965), J.N. Medical College, Belgaum (1963) and M.R. Medical College, Gulbarga (1963).

Devraj Urs Phase

The trend of private professional colleges continued under Devraj Urs. His government gave legitimacy to the capitation fee system by formulating a fee structure for private colleges. Nine more capitation fee based engineering colleges and three medical colleges were established. Urs also sanctioned some private aided colleges which, because the government gave a grant for recurring staff and other expenses, were allowed to have 20 per cent of their seats reserved for those who paid capitation fees. The remaining seats were to be filled on the basis of merit.

However, some effort was made by Urs' government to regulate the system of charging capitation fees. In 1977, it issued an order fixing this fee for admission to private engineering colleges and 20 per cent of the management quota of seats in aided engineering colleges (to control the charging of a higher rate of capitation fees) as follows:[20]

I. *Capitation Fee in Aided Engineering Colleges: 1977*
    (*a*) Karnataka domiciled students   Rs. 6,000
    (*b*) Other than Karnataka students   Rs. 12,000
II. *Capitation Fee in Private Engineering Colleges: 1977*
    (*a*) Karnataka domiciled students   Rs. 5,000
    (*b*) Other than Karnataka students   Rs. 10,000

Since the aided colleges were granted only 20 per cent seats as the management quota, they were allowed to charge a higher fee from students as compared to fees in private colleges where the management quota was higher. The government in the same order directed that 40 per cent of the seats in private engineering colleges would be filled by students chosen by the selection committee constituted by the government on a merit-cum-capitation basis. The remaining 60 per cent of the seats would be filled by the students selected by the management at their discretion.

Against this order, some of the managements of the private engineering colleges filed writ petitions and obtained stay orders. The State government kept the order in abeyance on the advice of the Advocate General. In the meantime, the capitation fee fixed by the government in respect of the 20 per cent of the seats in aided engineering colleges was implemented.[21]

In 1978, Urs' government stated that it had the major task of ensuring the satisfactory working of private medical colleges in the State, especially those enjoying clinical facilities in Government hospitals; namely: Kasturba Medical College, Mangalore; J.N. Medical College, Belgaum; J.J.M. Medical College, Davangere; and M.R. Medical College, Gulbarga. The government, at the same time, took a decision regarding admission of students to the first M.B.B.S. course in the government and private medical colleges in the State. The government also took a decision in regard

---

[20] Government of Karnataka, *White Paper on Professional Colleges and Institutions*, op. cit., pp. 19–20.
[21] Ibid.

to the system of capitation fee as related to private medical colleges which was as follows:[22]

1. Management seats   10%
2. Of the remaining 90% seats
     (a) Karnataka merit students not
         paying capitation   45%
     (b) Outside Karnataka students paying
         capitation fee of Rs. 50,000   22.5%
     (c) Non-resident Indians paying a fee
         of $15,000   22.5%

While this decision was quoted in the Legislative Assembly by Mr. M. Malappa, the then Minister for Health and Family Welfare, the Chief Minister, Devraj Urs, remarked: 'We have not been able to pay even a single paisa towards recurring charges to these institutions except the hospital facilities and nothing else is given to them. Either we allow them to run on the funds collected by them or we have to provide them from our source. It is also our responsibility to see that they run properly. You cannot ask the trustees to pay from their pockets. At least you must see that these colleges are run by the capitation fee.'[23] The protective tone of the State government towards the private professional colleges was obvious.

Gundu Rao Phase

It was under Gundu Rao's government that the expansion of private professional colleges in Karnataka took place at a rapid pace. Commercialisation of education took a sharp turn. There was enough academic protest, including the detailed Dr. K.N. Raj Commission Report on the working of the Mysore, Bangalore and Karnataka universities to prove that while admission rates had mounted and the Chief Minister had laid more foundation stones, the standards of professional engineering and medical education

[22] *Karnataka Legislative Assembly Debates*, Vidhan Soudha, Bangalore, 13 July 1978, pp. 337–41.
[23] Ibid.

had been falling rapidly.[24] The proliferation of private professional colleges under Gundu Rao continued, and within 3 years, during 1980–83, 13 colleges were established—one medical college and 12 engineering institutions. This was a significant phase in the expansion of capitation fee based colleges. The then Minister for Health, Mr. Abdul Samad, while replying to a question regarding government regulation on the capitation fee amount to be collected by the management, said that this amount would be 'absolutely under the discretion of the management, because the founding fathers of these institutions have dedicated themselves for the cause of these institutions and have worked hard for their improvement. In that background, the issue relating to collection of capitation fee comes entirely under the discretion of the management.'[25] This indicates the control exercised by the management.

It was openly stated by the Gundu Rao government members in the House that US $20,000 were to be collected from foreign students as capitation fees in private medical colleges to earn foreign exchange.[26] They were out to prove that their policy and reservation of seats vis-à-vis medical colleges was 'more progressive' compared to the policy of the previous government under Urs.[27]

Interestingly, while sanctioning a large number of private professional institutions, the State government under Gundu Rao also issued an order in September 1981 for the abolition of the system of charging capitation fees in private engineering colleges in a phased manner. Apparently, this may have happened because State elections were in the offing at that time. According to this order, the capitation fee was to be abolished within a period of five years in private colleges and within a year in aided colleges. Accordingly, the government directed that the distribution of seats between the merit pool and the management pool in the aided and un-aided engineering colleges should be regulated as indicated in Table 4.1.

It was decided that the management of both aided and un-aided colleges would fill 10 per cent of the seats at their discretion. The other seats in the management pool would be filled up by the selection committee appointed by the government on the basis of

---

[24] *Universities in Karnatka, Report of Review Commission*, 1980.
[25] *Karnataka Legislative Assembly Debates*, Bangalore, 9 July 1980, p. 173.
[26] Ibid.
[27] Ibid., pp. 163–76.

Table 4.1
Distribution of Seats in Engineering Colleges

Year	Merit pool (Percentage)	Manage-ment pool (Percentage)	Capitation fee
A. *Aided colleges*			
1981–82	80	10	10% at Rs. 30,000 per seat
1982–83	90	10	Nil
B. *Unaided colleges*			
1981–82	20	10	30% at Rs. 5,000 for students of Karnataka who satisfy the eligibility and domicile conditions stipulated in Rule 3 of Karnataka Engineering Colleges and Technological Institutes (Selection of Candidates for Admission) Rules. 40% at Rs. 30,000 per seat for others.
1982–83	40	10	20% at Rs. 5,000 for students of Karnataka who satisfy the eligibility and domicile conditions stipulated in Rule 3 of Karnataka Engineering Colleges and Technological Institutes (Selection of Candidates for Admission) Rules. 30% at Rs. 30,000 per seat for others.
1983–84	60	10	10% at Rs. 5,000 for students of Karnataka who satisfy the eligibility and domicile conditions stipulated in Rule 3 of Karnataka Engineering Colleges and Technological Institutes (Selection of Candidates for Admission) Rules. 20% at Rs. 30,000 per seat for others.
1984–85	80	10	5% of Rs. 5,000 for students of Karnataka who satisfy the eligibility and domicile conditions stipulated in Rule 3

(Contd.)

Table 4.1 (Continued)

Year	Merit pool (Percentage)	Management pool (Percentage)	Capitation fee
			of Karnataka Engineering Colleges and Technological Institutes (Selection of Candidiates for Admission) Rules. 5% at Rs. 30,000 per seat for others.
1985–86	90	10	Nil

Source: *White Paper on Professional Colleges and Institutions*, op. cit., pp. 72–73.

capitation fee-cum-merit. The order also prescribed the scale of capitation fee to be collected during the first four years into the general merit pool (without capitation fee). The moneys collected towards the capitation fee would be credited into a special account in a scheduled bank in the name of the Committee which would be constituted by the government. The Commission for Public Instruction and the Director of Technical Education, who would be members of the said Committee, would operate the bank account jointly and release funds to each of the engineering colleges for development expenditure to be incurred by it as per the decision of the Committee. All the aided and unaided private engineering colleges would restrict admission to the sanctioned intake and not exceed it under any circumstances.

The managements of private colleges filed a writ petition against the Government Order in 1981 and obtained a stay. The Karnataka State High Court quashed the Government Order 'as being without the authority of law and beyond the executive power of the State'.[28] The Government Order of 1981 was kept in abeyance because of the stay order, and during 1981–82 and 1982–83 the procedure of charging capitation fee as also the procedures for admission were continued as prevailing prior to 1981. In any case, an important feature of the Gundu Rao phase was the increase in fees and the quantum jump from Rs. 10,000 to Rs. 30,000 as regards the capitation amount for non-Karnataka students.

[28] L.S. Chandrakant, op. cit., p. 15.

In the case of private medical colleges, Gundu Rao's government issued orders in 1981 fixing a special tuition fee of Rs. 60,000 for a Karnataka student and Rs. 1,60,000 for a non-Karnataka student. These fees were to be reduced in a phased manner over a period ranging from three to seven years (see Table 4.2). At the same time, the merit-cum-reservation pool was to be increased while the special management seats were to be held constant at 10 seats for all colleges.

The order in respect of the newly started medical colleges— namely, M.S. Ramaiah Medical College, Dr. Ambedkar Medical College and Kempegowda Institute of Medical Science—reduced the seats under the special tuition fee of Rs. 60,000 and the number of seats to be allotted by the government in a phased manner over six years, and the seventh year onwards, retaining only the number of seats to be allotted on the merit-cum-reservation pool and management quota. Similarly, in respect of the old private medical colleges (M.R. Medical College, Gulbarga, J.J.M. Medical College, Davangere, J.N. Medical College, Belgaum and Karnataka Medical College, Mangalore section), the number of seats under special tuition fee of Rs. 60,000 and Rs. 1,60,000 were reduced in a phased manner over a period of three years, and from the fourth year onwards the total seats were distributed under two categories: (a) the number of management seats, and (b) the number of seats to be allotted to the students of Karnataka by the selection committee constituted by the government.

It was further instructed that the amount collected in the form of special tuition be credited to a special account opened in any scheduled bank in the name of Joint Director, Directorate of Medical Education, Bangalore, and drawn, after the approval of the government, by presenting budget requirements by the management concerned for the specific requirements. This fact was challenged by the management of private medical colleges and these orders were also kept in abeyance in view of the stay orders from the High Court.

In 1979–80, except for Ramaiah Medical College, in the other private colleges, 50 per cent of the seats were left to the discretion of the college managements, 15 per cent of the seats were allotted to candidates paying capitation fees of Rs. 50,000 (with preference for Karnataka students), and 25 per cent of the seats were allotted to candidates (including foreigners) paying capitation fees of

Table 4.2

Scheme of Phased Abolition of Capitation Fee in Medical Colleges Issued in 1981

I. Kasturba Medical College, Manipal

Out of a total of 125 seats, 62 to the merit-cum-reservation pool for allotment of seats to Karnataka students by a Committee constituted by the Government of Karnataka. 63 seats to be allotted on merit on special level of fees.

II. M.R. Medical College, Gulbarga
J.J.M. Medical College, Davangere
J.N. Medical College, Belgaum
Kasturba Medical College, Mangalore

	1981–82	1982–83	1983–84	1984–85 onwards
1. Total number of seats	100	100	100	100
2. Free seats in merit-cum-reservation pool	65	75	85	90
3. Allotted by management	10	10	10	10
4. Allotted by special tuition fee of Rs. 60,000 for Karnataka students	10	5	—	—
5. Allotted on special tuition fee of Rs. 1,60,000	15	10	5	—

Note: Allotment of seats under 2, 4 and 5 was to be done by a Committee constituted by the State government.

III. M.S. Ramaiah Medical College, Bangalore
Kempegowda Institute of Medical Sciences, Bangalore
Dr. Ambedkar Medical College, Bangalore

	1981–82	1982–83	1983–84	1984–85	1985–86	1986–87	1987–88 onwards
1. Total number of seats	100	100	100	100	100	100	100
2. Merit-cum-reservation pool	25	35	45	55	65	75	90

3. Allotted by management	10	10	10	10	10	10	10
4. Allotted by government	10	8	6	4	2	—	—
5. Allotted on special tuition fee of Rs. 60,000 for Karnataka students	5	7	9	11	13	15	—
6. Allotted on special tuition fee of Rs. 1,60,000	50	40	30	20	10	—	—

Note: Allotment of seats under 2, 5 and 6 was to be done by a committee constituted by the State government.

Source: *White Paper on Professional Colleges and Institutions*, op. cit., p. 76.

Rs. 1,25,000. In Kasturba Medical College, Manipal section, 30 per cent of the seats were reserved for students of Karnataka without capitation fees and 70 per cent of the seats were filled by the management. In M.S. Ramaiah Medical College, Bangalore, 90 per cent of the seats were left to the discretion of the management without any restriction on capitation fees.[29]

Tables 4.3 and 4.4 give the actual distribution of seats in private medical colleges from 1979 to 1983. We may observe from these that there has been an increase in student intake in some of the private medical colleges. Thus, in M.S. Ramaiah Medical College, the intake increased from 100 in 1979 to 125 in 1982–83, i.e., an

Table 4.3

Distribution of Seats in Government Medical Colleges (Mode of Selection)

Name of college		Intake	Reserved seats	Balance to be filled by selection committee on the basis of merit-cum-reservation
Bangalore	1979–80	101	5	95
Medical College	1980–81	150	8	142
	1981–82	153	6	147
	1982–83	153	9	149
Medical College, Mysore	1979–80	100	4	95
	1980–81	100	4	96
	1981–82	109	8	97
	1982–83	101	7	94
K.M.C., Hubli	1979–80	100	4	96
	1980–81	100	4	96
	1981–82	100	7	93
	1982–83	102	5	97
Medical College, Bellary	1979–80	100	4	96
	1980–81	100	4	96
	1981–82	100	6	94
	1982–83	102	4	98

Source: *White Paper on Professional Colleges and Institutions*, op. cit., p. 47.

[29] Details explained by Mr. A.K. Abdul Samad, Minister for Health and Family Welfare on 9 July 1980 in the Vidhan Soudha. See *Karnataka Legislative Assembly Debates*, op. cit., 9 July 1980.

increase of 25 per cent. In Kasturba Medical College, there was a 27.3 per cent increase in intake, from 220 to 280 in the same period. In J.J.M. Medical College the increase was from 125 to 135 students, an increase of 8 per cent. Again, in St. John's Medical College, M.S. Ramaiah Medical College, Ambedkar Medical College and K.M.C., a large number of seats were under the management quota, except for K.M.C. where the intake was nearly doubled in 1981–82.

We can observe three noticeable trends in this period, the most conspicuous being the constant increase in fees charged. This was allowed because the political leaders wanted the enterprises to succeed. Besides, from the amounts procured from capitation fees the education of merit students could be financed.

The second trend observed in these colleges was that besides the management quota, there were also non-capitation fee (merit) seats. Such placatory measures have often been adopted to strengthen state legitimacy. The state has to meet pressures of mass politics or else face loss of legitimacy.

The Karnataka/non-Karnataka distinction in the allotment of seats, which was a carry-over from the Urs period, was another significant trend. We can find an explanation for this in terms of political needs to reconcile and protect local interests, while at the same time, allowing private enterprise to succeed by taking higher fees from non-Karnataka students.

The Hegde Phase

The Janata Party, on assuming office, pledged the phased abolition of the capitation fee. This pledge which had held a prominent place in its January 1983 Assembly election manifesto found fulfilment in the Karnataka Educational Institutions (Prohibition of Capitation Fee) Act, 1984, which was preceded by an ordinance bearing the same title in 1983, soon after the Hegde government was inducted into office. What is of significance here is the fact that after having once rejected the system outright, the ruling party later tried to compromise and gave it further legitimacy. The Preamble of the Act of 1984 stated:

Table 4.4

Distribution of Seats in Private Medical Colleges (Mode of Selection)

S. No.	Name of the medical college	Total seats	No. of seats for the students of Karnataka without capitation fee	No. of govt. seats	No. of management seats	No. of seats with a capitation fee of Rs. 50,000	No. of seats with a capitation fee of Rs. 1,25,000
1	2	3	4	5	6	7	8
1979–80							
1.	J.N. Medical College, Belgaum	105	50	—	15	15	25
2.	J.J.M. Medical College, Davangere	125	50	—	35	15	25
3.	M.R. Medical College, Gulbarga	105	50	—	15	15	25
4.	K.M.C., Manipal/Mangalore	220	81	—	95	17	27
5.	St. John's Medical College, Bangalore	60	—	—	60	—	—
6.	M.S. Ramaiah Medical College, Bangalore	100	—	10	90	—	—
1980–81							
1.	J.N. Medical College, Belgaum	114	65	—	24	20	5
2.	J.J.M. Medical College, Davangere	125	65	—	35	20	5

	College						
3.	M.R. Medical College, Gulbarga	114	58	—	33	19	4
4.	K.M.C. (a) Manipal	225	105	—	95	20	5
	(b) Mangalore						
5.	St. John's Medical College, Bangalore	60	—	—	60	—	—
6.	M.S. Ramaiah Medical College, Bangalore	100	—	10	90	—	—
7.	Dr. Ambedkar Medical College, Bangalore	105	—	10	90	—	—
8.	Kempegowda Institute of Medical Sciences, Bangalore	100	—	10	90	—	—

1981–82

	College						
1.	J.N. Medical College, Belgaum	113	65	—	23	5	20
2.	J.J.M. Medical College, Davangere	134	65	—	44	5	20
3.	M.R. Medical College, Gulbarga	110	65	—	22	4	19
4.	K.M.C. (a) Manipal	245	65	—	155	20	5
	(b) Mangalore		(in Mangalore)				
5.	St. John's Medical College, Bangalore	60	—	—	60	—	—
6.	M.S. Ramaiah Medical College, Bangalore	100	—	10	90	—	—
7.	Dr. Ambedkar Medical College, Bangalore* (A.M.C.)	215	16	10	189	—	—
8.	Kempegowda Institute of Medical Sciences, Bangalore	110	—	10	100	—	—

Cont.

Table 4.4 *(Continued)*

1	2	3	4	5	6	7	8
1982–83							
1.	J.N. Medical College, Belgaum	114	65	—	24	5	20
2.	J.J.M. Medical College, Devangere	135	65	—	25	5	20
3.	M.R. Medical College, Gulbarga	110	65	—	22	4	19
4.	K.M.C. (*a*) Manipal (*b*) Mangalore	230	65	—	190	20	5
5.	St. John's Medical College, Bangalore	60	—	—	60	—	—
6.	M.S. Ramaiah Medical College, Bangalore	125	—	10	115	—	—
7.	Dr. Ambedkar Medical College, Bangalore	130	—	10	120	—	—
8.	Kempegowda Institute of Medical Sciences, Bangalore	130	—	10	120	—	—

Source: *White Paper on Professional Colleges and Institutions,* op. cit., pp. 48–51.

* In A.M.C., one more batch of 98 students was admitted which was approved by the government vide GTO No. HFW 209 MME 81 dt. 19.3.83 subject to the approval of M.C.I.

Whereas the practice of collecting capitation fee for admitting students into educational institutions is widespread in the State and whereas the undesirable practice besides contributing to large-scale commercialisation of education, has not been conducive to the maintenance of educational standards and whereas it is considered necessary effectively to curb this evil practice in public interest by providing for prohibition of collection of capitation fee and matters relating thereto be it enacted by the Karnataka State Legislature . . . .[30]

It is of interest to note that the questions of 'standards' and 'public interest' are in fact related to the broader issue of state legitimacy. As such, the state has conceded to mass demands. Ruling elites have also given a broad definition of educational institutions to cater to all kinds of interests to strengthen their support base.

Clause 3 of the enactment stated: 'Notwithstanding anything contained in any law for the time being in force, no capitation fee shall be collected by or on behalf of any educational institution or by any such person who is incharge of or is responsible for the management of such institutions.'[31]

At the same time, the legislation by the State government permitted any educational institution charging capitation fees and established before the date of commencement of the above enactment to continue to receive capitation fees or deposits for a specific period but not beyond five years.[32] It was also laid down that the government would specify the number of government seats, management seats and cash deposit seats.[33] This provision for the substitution of capitation fee with a refundable deposit was only for Karnataka students. The government relied on this provision as their trump card to placate the Karnataka students.[34]

The enactment also stated that the government would regulate

[30] See *Karnataka Gazette*, No. 425, Law and Parliamentary Affairs Secretariat, Bangalore, 9 July 1984, p. 5.

[31] Ibid.

[32] Ibid.

[33] Government seats were merit seats. Cash deposits were refundable after four or five years without any interest. In the case of medical colleges, this amount was Rs. 50,000. In engineering colleges, the ratio of merit–management seats was 40:60. In the case of private medical colleges the number of government/management seats was specified each year by the State government.

[34] *The Hindu*, Madras, 30 October 1986.

the tuition fee and any other charges collected by any institution. The proviso obviously was intended as a transitory measure to avoid dislocation in the existing capitation fee institutions by a blanket ban on capitation fee. It was also laid down that no educational institution should collect any fees or accept deposits in excess of the amount notified and that they should issue official receipts for them.[35]

When the State government decided to abolish capitation fee in phases, it was explained that the other alternative was to nationalise the capitation-charging colleges. This alternative was found to be expensive, involving a payment of Rs. 100 crore in compensation, a proposition which the government could not countenance.[36]

In fact, the Janata government, while trying to abolish capitation fee in this phased manner, permitted the continued collection of capitation fee for 5 years for the existing institutions to enable them to stabilise themselves and to develop a satisfactory infrastructure necessary to maintain minimal academic standards.[37] The State government, as we explained earlier, could not afford any financial commitment on its part.

In exercise of the powers conferred by the Karnataka Educational Institutions Act (1984), the Government of Karnataka fixed the capitation fee to be charged by private unaided medical colleges at the rate of Rs. 1.5 lakh per student for those who were not foreign students or non-resident Indians, and Rs. 2 lakh per student in any other case for a maximum period of five academic years beginning from 1983–84. Such colleges could also collect cash deposits not exceeding Rs. 50,000 per seat, 'subject to the refund of such deposit without interest to the student concerned, at the end of a period of ten years'[38] (see Table 4.5). However, by 1987–88 in almost all private medical colleges the total intake of seats had increased (see Table 4.6). It may also be observed from Tables 4.5 and 4.6 that the management seats increased while the number of merit/government seats declined in some colleges. However, the cash deposit seats continued to remain the same during these years.

[35] *Karnataka Gazette*, op. cit., p. 7.
[36] Personal interview with professor B.K. Chandrashekhar, the Janata Party Member of the Legislative Council.
[37] See *Indian Express*, New Delhi, 2 July 1987.
[38] *Karnataka Gazette*, op. cit.

Table 4.5
Distribution of Seats in Private Medical Colleges in 1984–85

Name of college	Government seats to be filled by a selection committee constituted by the Government under Rule 8 of the Karnataka Medical Colleges (Selection of Candidates for Admission) Rules, 1984	Karnataka students on payment of a deposit of Rs. 50,000 per student, free of interest, to the colleges, refundable at the end of ten years	Seats on payment of capitation fees not exceeding Rs. 1.5 lakh per student for students other than foreign students and Rs. 2 lakh for foreign students and non-resident Indian students	Total no. of seats
J.N. Medical College, Belgaum	58	10	47	115
J.J.M. Medical College, Davangere	75	10	65	150
M.R. Medical College, Gulbarga	58	10	47	115
Kasturba Medical College, Mangalore Section	65	10	55	130
M.S. Ramaiah Medical College, Bangalore	20	10	100	130
Kempegowda Institute of Medical Sciences, Bangalore	20	10	100	130
Dr B.R. Ambedkar Medical College, Bangalore	20	10	100	130

Source: Government of Karnataka, Health and Family Welfare Department, *Rules for Selection of Candidates to 1st M.B.B.S. Course in Government/Private Medical Colleges, 1984–85*, pp. 20–21.

Table 4.6

*Break-up of Seats Available in 1987–88 under the Government Merit Pool, Cash
Deposit and Management Quota in Private Medical Colleges in Karnataka*

Name of college	Govt./merit pool seats	Cash deposit seats	Management/ capitation quota	Total no. of seats
J.N. Medical College, Belgaum	56	10	90	156
J.J.M. Medical College, Davangere	60	10	170	240
M.R. Medical College, Gulbarga	57	10	93	150
Kempegowda Inst. of Medical Sciences, Bangalore	45	10	95	150
Dr. Ambedkar Medical College, Bangalore	45	10	95	150
J.S.S. Medical College, Mysore	37	10	113	160
Al-Ameen Medical College, Bijapur	30	Nil	90	120
Adichunchanagiri Institute of Medical Science, Mandya	30	10	110	150
Devraj Urs Medical College, Kolar	26	10	94	130
K.M.C., Mangalore	120	10	70	200

Source: Information provided by the Directorate of Medical Education, Government of Karnataka, Bangalore.

The State government allowed private medical colleges to collect
an annual tuition fee of Rs. 5,000 from any category of students
admitted to the college, in addition to the capitation fee. In
comparison, the government medical colleges charged only an
annual fee of Rs. 500 per student. The amount of capitation fee
collected in private medical colleges was also much more than the
amount specified by the government, ranging from anything between Rs. 2 and 4 lakh.[39] In the case of engineering colleges also,
according to the Act of 1984, the State government prescribed the

---

[39] Based on data collected through questionnaires and interviews. See Chapter 8,
'The Students'

amount of tuition and capitation fees to be collected. All such amounts had to be deposited in the account of the college. In each college there were a specified number of seats which were reserved as government seats without capitation fee.

The State government prescribed the number of seats that may be filled by the college management from among the Karnataka students on the basis of merit, on payment of refundable cash deposits. The government also laid down the number of seats to be filled wholly by the management at its own discretion. Not less than 50 per cent of the admissions to the government seats and management seats were to be from among the Karnataka candidates.[40]

An important consequence evident from the Act was that the State government enjoined private enterprises to run their institutions partly for the benefit of the government-nominated students without any financial involvement to the State exchequer. Following the Act, the Karnataka government ordered that 60 per cent seats would be reserved in the 1985–86 academic year for government-nominated students. It also prescribed the following tuition and capitation fees:

Tuition fee: Rs. 2,000 for Karnataka students
Rs. 3,000 for non-Karnataka students
(In State engineering colleges, the tuition fee was Rs. 300 per year.)
Capitation fee: Rs. 5,000 for Karnataka students
Rs. 30,000 for non-Karnataka students

Since the State government's orders practically knocked out the basis on which private institutions had been operating, they appealed to the Karnataka High Court. Nearly all educational societies of the engineering colleges filed a writ petition[41] seeking to strike down the provisions of the Educational Institutions (Prohibition of Capitation Fee) Act, 1985 as being unconstitutional and arbitrary,

[40] Information collected from the Directorate of Technical Education, Government of Karnataka. Also through personal interviews with the Joint Director, Technical Education, June 1986 and November 1987.

[41] See *Bapuji Education Association* vs. *State of Karnataka Davangere (Chitradurga District)*, *Indian Law Reports*, 1985, Karnataka, p. 80.

and also directing the respondents[42] not to interfere with the selection and admission of students or with the collection of capitation fee in their respective colleges. In an interim order the court allowed only 40 per cent seats to the government and set aside the capitation fee limits as prescribed by the government for the rest of the 60 per cent seats.[43]

The State government had also brought eight engineering colleges of the private sector under the fold of the State grants-in-aid system. In these colleges, 80 per cent seats were reserved as general quota to which admissions were made by the government. The rest of the 20 per cent seats were to be filled by the managements at their discretion, implying thereby that capitation fee may be collected for those seats.[44]

Though the Janata Party under Hegde had declared in its election manifesto in 1983 that it would end the system of capitation fee, it had to make several compromises on this score after coming to power. As a ruling party, it made bold promises including providing for prohibition of capitation fee, but after assuming office, it succumbed to pressures from sectional and minority interests. Soon after coming to power, Chief Minister Hegde justified the government's decision to sanction new private colleges in view of the new developments taking place.[45] Under the government's decision, there was an arrangement for a gradual takeover of the seats in those medical and engineering colleges charging capitation fees to the government/merit pool over the next 5 years, plus leaving minimal seats for the management. The private managements challenged this in the court and the scheme had a chequered career. In engineering colleges, the government was not able to secure more than 40 per cent seats, while in medical colleges, the numbers varied each year (see Tables 4.3 and 4.4). At the same time, the government also declared that it would prohibit new private engineering and medical colleges. While no new engineering colleges were allowed immediately, four private medical colleges were permitted before 1986, and later five more engineering colleges were also set up. Thus, the policy on capitation fees was one area

[42] The respondents in all the petitions were the Secretary, Education Department (State of Karnataka) and the Director of Technical Education, Bangalore.
[43] The High Court of Karnataka at Bangalore: Order dated 14/16th day of August 1985, before Hon'ble Justice Chandrakantaraj Urs.
[44] Information collected from the Directorate of Technical Education, Government of Karnataka.
[45] *Indian Express*, 18 October 1985.

where the Hegde government was on the defensive. From its election promise to continuously try to abolish these fees completely in course of time, it shifted to become one of the ardent proponents of this culture.[46] In fact, Mr. M. Raghupathy, one-time Education Minister in Hegde's cabinet, stated that he was restrained from putting an end to the system of capitation fees when he was in the State cabinet.[47]

The Karnataka government subsidised several of the medical colleges under private management by providing the facilities of government hospitals along with the teaching staff for clinical instructions to students. The government also, from time to time, deputed medical teachers from its own colleges to bail out students from these private institutions. There were cases when students of government medical colleges went on strike, as in the case of the Bangalore Medical College strike in July–August 1987, because their hospital beds were being shared by private medical college students and their teachers were lent to private colleges. Thus, while medical education was commercialised, the government also lent material support to those engaged in this process. In lieu of the hospital facilities the government gave, it received some merit pool seats for students (selected through the State entrance examination) in private colleges.

The Post-Hegde Phase

The State government and managements of private engineering and medical colleges finalised in May–June 1989 the fee structure which came into effect from 1989–90. This scheme, in the garb of putting an end to the practice of capitation fee, gave official sanction to the commercialisation of professional education. The Karnataka Educational Institution Act had conferred on the State government the powers to regulate tuition fees charged by private professional colleges. The State administration under President's rule drew up a scheme that succeeded in merely staggering the payment of capitation fee over the entire course in the form of tuition fees.

In this scheme, a student from Karnataka joining a private medical college would pay Rs. 1.5 lakh (Rs. 25,000 annually), a non-Karnataka student over Rs. 3 lakh (Rs. 60,000 annually), and a foreign student as well as a non-resident Indian student over

[46] See *The Economic Times*, Bangalore, 29 June 1987, and *The Times of India*, Bangalore, 26 April 1987.
[47] *The Hindu*, 16 October 1986.

Rs. 4 lakh (Rs. 80,000 annually). A seat in a private engineering college would cost between Rs. 25,000 to Rs. 40,000 for a Karnataka student, and Rs. 60,000 for a non-Karnataka student.[48] Candidates in the merit pool would pay the same fee that was charged in government colleges, i.e., Rs. 2,000 per annum in medical colleges and Rs. 1,200 in engineering colleges.

The new scheme worked to the disadvantage of a large number of students by making professional education prohibitively expensive. The private institutions that stood to benefit from this welcomed the scheme as being very practical, though they were not satisfied with the sum they could profitably collect in the name of imparting education. While the official fee was steep, the managements could unofficially charge even more. In this way considerable black money was generated. The managements controlled the admission of non-government quota students, and whoever was willing to pay more could gain admission.

In July 1991, the Karnataka education minister Veerappa Moily, remarked that the State government would not hesitate to derecognise engineering colleges whose courses and infrastructure were found below standard. He added that the Srinath and the Rame Gowda Committees had been set up to review the infrastructure and the syllabi and their reports would be implemented to improve the standard of engineering education in the region. Chief Minister Bangarappa's cabinet minister Moily again stated that since capitation was a menace to the medical profession his government would strictly implement the Anti-Capitation Act. A Cabinet sub-committee had been formed to look into the different facets of the problem of capitation fees and an effort would be made to implement its recommendations.[49]

However, in the following month, Bangarappa's Health Minister, G. Puttaswamy Gowda pointed out that a cabinet sub-committee would take a decision on sanctioning more private medical colleges in the State after processing 18 pending applications seeking approval of the government.[50] Such self-contradictory positions on the issue have been the hallmark of almost all the governments in the State.

[48] See Proceedings of the Government of Karnataka, Government order on fee structure in engineering colleges, 26 May 1989; and Government of Karnataka, Notification on fixation of tuition fee and other fees and deposits to be collected by private medical colleges with effect from the academic year 1989–90, 5 June 1989.

[49] *Deccan Herald*, Bangalore, 2 and 16 July 1991.

[50] *Deccan Herald*, Bangalore, 20 August 1991.

In fact, in August 1992, Bangarappa divested Moily of the important Education portfolio for his criticism of certain decisions concerning the Education Department, in particular, the sanctioning of professional colleges to individuals and institutions of the Chief Minister's choice. Although the Karnataka High Court in September 1992 stayed the sanction granted by the State government to start nine new engineering colleges, Bangarappa went ahead to announce that his government was inclined to start a few more medical colleges in the region. Later, in October the same year, in the wake of increased pressure on Chief Minister Bangarappa in the form of a spate of ministerial resignations, including Veerappa Moily's, and the relentless campaign of the dissidents, as well as to save himself the kind of embarrassment that befell Andhra Pradesh Chief Minister Janardhan Reddy, he announced the withdrawal of the government order of September 1992 sanctioning fresh capitation fee colleges. Bangarappa then went on to state that the managements of these colleges had failed to obtain permission from AICTE which is now mandatory, and therefore, the permission was withdrawn.[51] This illustrates the vacillating stance of the Chief Minister in the absence of specific guidelines and effective controls.

An Overview

We have observed that the capitation fee institutions registered considerable growth in the 1980s. Also, during this period, university control vis-à-vis private-based colleges steadily eroded. What is of significance is that despite policy announcements and promises at the time of elections to stop further growth of these institutions, the government policy has essentially been directed at regulating the fee structure. However, the steady increase in fees was a constant trend in all the phases studied. The government was successful only with regard to regulating the tuition fee. Private colleges did not always adhere to the government formula of charging capitation fees and, as we will see later, often took larger donations than those prescribed by the State government. It was Urs who legitimised the system by regulating the fee structure. Gundu Rao's policy of granting sanctions to a large number of private colleges gave momentum to the process of commercialisation

[51] *The Times of India*, New Delhi, 26 August, 26 and 28 September and 29 October 1992.

that had crept into the system of education. These trends continued under Hegde and have not changed in the post-Hegde period.

Capitation fee colleges have thus become an integral part of Karnataka. Successive governments have actively encouraged the growth of private enterprise in engineering and medical education.[52] Whether it has been the Janata or the Congress Party in power, the capitation fee system has persisted. The reason for this has been partly explained by Manor: 'The social correlations both the Janata and the Congress seek to cultivate are identical. The two political parties in Karnataka do not have a different social base.'[53] In fact, irrespective of party changes, there has been a substantive continuity vis-à-vis the sanctioning of such new institutions. The various governments' interventions in regulating fees or raising their quantum have only succeeded in legitimising the system of capitation fee and have been quite in tune with their general thrust towards privatisation.

The State government has apparently not drawn any well-defined policy in respect of technical or medical education based on a correct perspective of technological and medical personnel requirements. Instead, the government has yielded to political compulsions of one form or another, caste and communal pressure groups, regional demands, and so on. The Supreme Court verdict in the *Mohini Jain* Vs. *State of Karnataka* case declaring the right to education for all levels an enforceable fundamental right and quashing the Karnataka government notification permitting private medical colleges in the State to charge exorbitant capitation fees from students,[54] has brought a new twist to the issue. It remains to be seen what the verdict will finally achieve or whether it will remain just a pious declaration.

The central government's reactions to the unplanned and un-coordinated expansion of engineering and medical education through the State government's direct encouragement to private enterprise have also not been clear. The National Policy on Education (1986) stated that in the interest of maintaining standards 'the commercialisation of technical and professional education will be curbed.'[55]

[52] Lalitha Natraj, 'Of Felicitation and Agitations,' *Economic and Political Weekly*, Vol. XVI, No. 7, 14 February 1981, p. 271.

[53] Personal interview with James Manor, Delhi, 31 August 1988.

[54] *The Times of India*, New Delhi, 31 July 1992.

[55] Government of India, *National Policy on Education*, Ministry of Human Resource Development, New Delhi, 1986, p. 20.

But no concrete steps have been tàken by the Centre in this respect, nor has it been able to intervene effectively whenever such action was called for. The Human Resource Development Ministry may have dubbed these institutions as 'unapproved' and may even have denied them central funds for quality improvement, but as we have seen in this chapter, these measures have not had any significant effect. Not only have such institutions not ceased to exist, but their number has increased considerably over the years. The National Front Government had promised abolition of capitation fee in its election manifesto. However, the then Union Minister of State for Human Resource Development had stated that abolition of capitation fee was a difficult task as the government could not provide funds for all the needy colleges, and therefore, only the rules pertaining to it would be tightened.[56] Narasimha Rao's government reemphasized the 1986 National Policy on Education and went on to state that although some people would like to condemn private schools and colleges as 'teaching shops', it was also a fact that the state alone could not take on the entire burden of education.[57] The Supreme Court's July 1992 verdict had its ramifications for the State reeling under a resource crunch.[58] The Court reiterated the role of the state in providing education for all, but the moot question that remained was: How does the state reconcile the judgement with the ongoing privatisation of education?

Besides the administrative shortcomings in the functioning of capitation fee colleges, socio-political dynamics have also been at play. Middle-caste elites, sectional, minority and entrepreneurial interests, and pressures of mass politics have prevailed, and the government at best has only been able to perform a balancing act between the different pressure groups. Government policy has hardly been able to alter the logic of the capitation fee system. With the various groups clamouring for educational institutions for their own specific reasons, it has not been surprising that the capitation fee phenomenon has proliferated to such proportions. In the next chapter, we will examine the functioning and management of private colleges.

[56] *Indian Express*, New Delhi, 6 August 1990.
[57] *Indian Express*, New Delhi, 7 July 1991.
[58] Ajaz Ashraf, 'Right to Learn: Who Pays?,' *The Pioneer*, 30 August 1992.

5

THE MANAGEMENT PROCESS

In this chapter we will examine the organisational structure of private colleges, their actual functioning and, to some extent, the management of their finances. We will also study, more comprehensively, the composition of the management boards and the socio-economic background of the members. The main purpose is to explore the linkage between state, society and education as seen in the organisational setup, the decision-making process, the operation and management of finances, and the admission policy of these colleges. The information in this chapter is based on personal interviews with principals, students, faculty members and members of managing boards. The criteria for selecting the colleges studied have been outlined in the next chapter.

The Organisational Structure

In all the colleges studied, the managing board or the executive committee was the policy-making body. The Principal of the college was responsible for implementing the decisions of the management. The executive committee also controlled all financial matters. In most Lingayat- and Vokkaliga-run colleges, elections were held to select members to this committee, but in the case of some minority-run colleges, the members were nominated. Although the government order has specified that 'not more than two persons who are close relations shall be nominated as members of the managing committee,'[1] it was observed that private entrepreneurs usually had several other family members on their management boards, and it was largely the family which formed the managing or executive committee. This committee was also referred to as the governing body in some cases, as in the Sree Siddhartha Institute of Technology, Tumkur. No employee of the private institution, other than its academic head, could be chosen as the Secretary of the managing committee. According to the Education Bill of 1983, the Secretary, 'subject to the general superintendence and control of the managing committee, [would] be the Chief Executive of the institution in all matters pertaining to the private educational institution . . . .' Further, the Bill states that 'the Secretary shall also be the custodian of all its property and records and shall be responsible for their proper custody, maintenance and safety.'[2]

Academic matters were generally taken care of by the governing council of the college—a body which consisted of some members of the management, the Principal, two nominees of the State government (in the case of medical colleges), some heads of departments from the institution (generally two representatives from the staff), and a few leading academic experts, either from the university or from outside. The last mentioned make their appearance at meetings on certain occasions but the final decision-making authority rests with the managing or executive committee. Some professionals, like doctors and engineers, would sometimes also be included, as in the case of the Vokkaligara Sangha and the Ramaiah colleges. This was done largely as a pretence of representing academic interests but in reality policy decisions hardly rested with them.

The governing council had to seek the approval of the executive committee for any purchases, including that of equipment required for the college. The budget had to be cleared by the executive committee. Sometimes, there also existed an intermediary finance committee. For instance, the colleges run by the Vokkaligara Sangha had such a committee which was headed by the Sangha

---

[1] See the *Karnataka Education Bill 1983*, p. 41.
[2] Ibid., p. 42.

Treasurer. This body controlled all financial matters but it too had to have the final approval of the executive committee. Important administrative decisions—such as recruiting staff members and laying down their working conditions, or selecting students for filling up the seats in the management quota—were also taken by the executive committee. Owing to heavy interference from the management, there was no rigid adherence to any procedures for admissions or the amount of capitation fee to be collected. Besides the executive committee and the governing council, in some colleges like the Kempegowda Institute of Medical Sciences, the general administration of the college was in the hands of the Principal who was aided by a consultative body, known as the college council, consisting of all the professors and heads of departments. But the executive committee remained the highest body in all matters of decision-making. The organisational hierarchy in these colleges was as follows:

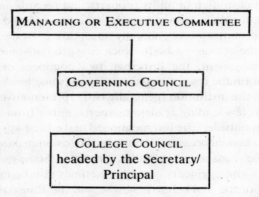

In colleges run by the dominant castes, the executive committee and governing council were often both headed by the religious head of the *mutts*.

Thus we see that while the managing or executive committee was the apex body taking all major decisions, the governing council only took decisions pertaining to academic affairs. The Principal was responsible for day-to-day administration. In caste-based institutions supported by *mutts*, the *swamijis* of the *mutts* headed all committees. Through their donations, the *mutts* maintained their links with the institutions and received support from their communities.

Operation and Finance

The managements relied heavily on the support of politicians and bureaucrats to run these institutions. Individual entrepreneurs particularly, although they kept shifting their loyalties to the party in power, made use of money power to get the required support.[3] While the extent of corruption involved becomes difficult to ascertain, it was more than apparent that the capitation fee phenomenon linking business entrepreneurs, the bureaucracy, dominant landed castes and politicians did foster a black economy. A good example was the dual fee structure prevalent in all private colleges. For the minimal facilities provided in most of these colleges, almost all the managements charged a capitation fee much higher than that prescribed by the State government. Even the tuition fee charged in private institutions was much higher than in government colleges. In some colleges, like the Kempegowda Institute of Medical Sciences, two separate receipts were issued for the money collected—one, for the amount permitted by the Karnataka government to be charged as capitation fee, and the other, for voluntary donation.[4] Often, the capitation fee transactions were cash transactions. Details of the fee charged by a non-dominant caste college, the R.V. College of Engineering, are given here in a copy of the letter (Exhibit 5.1), which was circulated to parents eager for seeking admission for their children. In such cases, any amount specified by the government loses all meaning.

The sources of finance for private professional colleges were largely donations and capitation fees. Vokkaliga- and Lingayat-run colleges were supported by *mutts*; the Vokkaligara Sangha or registered Lingayat societies received huge public donations, and if there was any deficit in the college finances, the organisations took care to meet some expenses. There were people who sold land and gave donations to the *mutts* and the Sangha with the aim of promoting education amongst their caste members. Contributions to educational trusts were also exempted from income tax.[5] It was

[3] Interview with the Director, Medical Education, November 1987, and the Director, Technical Education, June 1988.

[4] Personal interview with the Treasurer, Vokkaligara Sangha, Bangalore, June 1988.

[5] See *Prospectus*, A.I.M.S., 1987–88.

Exhibit 5.1

R.V. College of Engineering
Mysore Road, Bangalore 560 059
Rashtreeya Sikshana Samithi Trust
Jayanagar, Bangalore 560 011

No. RVE/   85–86   *Date: 29th May 1986*

Dear Parent,

Sub: Admission to Engineering Course 1986–87

With reference to your enquiry regarding admission to your ward, I would like to clarify the following:

Admission is open for a very few seats in the following courses of engineering faculties:

1. Civil Engineering   2. Mechanical Engineering
3. Electrical Engineering   4. Electronics Engineering
5. Industrial Prodn. Engg.   6. Instrumentation Tech.
7. Chemical Engineering   8. Computer Science

The course on Computer Science & Electronics will be offered if the candidate has secured more than 70% marks in PCM. The course on Mechanical Engineering will be offered if he has secured more than 60% marks in PCM. The remaining courses will be offered if he has secured more than 55% marks in PCM.

The candidate must have passed Pre-University of Karnataka or equivalent to that, i.e., 10 + 2 examination in English medium. The following will be the Capitation/Donation:

Computer Science & Electronics	Rs. 70,000
Mechanical Engineering	Rs. 65,000
Civil, Electrical, Industrial Prodn.,	
Chemical & Instr. Technology	Rs. 50,000

If you are agreeable to pay the above Capitatioin/Donation you can straight away come down to the College or to the Rashtreeya Sikshana Samithi Trust office and meet the undersigned or the

Hon. Secretary immediately, with the original marks cards, etc. You must also bring a local person as Local Guardian of your ward.

Only a few seats are available and will be filled up on 'first come first served' basis. We are not responsible if you meet us at a later date. All the seats will be filled up only on the 'first come first served' basis.

1. Application form is attached/not attached.
2. Please send Rs. 50 towards Application form through DD or PO in favour of the Principal.
3. No further correspondence will be done regarding admission for the year 1986–87.

Yours faithfully

Sd/-

D.A. PANDU   M.R. HOLLA
Hon. Secretary   *Principal*
RSST, R.V. Teacher's College Building   *R.V. College of Engg.*
Jayanagar, Bangalore 560 011   *Bangalore 560 059*

---

difficult to determine the extent to which these finances were utilised for the development of private colleges. The Vokkaligara Sangha, the Siddaganga *mutt* and the Karnataka Liberal Education Society all maintained that their institutions were not run by single individuals, and therefore, all money collected from students was accounted for.[6] Since the *mutt* accounts were not open to public scrutiny, it was difficult to verify the amount that was actually collected and spent,[7] though there were adequate grounds to believe that considerable profits were made.

It was explained in Chapter 3 that the capital expenditure required to set up an engineering degree college was about Rs. 8 to 10 crore and the recurring expenditure about Rs. 80 to 100 lakh.[8]

[6] Personal interviews with the Treasurer, Vokkaligara Sangha, Secretary, K.L.E. Society and the Principal, S.I.T., Tumkur.

[7] Personal interview with the Resident Editor, *The Times of India*, Bangalore, June 1988. Evidence from the Legislative Assembly Debates in Chapter 3 had also substantiated the profitability aspect in the running of private colleges.

[8] Interview with the Head of the Mechanical Department, Visvesvaraya Engineering College, Bangalore, June 1988.

Private enterprise would raise this money from students and to equip a college with the required facilities it would take about five to six years. The capitation fee would be hiked from Rs. 80,000 to Rs. 1 lakh and a high tuition fee would be charged (about Rs. 10,000 to 15,000) to cover the recurring costs. While the intake of students would be increased, the private management economised by not providing the necessary facilities and amenities. Most of these colleges at the time of inception provided minimal infrastructural facilities. They relied heavily on the capitation fee received from the students, and even here it was not that the entire capitation fee amount collected went into the development of the college. Thus, even after a period of eight to 10 years such colleges were only able to provide some of the basic amenities.

In the case of engineering colleges, for instance, though the government stipulation for the capitation amount was Rs. 5,000 for Karnataka students and Rs. 30,000 for non-Karnataka students, the average capitation fee taken from Karnataka students was Rs. 40,000 to Rs. 50,000 and from non-Karnataka students it was anything between Rs. 50,000 to Rs. 1 lakh. The balance was taken as donations to the trust managing the college for which some of the donors stated they had managed to get income-tax rebate.

In particulars concerning finance furnished to an Expert Committee in June 1987 by an engineering college it was stated that a collection of Rs. 40,15,600 as tuition and special fees was made for 1985–86. The amount collected as capitation fees from students for that year was stated as 'Nil' and donations were also shown as 'Nil'. However, capitation fees must have been collected, since from interviews with students it was found that a majority of them had paid over Rs. 50,000 on an average as capitation fee. But this amount was not shown as receipts by the college. Accounts can thus be easily manipulated.

In *mutt*-supported colleges, it was observed that while some concessions in the capitation fee may have been made for a few needy students from the Lingayat or Vokkaliga castes, other students could gain admission only by paying much higher donations. A Vokkaliga student at the medical college in Mandya paid Rs. 30,000 as capitation fee for which his father had to sell his land. This 'lower' fee was accepted by the college only after the student had made a special appeal to the *swamiji* at Nagmangala to allow this concession, considering his economic condition. The other students in the college had to pay between Rs. 1 lakh to 3 lakh as capitation. In another similar case, at the Siddaganga Institute of Technology, one student was given admission after paying only Rs. 8,000 as capitation fee on the intervention of the Tumkur *swamiji*. Instances such as these were however rare, for even amongst the dominant castes, few students stood to benefit from such institutions run by their own caste. A large majority were unable to pay the large capitation fee, and it was mainly the upper crust of their caste that reaped the benefits.

The prospectus of the Adichunchanagiri Institute of Medical Sciences (A.I.M.S.) presents an interesting case for promotion of professional education for rural students. They claim that since educational facilities in rural areas are poor, the *swamiji*, 'in order to help the under-privileged youth' in villages, started a medical college at Nagamangala Taluka.[9] However, in reality, through interviews conducted in the college, a different picture emerged. Of the 20 student respondents, only four came from a rural background, while the other 16 students came from towns many of whom were from different parts of the country. Most of them had paid over Rs. 1.5 lakh to gain admission. Of the four village-bred students, one from Kerala had paid Rs. 1.5 lakh and another two from within Karnataka had also paid Rs. 80,000 and Rs. 30,000 respectively.

Thus, while caste and community objectives were professed by the managements of the colleges, they were not implemented in actual practice. Again, at the Ambedkar Medical College, of the 108 students interviewed, only six belonged to the scheduled caste group; at the Ambedkar Institute of Technology two students out of 21 were scheduled caste students. Similarly, of the 29 students interviewed at the Sree Siddartha Institute of Technology, only five belonged to the scheduled caste group. The remaining students had paid capitation fee to seek admission. Thus, the bulk of the management seats were capitation fee seats filled by fairly affluent students.

Some of these colleges were also attracted by the generous grants-in-aid extended by the State government. The management of the Ambedkar Institute of Technology, for instance, had

---

[9] *Prospectus, A.I.M.S., 1987–88,* p. 37.

approached the State and central governments for help under the special provision of the Constitution to convert the college into a grants-in-aid institution on the plea tnat this institution was primarily meant for scheduled castes and scheduled tribes and other backward classes.[10]

In the case of some dominant-caste colleges, while professing the aims of their caste openly, they also claimed that they ran a secular college and admitted 'everyone'—by everyone they meant those who had the money to pay a large fee. Not more than 20 to 30 per cent of the students belonged to the dominant castes in almost all the cases. The Principal of the Lingayat-run Siddaganga Institute of Technology stated that on an average not more than 30 per cent seats went to Lingayat students. The case in K.L.E.S. institutions was similar. At the Kempegowda Institute of Medical Sciences, the Principal, Dr. Somaiyya, stated that about 25 per cent of the seats went to the Vokkaliga students. Amongst the minority colleges, only the Islamiah Institute of Technology stood apart from other such colleges in that of all the students interviewed, about 80 to 85 per cent were Muslims.

In the Muslim minority institutions, the managements had greater freedom to function without paying much heed to state regulations. The Karnataka Education Bill, 1983, which sought 'to provide for better organisation, development, discipline and control of the educational institutions in the State',[11] in no way encroached on the freedom of the minority institutions. While the State government could take over the management of any educational institution 'in public interest or in order to secure the proper management of the said educational institution',[12] it could not take over any private educational institution under the management of a religious institution, endowment or a *wakf* 'without the prior consent of such management', since these managements enjoyed special privileges and protection. The same Act stated that 'nothing in the Act or the rules made thereunder shall apply to any minority educational institution to the extent they are inconsistent with the rights guaranteed under Article 30 of the Constitution of India.'[13]

---

[10] Dr. Ambedkar Institute of Technology, Bangalore, *Prospectus, 1987*.

[11] *The Karnataka Education Bill 1983*, Karnataka Legislative Assembly, Seventh Assembly, Third Session, p. 7.

[12] Ibid., p. 56.

[13] Ibid., p. 91. Article 30 of the Constitution allows the minorities, religious or linguistic, to establish and administer their own educational institutions.

The Manipal colleges claimed the linguistic minority status for themselves on the plea that as the Konkani-speaking people in Dakshina Kannada they formed a linguistic minority group. Surely, managements of institutions with a good repute did not need a minority status for themselves unless it served the purpose of circumventing government regulations. When questioned on the issue, a spokesman of the management in Manipal stated that the status was acquired soon after the government enacted legislation to ban capitation, and it was advantageous to avail of the privileges granted by the Constitution. But the spokesman hastily added, 'we are not asking for leniency in standards; we only want protection from interference by politicians.' However, a student remarked in an interview that in Manipal, 'the authorities were not giving admission to the Konkani-speaking minorities who cannot afford this education. It is money which buys admission here.'

It is interesting to detail here how the managements of capitation fee colleges justified themselves and constructed a rationale for the existing system. They felt that since the state was not able to fulfil the demand for higher professional education owing to paucity of funds, if there were parents who were willing to pay the price and send their children to private institutions, it should be considered perfectly justifiable. T.M.A. Pai, who established the first private enterprise in medical education, was among others who argued along the above lines. Dr. Chennabasappa, Principal of the Ambedkar Medical College, felt that since these institutions were purely private and unaided by the state, and since the expenses involved in setting up and running such professional colleges were enormous, it would be impossible to manage them without charging the students a capitation fee. Dr. Gangappa, Principal of the Kempegowda Institute of Medical Sciences, and Dr. Amrita Rai, Principal of M.S. Ramaiah Medical College, both felt that students who could afford to pay the money should be entitled to admission; more so, if they had some potential and felt interested.

The Pais of Manipal questioned the justification for heavily subsidising higher and professional education from government revenues for the benefit of people who were relatively better off and who had no obligation to serve the country in return.[14] Dr. Ram Das Pai, the Medical Director of Kasturba Medical College,

[14] See *Capitation Fee Institutions—Need for Rational Evaluation with National Objectives*, The Academy of General Education, Manipal (year not given).

also argued that the question of commercialisation or black-marketing would arise if the capitation fee charged was in excess of what the government itself spent on medical education in its colleges and the sponsors were self-seeking. If the money collected was not in excess of government expenditure from the exchequer and was scrupulously spent for the purpose for which it was collected, it did not amount to commercialisation or black-marketing. The university could lay down more rigid conditions for granting affiliation and to ensure that adequately high standards were maintained.

Some managements claimed that the money they received as capitation fee was sufficient to meet the recurring expenditure and the entire amount collected was utilised for the benefit of the students. In this regard, Principal Holla of R.V. College of Engineering remarked: 'The government is in fact not offering any concession or help and wants 40 per cent of the seats in engineering colleges for the merit pool students. How to pay the teachers a salary of Rs. 4.5 lakh and an electricity bill of over Rs. 1 lakh per month without charging capitation fee is a tricky question.'

The management also compared their institutions with government colleges and observed that while the latter were ill-equipped, they were, on the other hand, able to purchase the latest books and buy adequate equipment with the capitation and donation money. They stated that a large number of deserving students were denied admission in government colleges because of the policy of reservations, but through private institutions many such students were given an opportunity to get trained professionally.

They further justified the admission of richer students by saying that with the rich being able to pay for their own education, the limited funds of the state could be utilised for the poorer sections. Since some students joining these colleges were non-resident Indians or foreigners, a few managements claimed that these colleges were also a source of earning the much needed foreign exchange for the country.

Lack of Facilities

While the managements tried to build a case for charging capitation fees, their claim that they spent more money than they collected was not corroborated in the several interviews conducted with students and faculty members. As will be seen in the following two chapters, the majority of the respondents stated that the facilities in their colleges were average, inadequate or poor. The colleges were not imparting any training worth the name even after having collected large sums of money. Earning profits seemed to be their chief concern. The managements did not offer any stipends or financial aid to their students on the basis of their academic performance. Some, like the R.V. College of Engineering, the Manipal colleges and the K.L.E. Society colleges, did give small amounts as cash prizes, but by and large there were no incentives for students. Amongst the colleges surveyed, not a single college had maintained a systematic record of how their students had been faring after having qualified from their institutes; in most cases there was no alumni association either, yet almost all the managements stated that 'their students were doing very well.'

The college authorities, in fact, had managed to successfully circumvent all efforts of the government to enforce controls and regulations. Some of the medical and engineering colleges had even violated the intake policy prescribed by the government by taking on more students and securing *post-facto* approval of the government (see Tables 5.1 and 5.2). High intake would tend to affect the facilities and standards adversely.

The Admission Process

For entrance to an M.B.B.S. course, the minimum eligibility conditions laid down by the Government of Karnataka for both government and private medical colleges are similar. No person was eligible to apply for admission to such a course unless he had passed

the second year of the two pre-university examination or any other examination declared as equivalent thereto by the concerned University in Karnataka with Physics, Chemistry and Biology as optional subjects and English as one of the languages; or B.Sc. degree examination of any university established by

Table 5.1

College-wise Figures in Respect of Government and Private Medical Colleges Regarding Annual Admission to M.B.B.S.

Name of medical college	Year of starting the college	Intake authorised by the Medical Council of India				Seats approved by the government				Actual number of candidates admitted			
		1979–80	1980–81	1981–82	1982–83	1979–80	1980–81	1981–82	1982–83	1979–80	1980–81	1981–82	1982–83
1	2	3	4	5	6	7	8	9	10	11	12	13	14
Government Medical Colleges													
Bangalore Medical College, Bangalore	1954	100	150	150	150	101	150	153	153	101	150	153	152
Medical College, Mysore	1924	100	100	100	100	100	100	103	101	100	100	102	102
Karnataka Medical College, Hubli	1959	100	100	100	100	100	100	100	102	100	100	99	101
Medical College, Bellary	1961	100	100	100	100	100	100	100	102	100	100	100	100
Private Medical Colleges													
St. John's Medical College, Bangalore	1963	60	60	60	60	60	60	60	60	60	60	60	60
Kasturba Medical College, Manipal	1953/1977	175	200	200	200	220	225	245	280	228*	226	225	280
J.J.M. Medical College, Davangere	1965	100	125	125	125	125	125	110	135	125	125	134	135

Institution													
J.N. Medical College, Belgaum	1963	75	100	100	100	105	114	113	114	105	114	109	113
M.R. Medical College, Gulbarga	1963	67	100	100	100	105	114	110	110	—	—	—	—
M.S. Ramaiah Medical College, Bangalore	1979	100	100	100	100	100	100	100	125	100	100	100	130*
Kempegowda Institute of Medical Sciences, Bangalore	1980	—	100	100	100	—	100	110	130	—	100	110	130
Dr. Ambedkar Medical College, Bangalore	1980	—	100	100	100	—	105	117	130	—	—	215*	130

Source: Government of Karnataka, *White Paper on Professional Colleges and Institutions*, Department of Education and Youth Services and Department of Health and Family Welfare, March 1983, p. 44.

The admission capacity is approved by the government and not by the Medical Council of India.

* Admissions exceeding the number approved by the government.

Table 5.2 Intake in Private Engineering Colleges (Full-time Courses)

Name of college	Affiliation orders issued on the recommendation of	Year of establishment	Course	1979–80		
				Initial intake	Additional intake	Total
M.S. Ramaiah Institute of Technology, Bangalore	M.U.	1962	C.E.M.	325	170	495
Manipal Institute of Technology, Manipal	M.U.	1957	C.E.M.EN.CH.AR.IPE.	359	60	419
R.V. College of Engineering, Bangalore	M.U.	1963	C.E.M.EN.	285	112	397
Sri Siddaganga Institute of Technology, Tumkur	M.U.	1963	C.E.M.EN.CH.	285	80	365
Dayananda Sagar College of Engineering, Bangalore	Committee	1979	C.E.M.EN.	220	75	295
Bangalore Institute of Technology	Committee	1979	C.E.M.EN.	200	42	242
Islamiah Institute of Technology, Bangalore	Committee	1979	C.M.	120	30	150
Sri Siddartha Institute	Committee	1979	C.M.	120	—	120
Bapuji College of Technology, Davangere	M.U.	1979	C.E.M.EN.IPE.	180	15	195
S.D.M. College of Engineering, Dharwar	K.U.	1979	C.E.M.	90	—	90
K.L.E. Society's Engineering College, Belgaum	K.U.	1979	C.E.M.	120	—	120
K.L.S. Engineering College	K.U.	1979	C.E.M.EN.	160	20	180
H.K.S. College of Engineering, Raichur	K.U.	1979	C.E.MT.TX.	120	—	120

Source: *White Paper on Professional Colleges and Institutions*, op. cit., p. 25.
Abbreviations: C: Civil, E: Electrical, M: Mechanical, EN: Electronics, CH: Chemical, AR: Architecture, IPE: Industrial Production, MT: Metallurgy, TX: Textiles

law in India in the case of those seeking admission to the seats, if any, reserved for those who have passed such examination with

1. Physics, Chemistry and Biology; or
2. Chemistry, Botany and Zoology as optional subjects.

He should have obtained not less than 40 per cent of the marks in the optional subjects in the qualifying examination (referred to in the above clause) if he belongs to any of the Scheduled Castes or Scheduled Tribes and 50 per cent in such subject in case of others.[15]

This, in fact, meant that with a mere pass percentage of 35 per cent and 50 per cent marks in Physics, Chemistry and Biology (in the case of scheduled castes and scheduled tribes it was 40 per cent), students were eligible to apply for the M.B.B.S. course. There was a common entrance test (conducted under the Karnataka Entrance Test) for admission to a medical course. From amongst those students who passed this test, the top few got into the four government colleges in Karnataka. There were also students who had secured a fairly high percentage in the range of 80–90 per cent at the pre-university examination. Those lower on the merit list were allocated to the private professional colleges. Their percentage was in the range of 50–70 per cent.

For engineering colleges too, a minimum of 50 per cent in Physics, Chemistry and Mathematics was necessary. Many students bordering on this minimum percentage sought admission to private engineering colleges. The average percentage of marks of students paying capitation fee (who were interviewed) was between 53 and 70 per cent, while most students in the merit quota had secured above 80 per cent in the pre-university examination. With this distinction in view, there was bound to be a qualitative difference between the two categories of students, invariably affecting standards of professional education. However, the managements of private colleges were only interested in limiting the merit quota of students as they were unable to get any capitation fee from this group.

The decision-making power, as we have seen, rested with the

[15] Government of Karnataka, *Rules for Selection of Candidates to Ist M.B.B.S. Course in Government/Private Medical Colleges 1984–85*, Bangalore.

executive committee. Academic matters stood secondary to financial concerns. The financial control was with the managing committee, manifesting the operation of the power structure in private colleges. In private colleges where members were nominated to the executive committee and where it was essentially a 'family enterprise', decision-making was only at the top indicating a lack of democratic functioning. The charging of capitation fee was arbitrary. *Mutts* funding educational institutions maintained their connections with the colleges and received the support of their respective castes as well.

Thus, we see the clear linkage between the state, society and education in the setting up of private colleges. Various institutions received the government's sanction on the basis of their caste or community strength. Politicians and bureaucrats influenced decisions regarding the establishment of such colleges. These institutions also ensured social prestige, a stable vote bank, political power, and influence for caste and political leaders.

The Management: A Socio-Economic Profile

As we have seen in the earlier chapters, the various pressure groups involved in private enterprise in higher education in Karnataka ranged from different caste groups, sects and communities to private entrepreneurs, industrialists and the rich peasantry. That there was adequate political support for this system can be seen from the presence of political figures on the management bodies of these institutions, as also from the fact that various governments in the State, even while publicly criticising the system, have defended it in one way or another.

In Karnataka colleges charging capitation fees may be grouped into three categories: the first, comprising the dominant-caste colleges, run by Vokkaligas and Lingayats; the second, belonging to minority groups like the scheduled castes and religious and linguistic minorities; and the third, colleges managed by private entrepreneurs. We will now discuss the main funding bodies and management of each of these categories separately, and present a socio-economic and political profile of the people running these institutions.

Colleges Run by Dominant Castes

Amongst the Lingayat- and Vokkaliga-run colleges, there were also socio-religious institutions supported by *mutts*, which performed the role of a mediating agency between the caste and its educational institutions.

The Bangalore Institute of Technology (B.I.T.) and the Kempegowda Institute of Medical Sciences (K.I.M.S.), both situated in Bangalore, were two of the Vokkaliga-run colleges studied. Table 5.3 presents some details of the members on the management board of these colleges. Both these were purely caste-based institutions run by the Vokkaligara Sangha (the main funding body). The Sangha came into existence in the early years of this century, 'to cater to the needs of the ryot communities of this State' and one of the objectives of the Sangha had been to promote the progress of the social, cultural and educational heritage of the State.[16]

Karnataka has a tradition of *mutts* (run by both the Lingayats and the Vokkaligas) taking an interest in educational activities. Colleges belonging to the same caste, for example, two Vokkaliga colleges, can be run by different *mutts* of the same caste. Some of these *mutts* have formed their own educational trusts and societies like the Mysore Lingayat Education Fund Association (M.L.E.F.A) and the Vokkaligara Sangha. Both these associations, as we saw in Chapter 2, worked for the educational advancement and general betterment of the two communities across the State.[17] Large donations were collected by the caste followers in their respective *mutts*, which allocated funds to their educational trusts and societies running private professional colleges. Many such trusts were exempted from payment of tax.[18] However, the motive in several cases was not purely philanthropic in the interest of caste members, but also included profit-making.

[16] *Prospectus 1986–87*, Bangalore Institute of Technology, Bangalore.

[17] See James Manor, 'The Evolution of Political Arenas and Units of Social Organization: The Lingayats and Okkaligas of Princely Mysore' in M.N. Srinivas (Ed.), *Dimensions of Social Change in India*, Allied Publishers, New Delhi, 1977, pp. 170–87.

[18] Contributions—for instance, to the Adichunchanagiri Shikshana Trust—were exempted from income tax as per order No. PRO/718–35/74/C17–111 dated 9.4.86 from the Commissioner of Income Tax, Bangalore. See *Prospectus 1987–88*, Adichunchanagiri Institute of Medical Sciences.

Table 5.3

Composition of the Management Board[a]

Name of the College: K.I.M.S., B.I.T.

Type: Dominant Caste—Vokkaliga

Member's name	Castel Community	Educational qualifications	Political affiliation	Occupation	Remarks
Dr. M.H. Marigowda	Vokkaliga	—	—	Ex-Director of horticulture	—
B.T. Parthasarathi	"	B.A. LL.B.	—	Advocate	—
A. Ananthappa	"	—	—	Landlord/Agriculturalist	—
G. Gowda	"	—	—	Retired bureaucrat	—
D.B. Basavgowda	"	B.A. LL.B.	—	Advocate	—
H. Srinivasaiah	"	B.E.	—	Retired government engineer	—
V. Papanna	"	—	—	Business	—
K.V. Gowda	"	—	—	Educationist/ Businessman	Runs colleges; is also a landlord
S.T.N. Gowda	"	B.E.	—	Engineer/Contractor	—
K.S. Sachithananda	"	Educated	Janata	Politician	A Janata Party supporter; contested for a seat in the Legislative Council from the teachers' constituency from south Karnataka, his father was the former education minister from Karnataka.

Name			
R. Manujunath	Congress-I	Politician/Businessman	Congress-I supporter; has won 3 times a seat in the university senate
Dr. C. Vittal	"	M.B.B.S., M.S.	Private medical practitioner
B. Shivanna	Janata	Politician	A Janata supporter. His brother is an M.L.A.
K.B.M. Reddy	"	Educated	Rich landlord/Politician
N. Narayanaswamy	"	"	Landlord

• All information regarding educational and occupational background of the members has been provided by Mr. H. Srinivasaiah, Treasurer, Vokkaligara Sangha, Bangalore. Information as of June 1988.

A Vokkaliga *mutt*, the Sree Adichunchanagiri *mutt*, situated in Nagmangala Taluk, ran a medical college in Nagmangala and an engineering college in Chikmagalur. The trust maintaining these colleges was the Adichunchanagiri Shikshana Trust. At the time of this study, the head of the *mutt* was Jagadguru Sri Balagangadharantha Swamiji who ascended the Sidda Simhasana in 1974. The *mutt* was engaged not only in the propagation of spiritualism but also in educational activities which had increased particularly since the swamiji became its head. There were 12 branches of the *mutt* with 58 educational institutions (including hostels) under it. There were about 1600 students studying in the general and technical educational institutions run under the aegis of the *mutt* including the Adichunchanagiri Institute of Technology at Chikmagalur. Sri Balagangadharantha Swamiji had felt concerned about the lack of medical services in this rural belt, and had urged that the educational facilities for rural people should be expanded.[19] The Adichunchanagiri Institute of Medical Sciences was thus established.

Table 5.4 gives the composition of the various members on the management board of the two colleges run by the Adichunchanagiri Shikshana Trust. From Tables 5.3 and 5.4 it may be seen that all the members of the board without exception belonged to the Vokkaliga community. The members of both the managing committees included businessmen, politicians, landlords, government officials, engineers and medical practitioners. Thus, capital was acquired through businessmen and landlords, while the politicians and officials gave them political leverage, and it was left to the engineers and doctors to form the skill component of these managing bodies. This provided the linkage between capital, skill structure and the political process. The presence of advocates is worth noting. In view of the frequent disputes between these colleges and the government, the managements preferred to retain a couple of advocates to tackle legal complications. Another interesting feature of the composition was that the members had affiliations with both the then ruling Janata Party (1988) and the opposition Congress (I) Party in Karnataka. In this way, irrespective of which party came to power, they were able to have continued support for their functioning.

The other dominant caste in Karnataka, the Lingayats, also ran

---

[19] *Prospectus 1987–88*, Adichunchanagiri Institute of Medical Sciences.

Table 5.4
*Composition of the Management Board**
Name of the College: A.I.T. & A.I.M.S.
Type: Dominant Caste—Vokkaliga

Member's name	Caste/Community	Educational qualifications	Political affiliation	Occupation	Remarks
K.S. Kallegowda	Vokkaliga	S.S.L.C.	—	Coffee planter	Ex-president, Vokkaligara Sangha, Chikamagalur; is a landowner also
U.P. Shivaraman	"	B.A., L.L.B.	Janata	Advocate	—
A. Chowdri Shanker	"	B.A., L.L.B.	Janata	Advocate	—
G. Govindaraju	"	B.E.	—	Retired government official	Retired Executive Engineer, P.W.D., Mysore
K. Singari Gowda	"	B.A., L.L.B.	Janata	Politician	Ex-M.L.A., Mandya
R. Reddy	"	S.S.L.C.	—	President, Vokkaligara Sangha, Kolar	—
K. Ramagowda	"	B.A., L.L.B.,	—	Advocate	—
P.M. Chikkaboraiah	"	B.A., L.L.B.	Janata	Advocate	—
H.C. Srikantaiah	"	B.A.	Congress-I	Politician	M.L.C., Bangalore
G. Madegowda	"	B.A., L.L.B.	Congress-I	Politician	Ex-Minister for Forest Resources
H.D. Devegowda	"	L.C.E.	Janata	Politician	Ex-Minister for P.W.D., Karnataka
H.N. Nanjegowda	"	B.A.	Congress-I	Politician	M.P.
H. Srinivasaiah	"	B.E.	—	Retired official	Retired D.G.M., B.E.M.L.

* All information as of September 1988. Some details are available in the Prospectus of A.I.T.,1988, and other information has been obtained from the Principal of A.I.T. through the help of the Deputy Commissioner's office, Chikamagalur.

their own private professional colleges. These institutions were either funded by *mutts* or run by registered societies. The Siddaganga Institute of Technology in Tumkur was managed by the Siddaganga Education Society of the Siddaganga *mutt*, which was established in the fifteenth century.[20]

Sree Shivakumara Swamiji was the head of the *mutt* which ran a free boarding house and a Sanskrit Pathshala which had been started in 1917. The *mutt* also ran a nursery, primary and higher secondary schools, and colleges of arts, science and commerce in many rural parts of Karnataka with the object of providing opportunities to rural children. There were also teacher-training institutes being run by the *swamiji*. The *mutt* took care to state that all these institutions were non-profit-making and service-oriented. Sree Swamiji had also opened small-scale general hostels in various parts of Karnataka where boys were provided with free boarding and lodging facilities. According to the *mutt*, the boarding expenses, which included free feeding of 3,000 students and other pilgrims everyday, were mainly met out of the large donations in kind and cash from the public.[21]

Sree Swamiji also started an engineering college in 1963 in Tumkur. He was also the President of the Siddaganga Education Society running this college. As in the case of colleges run by the Vokkaligas, the society had, as its members, a large number of businessmen, industrialists and merchants who were also land-owners. Some of them were supporters of political parties (see Table 5.5). An interesting aspect of the composition here was that two of its members were non-Lingayats. It may also be noted that three of the board members had no educational qualifications and four others had only high school certificates.

The Jagadguru Sri Shivaratheeswara (J.S.S.) Medical College in Mysore was one among the hundred and odd educational institutions of J.S.S. Maha Vidyapeetha, an establishment of Sri Suttur Veerasimhasana Mutt, another Lingayat *mutt*. It was established during the second half of the tenth century by Adijagadguru Sri Shivaratheeswara Bhagwathpadaru and was supported by the Chola kings. His successors contributed to the development of literature and progress in socio-economic and educational fields.

[20] *A Brief Note on Sri Siddaganga Mutt and Its Activities*, Sree Siddaganaga Mutt, Tumkur, 1982.
[21] Ibid.

Jagadguru Sri Shivarathee Rajendra Maha Swamigalavaru, the twenty-third pontiff of Sri Suttur Veerasimhasana Mutt, was the architect of the J.S.S. Maha Vidyapeetha. He established Maha Vidyapeetha in 1954, 'with the purpose of spreading education and enlightenment among the masses'.[22] Under his stewardship, it was running more than 100 institutions, ranging from kindergarten to postgraduate courses in arts, science, commerce and technology. As in the case of other colleges, the J.S.S. Medical College had on its management board important leaders belonging to different political parties. Some significant members in 1987–88 were Mr. M.S. Gurupadaswamy, then leader of the Janata Party in the Rajya Sabha, Mr. H. Gangadharan, a B.J.P. M.L.A. from Mysore city, and Mrs. R.S. Nagaratnamma of the Congress-I, leader of the opposition in the Karnataka Legislative Assembly.[23]

Although Sri Jayachamarajendra College of Engineering (S.J.C.) Mysore was a grants-in-aid college, it was also run by the J.S.S. Mahavidya Peetha. Twenty per cent of the students here were given admission on the basis of capitation fee.

The Karnataka Liberal Education Society (K.L.E.S.)[24] in Belgaum ran one medical college, the Jawaharlal Nehru Medical College (J.N.M.C.) and an engineering college, the K.L.E. Society's Engineering College, both in Belgaum. The Society was founded in 1916, and starting with a high school, it built a junior college, some arts, science and commerce colleges, and teachers' training colleges.

With the reorganisation of the States in 1956 on a linguistic basis, the four northern Karnataka districts of Belgaum, Dharwar, Bijapur and Karwar merged into the enlarged Mysore (now Karnataka) State. With the exception of three high schools in the Sholapur district, which remained in Maharashtra, all the other institutions of K.L.E.S. came into the Mysore State. After that, the society began to impress upon the State government the importance of private enterprise in the sphere of education, which till

[22] *Prospectus 1986–87*, J.S.S. Medical College.

[23] Information obtained through interviews with S. Murthy, Correspondent, *The Week*, Bangalore, and the Director, Medical Education, Karnataka, June 1988 and November 1987.

[24] This society was till 1949 called the Karnataka Lingayat Education Society. After Independence, the society keenly felt that it should also become fully secular by altering its name. See *K.L.E.S. Diamond Jubilee Souvenir*, 1979, p. 10.

Table 5.5

Composition of the Management Board*

Name of the College: S.I.T.

Type: Dominant Caste—Lingayat

Member's name	Caste/ Community	Educational qualifications	Political affiliation	Occupation	Remarks
Sree Shivakumar	Lingayat	B.A.	—	Head of *mutt*	
M. Mariswamiappa	"	Nil	—	Contractor	Has donated buildings to the Siddaganga Education Society; also owns land
G. Shivappa	"	School level	—	Merchant	Does business in fertilisers, seeds, chemicals, grains; is a landowner
T.K. Nanjundappa	"	B.A.	—	Business/Rich farmer	Deals with petrol kerosene, cement, hardware
N.R. Jagadeesh	"	School level	Congress-I	Industrialist	Does business in oil; owns land; father was an agriculturalist
K.R. Pai	Brahmin	High school	Congress-I	Industrialist	Business in soap
V.L. Shivappa	Lingayat	—	—	Landlord	Owns coconut plantation, Ex-M.L.A.
G.B. Chidanand	"	Nil	—	Business	A merchant in grains, oil and seeds; owns land
Dr. T.S. Malikarjunaiah	"	M.B.B.S.	—	A medical practitioner	Sons own land and factories

Name	Education	Caste	Political party	Occupation	Other
Dr. T. Anantharamasetty	Nil	Vysya	—	Business	Deals with cloth, owns land
C.P. Sadashivaiah	High school	Lingayat	—	Businessman/Industrialist	Owns agricultural tools factory
C.P. Chikannaippa	B.E.	Lingayat	Congress-I	Retired Chief Engineer (Govt.)	Former Principal of S.I.T.; owns some buildings
S. Diddagangaiah	B.A.	"	—	Auditor (Govt.)	Owns land
Dr. M.N. Chamabesappa	Ph.D.	"	—	Professor	Head of the Department of Mathematics, K.R.E.C., Surathkal; father owns land
D. Rudraiah	B.A.	"	—	Business	A paddy merchant; does business in foodgrains; owns land

• Information as of June 1988 provided by Mr. C.P. Sadashivaiah and Mr. C.P. Chickannaiyappa, members of the management board of S.I.T.

then had played a negligible role. The society urged the State government to look upon private enterprises 'as partners in the task of educating the people in a free country' and made frequent appeals for a liberal grant-in-aid code 'since the State alone can at no time in the near future shoulder the entire responsibility of educating the vast masses'. The aims of the society were to spread education in general and to take over the management and control of colleges and schools managed by other similar societies.[25]

The K.L.E. Society set up its medical college in 1963 with the help of S. Nijalingappa, the then Chief Minister, and obtained 100 acres of land from the Belgaum Borough Municipality at the cost of Rs. 500 per acre through the help of the Divisional Commissioner and the support of officers of the government. The engineering college in Belgaum came up in 1979. All the board members were Lingayats. The management board consisted of 15 elected members (see Table 5.6). Again, like the Vokkaliga colleges, it had a combination of rich businessmen, landlords, politicians, advocates, scientists, doctors and government officials.

Colleges Run by Minority Groups

In this category seven colleges were studied: three managed by scheduled caste and scheduled tribe trusts, one run by a Muslim trust, two colleges managed by the T.M.A. Pai Foundation (a linguistic minority—Konkani—trust), and one M.V.J. College which had also acquired the status of a linguistic minority (Tamil) college. The scheduled castes and scheduled tribes together comprise roughly 22 per cent of Karnataka's population.[26] Within Bangalore itself, the Ambedkar Institute of Technology and the Ambedkar Medical College were being run by the Panchajanya Vidhya Peetha Welfare Trust and the Ananda Social and Educational Trust respectively with wholly scheduled caste managements. As in the case of Vokkaliga and Lingayat management boards, we observed

[25] K.L.E. Society Diamond Jubilee Souvenir, 1979, pp. 12 and 19.
[26] The scheduled castes form 16.7826 per cent of the population in Karnataka while the scheduled tribes form 6.7254 per cent. See Government of Karnataka, Report of the Karnataka Third Second Backward Classes Commission, 1990, Vol. I, p. 45.

a similar combination of people on scheduled caste and scheduled tribe college managements. By and large, they were economically well-placed. Being scheduled castes enabled them to acquire special facilities from the government.

The Ananda Social and Educational Trust running the Ambedkar Medical College was a registered organisation 'funded by a few like-minded, educated friends of Karnataka, scheduled castes and scheduled tribes, and other backward communities inspired by the ideals of Lord Buddha'.[27] It was established with the main objectives of working for the educational, cultural, social and economic progress of the scheduled castes and scheduled tribes and other people belonging to the down-trodden communities of Karnataka 'by providing educational facilities on a large scale'.[28]

The Ananda Social and Educational Trust in its aims and objectives stated that not merely in Karnataka but in the country as a whole there were no professional colleges maintained by scheduled caste and scheduled tribe organisations to provide educational facilities to their children. 'Realising the absolute need to provide professional educational facilities to the children of these weaker sections, the Ananda Social and Educational Trust has established this medical college at Bangalore. There are about a lakh and odd doctors, but there is not even one per cent of them belonging to SC/ST and other weaker sections.'[29]

Mr. C.M. Armugham, a Republican Party M.L.A. who had been elected with Congress-I support in 1978, was the founder member of the Ambedkar Medical College. The permission to start the college was given by Mr. Gundu Rao, the then Chief Minister of Karnataka, to a trust of scheduled caste leaders headed by Mr. Armugham. Gundu Rao loaned the services of Dr. N.T. Mohan, an eminent professor who became the Principal of the college.[30] The trust running this institution comprised retired government officials, engineers, doctors, politicians and advocates. Mr. L. Shivalingaiah, the Chairman of the Trust, was the Chief Engineer of the Karnataka Water Board. Mr. V.S. Kuber was an influential lawyer. Mr. M.H. Jayaprakash Narayan was a politician,

[27] *Prospectus 1986–87*, Dr. B.R. Ambedkar Medical College, Bangalore.
[28] Ibid.
[29] Ibid.
[30] Interview with L. Shivalingaiah, Chairman, Anand Social and Educational Trust, June 1988.

Table 5.6

Composition of the Management Board[a]

Name of the College: J.N.M.C. & K.L.E.S. Engineering College

Type: Dominant Caste—Lingayat

Member's name	Caste/ Community	Educational qualifications	Political affiliation	Occupation	Remarks
P.B. Kore	Lingayat	B.Com.	—	Landlord/ Industrialist	Contested for M.L.A.'s seat but lost; Chairman of the K.L.E.S.
S.H. Koujalagi	"	B.Com. Ll.B.	—	Advocate	Janata M.L.A.; father was a minister; owns land
A.G. Bagewadi	"	B.A., B.Com.	Congress-I	Business/Landlord	Wholesale tobacco merchant Also a landlord
P.B. Patil	"	B.Sc., Ll.B.	Congress-I	Advocate	Owns land; is a cotton merchant and was the Taluk Development Board President
M.B. Munavalli	"	Intermediate	Congress-I	Business	
M.K. Kavatigamath	"	Intermediate	Congress-I	Chairman of a spinning-mill/ Landlord	Director of a sugar factory and of a bank, both under the Congress-I banner
Dr. N.S. Hambarwadi	"	M.B.B.S., M.S.	Janata	Doctor/Politician	Janata M.L.A.; is also a landlord
V.C. Hanji	"	B.A.	Janata	Forest contractor	Owns land
M.C. Kolli	"	B.A.		Landlord	—
V.M. Patted	"	B.A., Ll.B.		General Manager of a bank	—

R.M. Patil	"	Nil	Janata	Landlord	Runs a sugar factory
J.N. Metgud	"	B.Sc., Ll.B.	Congress-I	Advocate/Businessman	Runs an oil mill; is also a landowner
Dr. V.G. Nelivigi	"	M.Sc., Ph.D.		Scientist/College principal	
S.B. Patil	"	M.Sc.		Principal, science college	
B.C. Heskeri	"	M.Sc.		Principal, Science College, Hubli	

* Information as of June 1988, provided by the Principal, K.L.E.S. Engineering College and Mr. P.B. Patil, Member of the Managing Board of the K.L.E. Society, Belgaum.

an ex-MLA and Congress-I supporter. Almost all the trustees had landed property. According to Shivalingaiah, this was because 'all of us have landed/rural roots'. However, the students gave a different version, stating that many of the trustees had added to their assets, i.e., land and property, after acquiring membership of the management board.

Jayaprakash Narayan and L. Shivalingaiah were also on the managing board of the Ambedkar Institute of Technology, another college which proclaimed to be an institution 'primarily meant for SC/ST and other backward classes'.[31]

The Shri Siddharatha Institute of Technology (S.S.I.T.) in Tumkur had almost a similar combination of people in the management. We may observe from Table 5.7 that three of the politicians were also landlords. Two members were full-time politicians. As in the case of dominant caste colleges, politicians owing allegiance to different political parties were members of the board.

The Governing Council of S.S.I.T. had amongst its members Mr. Veeranna, the Minister of State for Small Savings and Finance in the Janata Government of Karnataka, and Mr. S.N. Shetty, a merchant. While influential government officials were a help in getting files to move faster, political contacts ensured the smooth functioning of the college. A combination of these influences was observed in the scheduled caste institutions that were studied. Businessmen, politicians, senior government officials and landholders were the decision-makers and managers of such private colleges.

Of the eight minority institutions in Karnataka in 1987, two were studied. The Islamiah Institute of Technology (I.I.T.) was a religious (Muslim) minority college in Bangalore. The college was established through the efforts of Haji Imtiaz Khan who was a recruitment agent for Middle East companies. Some serving and retired Muslim government officers and a few businessmen got together and, with financial help from the Gulf, started this college.[32] The college had on its management body some retired government officials (bureaucrats) and a few businessmen (see Table 5.8), all of whom were Muslims. As indicated in the study of other colleges the linkage between capital, the skill component and the state

[31] *Prospectus 1987–88*, Ambedkar Institute of Technology, Bangalore.

[32] Personal interviews with the Director, Technical Education, Government of Karnataka, and S. Murthy, Reporter, *The Week*, Bangalore, June 1988.

Table 5.7

*Composition of the Management Board***

Name of the College: S.S.I.T. (Tumkur) Type: Minority (Scheduled Caste) College

Member's name	Caste/Community	Educational qualifications	Political affiliation	Occupation	Remarks
M.M. Kharge	Scheduled Caste	B.A.	Congress-I	Politician	Deputy Opposition leader from Congress-I, sitting legislator
A.M. Gangadiraiah	"		Congress-I	Politician/Agriculturalist	Runs educational institution; owns land; ex-M.L.C.
J.P. Narayan	"	B.A.	Congress-I	Politician/Landlord	Ex-M.L.A.
M. Shankaraiah	"	B.A.		Retired government official	—
M. Puttathimaiah	"	M.A.	Janata	Landlord/Politician	Janata officer-bearer
D.R. Nanjaiah	"	Educated		Retired government official	Runs a newspaper
Sri Kumaraswamy	"	B.A. Ll.B.		Retired Sessions Judge	Practising in the High Court.
T.K. Ramaiah	"	Educated		Retired government official	Retired Assistant Engineer
G. Puttaswamy	"		Janata	Politician	Ex-Deputy Speaker Chikmagalur
Maruthy Male	"	B.A.	Congress-I	Secretary, Karnataka People's Education Society	—
Dr. G. Shivprasad	"	M.B.B.S., M.S.		Doctor	—
Dr. G. Parmeshwara	"	M.Sc. Ph.D.		Administrator of the S.S.I.T.	Son of Gangadiraiah, the owner of the college
Dr. G.L. Byriah		M.Sc. Ph.D.		Director, Collegiate Council	—

* Information as of June 1988. Interview with Dr. G. Parameshwara, Administrator, S.S.I.T.

Table 5.8
Composition of Management Board*
Name: Islamiah Institute of Technology
Type: Religious Minority

Father's name	Community	Educational qualifications	Occupation
A. Sharief	Muslim	B.E., M.E.	Retired government engineer; landowner
H.I.A. Khan	"	Literate	Business
A. Khayum	"	S.S.L.C.	Retired teacher; owns land
Col. Hussain	"	"	Retired army officer
S. Ahmad	"	"	Business
Sahabuddin	"	Educated	"
M. Ahmad	"	B.Sc.	Government service
A.M.J. Shaikh	"	"	Retired government official

* Information as of September 1988, procured with the help of a senior K.P.S.C. official, Mr. Nazeer Hussain, Planning Department, Government of Karnataka.

structure was brought into focus through the composition of its management, which was again a combination of businessmen, landholders, engineers and government officials. This linkage can also be seen in this institution (Table 5.8).

There were two rival factions in the management, each wanting to gain greater control over the affairs of the college. Abdullah Sharief, the former Principal of the college who led one of the factions, claimed that the land where the college building was situated belonged to him.[33] The High Court had appointed a receiver to administer the college affairs.

Amongst the linguistic minority colleges, the rise of the Kasturba Medical College, the first private enterprise in medical education in Karnataka, has been discussed earlier in Chapter 3. The college was started by a Brahmin trust. Dr. Pai, the founder of the college, 'in fact wanted to see all educational opportunities open to all castes'.[34] Although initially, the Kasturba Medical College might have been motivated by caste feelings (and members of other castes have been known to refer to it as a 'Brahmin college'), in

[33] Personal interview with Abdullah Sharief, November 1987.
[34] Personal interview with Ramesh Pai, Chairman, T.M.A. Pai, Foundation Trust, November 1987.

fact the Brahmins were never more than about a third of all the students.[35]

Both the K.M.C. and M.I.T. had the status of minority colleges, and the trustees were Konkani-speaking people. The object of the trust was to promote the development of the language and culture of the Konkani-speaking people, and work for their educational advancement.[36] The Konkanis, being a linguistic minority,[37] have been protected under Article 30 of the Constitution.

The T.M.A. Pai Trust running the Manipal Institute of Technology (M.I.T.) and the Kasturba Medical College (K.M.C.) was a family trust. The Pais who were running these colleges had wide-ranging interests. Their business enterprises included tile factories, a general construction company, roadways, a finance company, marketing for 30 companies (including Escorts motorcycles), agro-goods, pesticides, fertilisers, power presses, soft drinks, and surgical instruments. The Syndicate Bank which was nationalised in 1969 had been started by the Pais. The Canara Steel Limited, a mini steel plant in Mangalore, was also owned by them. Besides these industries, the Pais owned a considerable amount of land. T. Ramesh Pai, a nephew of T.M.A. Pai, was the Chairman of the Governing Council and also Chairman of the Industrial Credit and Development Syndicate, a company which had financed picture houses and hotels all over Karnataka. He was also the Managing Director of the Maharashtra Apex Corporation, an enterprise which carried on an extensive business in hire-purchase instalment loans.

The family had been able to wield considerable political influence. One of the nephews of Dr. T.M.A. Pai, Mr. T.A. Pai, became a Union Minister for Railways in 1972. He had earlier been elected by the Karnataka State Legislative Assembly to the Rajya Sabha.[38]

[35] Selden Manefee, *The Pais of Manipal*, The Academy of General Education, Manipal, 1969.

[36] *Dr. T.M.A. Foundation* vs. *State of Karnataka*, W.P. No. 12597 of 1984 dated 10 September 1984, *Indian Law Reports*, 1985, Karnataka.

[37] As regards the existence of such linguistic groups, the petitioners in the *T.M.A. Foundation* vs. *State of Karnataka* case stated that Konkani was a separate language spoken mainly in the districts of Dakshina Canara and Uttar Canara by about six lakh people. The percentage of persons whose mother tongue is Konkani as compared to the total population in the State is 1.96 lakh. See *Karnataka State Gazetteer, Part II*, p. 978 and *Karnataka State Gazetteer, Part I*, p. 439.

[38] Selden Manefee, op. cit.

The management board had amongst its members a retired bureaucrat, a journalist and an advocate (see Table 5.9). While the majority of the members on it were Brahmins, there were also two Christians including one advocate.

Table 5.9
Composition of the Management Board*
Name of the College: M.I.T. & K.M.C.
Types: Linguistic Minority

Member's name	Caste/ community	Occupation	Remarks
Ashok Pai	Brahmin	Industrialist	Youngest son of T.M.A. Pai; runs the Manipal Bottling Company; holds an engineering degree
Dr. T.R. Pai	"	Medical Director K.M.C. & Executive Director M.I.T.	Son of T.M.A. Pai; fully involved in college affairs
R.P. Kamat	"	Industrialist	Owns Kamat Group of Hotels, Hubli
G. Pai	"	Industrialist	Owns Bharat Beedi Works Private Limited
M.R. Pai	"	Business	—
Y.V. Pai	"	I.A.S. (Retired)	—
M.V. Kamath	"	Journalist	—
J.A. Sequeira	Christian	Advocate	—
P. Mallya	Brahmin	Hony. Secretary of the Konkani Bhasha Prachar Sabha, Cochin	
T. Ramesh Pai	"	Chairman, Governing Council, M.I.T.; Industrialist	T.M.A. Pai's nephew; fully occupied with college work

* Details made available in personal interviews with Dr. Ramdas Pai and Mr. T. Ramesh U. Pai, members of the management board and through the *Prospectus*, *M.I.T.*, *1987–88*. Information as of June 1988.

Colleges Managed by Private Entrepreneurs

Taking the cue from the success of caste- and community-based colleges, a large number of private entrepreneurs also entered the arena of private professional education in Karnataka, particularly in engineering education. In Chapters 2 and 3 we briefly discussed private enterprises seeking educational avenues for investing their surplus. Some of the colleges studied were being run by small entrepreneurs, while others like the Ramaiah colleges were large enterprises. While none of the managements of these colleges professed any caste aims, one of them, the M.V.J. College, had managed to acquire a linguistic minority status for itself. Such a status enabled the management to circumvent government rules and regulations regarding the functioning of private institutions.

M.S. Ramaiah, a contractor by profession, started the M.S. Ramaiah Institute of Technology in Bangalore in 1962. Fifteen years later, he set up a medical college in 1979. M.S. Ramaiah belonged to the Balija community, a backward trading class. However, he did not use the community label to get a 'backward' status for his college. He had made considerable profits as a contracter in Bihar and U.P.,[39] and he decided to invest in another lucrative and at the same time philanthropic activity—education. His additional asset was the 100 acres of family land he had inherited in Bangalore, now known as the Gokula Puram Extension, where both the engineering and medical colleges are located.

Ramaiah and his sons set up a number of industries with offices located in Bangalore. Their industries included a steel plant, called Brindaban Alloys, a cement plant (Gokula Cements) and the M.S. Ramaiah Construction and Engineering Company. They also owned over 400 acres of agricultural land about 25 miles away from Mysore city. The Ramaiahs ran a *mutt* and a *dharamshala* in Kaiwara, and also a free hostel in Bangalore.[40]

The Gokula Education Foundation which ran the Ramaiah medical and engineering colleges was a family trust. M.S. Ramaiah and his sons were on the management board (see Table 5.10).

[39] Information provided by students and teachers of Ramaiah colleges and Sri Kusumakar, Resident Editor, *The Times of India*, Bangalore.
[40] Personal interview with M.R. Jayaram, the eldest son of M.S. Ramaiah and Chairman of the Gokula Education Foundation, June 1988.

Table 5.10

Composition of the Management Board

Name of the College: M.S. Ramaiah Institute of Technology (M.S.R.I.T.), M.S. Ramaiah Medical College

Type: Private Entrepreneur's College

Member's name	Castel Community	Educational qualifications	Political affiliation	Occupation	Remarks
M.S. Ramaiah	Balija	F.I.A.E.	No open affiliation	Landlord/ Industrialist	Supports parties in power (information given by students)
M.R. Jayaram	,,	No formal degree	Ex-M.L.A. (Congress-I)	Ex-M.L.A./Politician	Resigned Congress-I membership in 1978; Chairman, Gokula Education Foundation
M.R. Sampangiramaiah	,,	B.Com.	—	Business	All are in family business; managing industries and college affairs
M.R. Sitharam	,,	B.Sc.	—	,,	
M.R. Raghuram	,,	B.A.	—	,,	
M.R. Pattabhiram	,,	B.Com.	—	,,	They own agricultural land also. Pattabhiram was the registrar in the medical college for some time (till early 1988)
M.R. Janakiram	,,	Degree in agriculture	—	,,	
M.R. Kodandaram	,,	M.Sc.	—	,,	
M.R. Anandaram	,,	B.Sc.	—	,,	
R. Ramaiah	,,	B.Com.	—	,,	

Information as of June 1988 collected from the *Prospectus M.S.R.I.T.*, interview with Mr. M.R. Jayaram, Mr. Pattabhiram, students and faculty members of the colleges.

Mr. Jayaram resigned his Congress-I membership in 1978, soon after the Janata government came into power in Karnataka. Almost all the board members, who were M.S. Ramaiah's sons, had graduate degrees and managed their own industries and businesses.

The R.V. College of Engineering was being run by an all-Vysya trust, the Rashtriya Sikshana Samiti Trust. The Chairman of the trust was M.K. Panduranga Chetty, a commerce graduate and a Governor of the Rotary Club of Bangalore district. He was a prominent industrialist and had a number of business interests. Panduranga Chetty ran the Krishna Flour Mills and owned some food industries besides having interests in real estate. He had no definite political alignment, though in early 1988 he was close to the then Chief Minister, Ramakrishna Hegde.[41] Mr. K.M. Nanjappa, the Vice-President of the management board, was the former mayor of Bangalore. The other members included Mr. D.A. Pandu, the Honorary Secretary of the Trust, who was a silk merchant, Mr. S.N. Shetty, the Treasurer, a businessman, and Mr. G. Shivappa who was a merchant and a landowner possessing large tracts of urban and agricultural land.[42] In the case of R.V. College it was noted that a majority of the management board members belonged to the prosperous merchant class, who were able to secure the required political support.

The Dayanand Sagar College of Engineering was started in 1979 by Dayanand Sagar, another private entrepreneur. He was an affluent Vokkaliga barrister, a prominent Congressman, who had been a Deputy Minister and a member of the Legislative Assembly and the Legislative Council.[43] The college was run by the Sagar family trust. When Dayanand Sagar died in 1987, his son Hema Chandra Sagar became the Chairman of the trust. The son became the *de-facto* Principal of the college and all decisions rested with him. H.C. Sagar was a medical practitioner but spent most of the time looking after the affairs of the college. He had no definite leanings towards any political party.

The M.V.J. College of Engineering, which was run by the

---

[41] Interview with C.P. Chickannaiyappa, Member Syndicate, Bangalore University, June 1988.

[42] Ibid.

[43] Information gathered in an interview with H. Kusumakar, Resident Editor, *The Times of India*, Bangalore and B.N. Krishnamurthy, Director, Technical Education, Government of Karnataka, June 1988.

Venkatesha Education Society, was started in 1982 by another private entrepreneur, M.V. Jayaram. A Tamilian Brahmin, Jayaram started a small high school, then a B.Ed. college, and finally managed to obtain permission during Gundu Rao's tenure for an engineering college in Bangalore. The Venkatesha Education Society he headed was a family trust, consisting of his sons and sons-in-law. He had no permanent political affiliation. Although M.V.J. College was sanctioned by Gundu Rao's government, Jayaram switched over his loyalty to the Janata Party under Hegde.[44]

Within a period of three years after its establishment in 1982, the M.V.J. College was granted a minority status by the High Court. The Venkatesha Education Society ran this institution for the benefit of the Tamil-speaking students in Karnataka.

The Karnataka High Court gave a ruling[45] on 14/16 August 1985 that the Tamil language could not be denied the status of a distinct and different language spoken by smaller sections of the people inhabiting the Karnataka State. Permission was granted by the court to the societies to promote the interests of the linguistic minorities which they represented. Such colleges were entitled to all the protection linguistic minority institutions enjoy under Article 30 of the Constitution.

The Managements: An Analysis

The study of the managements of the 19 colleges, which were representative of the various categories outlined earlier, provides a fair idea of the various interests involved in private professional education in Karnataka. There were many common noticeable threads in the respective management boards.

The first aspect we note is that almost all colleges had people with strong political ties. Significantly, in the same board there were members who were supporters of both the leading political parties—the Congress-I and the Janata. At the same time, the members had shifting loyalties—ever willing to change their affiliations when a new government came to power. Politics in the

---

[44] Interview with the Director, Technical Education, Government of Karnataka, June 1988.

[45] See *Deccan Herald*, 17 August 1985. Also see *Indian Law Reports*, 1986, Karnataka.

management, for instance, might not have been permitted by the *Swamiji* of the Adichunchanagiri Mutt, but politicians were members of the trust, and they were all utilised to further the cause of their community or caste, despite personal differences amongst themselves.[46] G. Parmeshwara, the administrator of the Shree Siddhartha Institute of Technology, also remarked in this context that to ensure the smooth functioning of a professional college, it was necessary to maintain 'an all-political party profile'.[47]

Often, the strategy of retaining the support of both the Congress-I and the Janata politicians worked, as we have seen in the case of Ambedkar Medical College where there was a clearly larger Congress-I representation on the management board. Although this college was sanctioned by Gundu Rao's government (Congress-I), once the Janata Party came to power, a group owing allegiance to a senior scheduled caste minister, B. Rachaiah, and comprising senior scheduled caste officials, came to exercise control. After that there was a great deal of discord between the old and new management members in their quest for power and financial control of the college affairs.[48] This change from the Congress-I to Janata supporting groups shows how the government in power exercises an influence on the shifting alignments in management boards.

The trend towards including politicians on the managing committees of private professional colleges is, in a way, indicative of the many contradictions existing in the larger political reality.[49] On the one hand, the State and central governments have been decrying the capitation fee system in colleges; on the other hand, politicians who operate the state machinery have been present, to a significant extent, in the management boards of private institutions.

The most striking feature of the college managements was that they were dominated by a single caste or community. With rare exceptions of one or two members not belonging to the majority groups in the colleges studied, it was the common caste or community factor that stood out. However, they were all operating in

[46] Interview with H. Srinivasaiah, Member, Adichunchanagiri Shikshana Trust, November 1988.

[47] Interview with G. Parmeshwara, November 1987 and July 1988.

[48] Interview with S. Murthy, *The Week*, Bangalore, July 1988.

[49] See Manoranjan Mohanty, 'Duality of the State Process in India: A Hypothesis' in Ghanshyam Shan (Ed.), *Capitalist Development: Critical Essays*, Popular Prakashan, Bombay, 1990.

a competitive situation and were using the educational arena to further their interests.

Another noticeable trend was a good mix of businessmen and industrialists, rich landowners and agriculturalists, government officials and advocates on the managing boards of the colleges studied. Advocates were always a help in pinpointing the legal loopholes and turning them to their own advantage, and a significant number of court rulings had gone in favour of the private managements.

For rich businessmen and industrialists, education was an extension of an industry or business. They were in a position to initially invest the minimum that was needed to start an institution. The managements, however, professed noble aims like promotion of education.[50]

For certain private entrepreneurs, investing in education was not only a 'philanthropic activity', but it also ensured social and political prominence. M.S. Ramaiah could have set up more industries on his 100 acres of land, but he preferred to run colleges. To ensure that there was tight financial control, private entrepreneurs had their family trusts managing college affairs.

On the strength of their money power, businessmen and industrialists were able to secure political support. In running private colleges, they were aware that they could not survive and grow without government help. Given the license- and sanction-granting authority of the bureaucracy, managing an educational institution demanded something more than initiative and foresight on the part of business entrepreneurs. A great deal depended on good public relations and the right political support. Although it was difficult to obtain verifiable evidence in interviews, some respondents stated that they had to keep politicians happy and make contributions to political parties during election time. Politicians always need businessmen to meet the high costs of campaigning in elections. Apart from electioneering, political parties need large finances to stage public meetings and rallies, and maintain their cadres for conducting their day-to-day business. Businessmen were

[50] M.R. Jayaram, Chairman of the Gokula Education Foundation, in a personal interview, June 1988, remarked that such private institutions were a response to the large number of applicants.

often only too willing to meet this need in the hope of being reciprocated at a later date.[51]

Political contributions from companies are perfectly legal. Till 1956, according to the Companies Act, apart from charitable donations no political contributions could be made by companies. However, after the 1957 ruling in the High Courts of Bombay and Calcutta, charitable donations could include those to political parties. But in 1969 when Mrs. Gandhi was in power, all donations were banned under section 293-A of the Companies Act. In 1985, this ban was lifted and companies could make political contributions provided they declared the name of the party they were contributing to and also the amount. But few companies would donate to parties openly. The corporate sector would surely not contribute out of a sense of philanthropy. And as Dilip Sarwate has remarked, 'there are expectations and that is why most companies hedge their bets by chipping into the election funds of both the ruling party and the opposition.'[52] Entrepreneurs running private colleges, to secure government help, need to keep politicians happy and shift their loyalties to the party in power.

The data collected in this study revealed that few business entrepreneurs openly aligned themselves to a single political party, but would often support the party in power. Pandurang Chetty and M.V. Jayaram both supported the Janata party, but M.R. Jayaram gave up his Congress membership in 1978, soon after the Janata party came to power in Karnataka. Individual entrepreneurs like M.V. Jayaram had to rely on political support as well as utilise bureaucratic channels to run their institutions. Money power was often used to manipulate the right kind of support needed at the appropriate time.[53]

Another important aspect observed was the presence of land-owners and agriculturalists on the managing boards of private

---

[51] See O. Tellis and M. Padmanabhan, 'Crony Capitalism: The Business–Politics Nexus,' *Sunday*, October 1988, pp. 23–29. Also see Moin Shakir, *State and Politics in Contemporary India*, Ajanta Publications, Delhi 1986, p. 48, wherein it is stated that leading business houses gave donations worth Rs. 36,38,408 to different political parties in 1969.

[52] See Dilip M. Sarwate, *Political Marketing: The Indian Experience*, Tata McGraw-Hill, New Delhi, 1990, p. 170.

[53] Interview with the Director, Technical Education, Karnataka, July 1988.

professional colleges. There was a small but significant percentage of investment in education from amongst the dominant castes, particularly from those engaged in agriculture. The rural rich tried to diversify into other profitable ventures.[54] Amongst the dominant agricultural castes, prosperous sections vied with one another to get more jobs for themselves and for places in institutions providing professional education. The need to acquire educational and professional qualifications for employment was strongly felt and so they were willing to train professional cadres from amongst themselves.[55]

Senior government officials, either retired or those in active service, were also to be found on management boards. Sanctions for starting private colleges had to come through such government channels. Having retired bureaucrats on the boards was a help because they knew their junior colleagues who would 'push files faster' in order to get permission for registering a trust, to find a suitable site, to procure cheap land, and finally, to start a college. Those who had been in active service were themselves valuable for such work. All the private colleges mentioned in this study had the support of a Chief Minister in Karnataka. The K.L.E. Society's medical college in Belgaum, for instance, came into existence in 1963, 'thanks to the far-sighted vision of the Chief Minister S. Nijalingappa—who was keenly interested in the all-round development of Belgaum'.[56] In addition, the senior bureaucrats had been of great help.

The most important and immediate problem for the medical college in Belgaum was to secure a large and suitable stretch of land near the Civil Hospital for the construction of the buildings. 'Through the good offices of Shri G.V.K. Rao, the then Divisional Commissioner of Belgaum, we were able to get 100 acres of land from Mal Maruti extension of Belgaum Municipality.'[57] Thus, while S. Nijalingappa sanctioned a medical college at Belgaum, G.V.K.

[54] 'Originally the management board members were all rural people with some landed property and they were financially sound. Now they have also got "mixed" into other professions', remarked Mr. Srinivasaiah, Treasurer of the Vokkaligara Sangha, Bangalore. Beyond the initial stage, as was observed earlier, there was no further investment required in the setting up of capitation fee based colleges; however, some agricultural surplus went into education.

[55] See A.R. Desai, *India's Path of Development*, Popular Prakashan, Bombay, 1984, pp. 187–90.

[56] *Prospectus 1988–89*, J.L.M.C., Belgaum.

[57] Ibid., p. 2.

Rao and the Belgaum Municipal Council enabled the Society to make the medical college a reality by making a suitable site available for it. In the case of the managing boards of some colleges there was a bid to control finance by different factions as was the case in Ambedkar Medical College where there were two rival factions, and also in the case of the Islamiah Institute of Technology. This revealed the interests of the groups involved in gaining a financial hold so that they could partake of the profits. The executive committee of the colleges run by the Vokkaligara Sangha in Bangalore consisted of elected members of the Sangha. 'During elections there are no classes but the college campus is like a battlefield. Social recognition and financial gains which you can achieve through such elections are very significant; hence a number of clashes occur. There are differences between members of the Sangha and occasionally you may come across Sangha dissidents,'[58] remarked a student of the Kempegowda Institute of Medical Sciences.

In some *mutts* (for instance, the Siddaganga Mutt running several institutions in Tumkur including the Siddaganga Institute of Technology), there was a dispute between the senior *swamiji* and the junior *swamiji*. The senior *swamiji*, Sree Shivakumar, was the religious head of the *mutt* and also the President of the Siddaganga Education Society. He had spent 40 years in building up educational institutions. Through the schools and colleges of the society as well as through donations, a fair amount of money, to the extent of 30–40 crores of rupees, had come into the *mutt*.[59] Hence, different factions were involved in a bid to corner the wealth of the *mutt*. The junior *swamiji*, who had been groomed as his successor by Sree Shivakumar himself, had levelled accusations against the latter of mismanaging the funds and of embezzlement. Sree Shivakumar, doubting the integrity of the junior *swamiji*, accused him of destroying institutions which had taken them years to build and no longer deemed him a worthy successor. Violent clashes between the two rival groups took the form of stone-throwing and burning of buses in Tumkur town and for some time it became a serious law-and-order problem. Caste and political

[58] A professor of economics at Bangalore University, formerly a member of the Vokkaligara Sangha, was one such dissident.

[59] Personal interview with the Deputy Commissioner, Tumkur, June 1988. There is also the Lingayat practice of Dasoha, i.e. feeding others. So, Lingayats donate both in cash and kind to the *mutts* as charity. *Mutt* accounts, as we have seen, were not open to public scrutiny.

elements also crept into this feud. Sree Shivakumar being a Lingayat was supported by the Lingayat group led by S.R. Bommai (former Chief Minister of Karnataka), as well as by the more wealthy industrialists. The junior *swamiji* was supported by the not-so-affluent industrialists, the local Congress-I leader, and another M.L.A. So in a way this rivalry also surfaced as a Janata–Congress clash. But, as we have pointed out earlier, such disputes arose primarily out of a desire for securing monetary gains. Implications of such feuds were deeper, and manifested patterns of political alignments.

After reading this analysis of members on the management boards of private engineering and medical colleges in Karnataka, it would not be incorrect to conclude that the members were able to wield a great deal of influence and pressurise any party in power through the combined strength of their money, power and caste or community backing as well as political support. Thus, the management boards also clearly reflected the intertwining of caste, class and politics in the sphere of professional education. Such then were the dominant social forces controlling education and influencing the government.

6

THE STUDENTS

With growing unemployment of the general arts and science graduates in India, the demand for professional education has been continually on the increase. Consequently, as we have seen, a large number of private professional colleges have been established in the country, especially in Karnataka. Students aspiring to become engineers and doctors, but unable to gain admission in the government-run colleges on their own merit, have sought admission in these private colleges which charge high rates of capitation fee.

In this chapter we will attempt a study of these students, their aspirations and motivations, and their socio-economic background. Also, we will analyse the background of their parents who have been paying large sums of money to ensure their wards' admission to these colleges. It would be interesting to relate this analysis with our earlier study of the management process and the board members (Chapter 5), and examine the interests the capitation fee system has been serving. We will also examine whether the quality of education imparted in private colleges, in the opinion of students, meets the minimum standards as regards the faculty and facilities provided, how it compares with government colleges, and whether it has been able to fulfil their aspirations.

Sampling for the Study

For the purpose of our study, we categorised the engineering and medical colleges into three groups: (*a*) colleges managed by the dominant castes, the Vokkaligas and Lingayats; (*b*) colleges run by minority groups; and (*c*) those run by private entrepreneurs. We selected 19 colleges permitting a balanced sample representative of these three categories. Information was obtained through questionnaires, interviews and documents available from the colleges.

Two types of samples were collected. One was the 'extensive' or initial sample (which we will refer to as Sample I) from 19 colleges to provide an overview of the capitation fee system in the State. The second was an 'intensive' sample (Sample II) of four colleges to obtain specific data pertaining to the colleges. To ensure as broad a sample as possible, we circulated questionnaires to different groups of students in terms of sex, caste and community and their parents' occupation. Rural/urban, capitation fee/non-capitation fee, Karnataka/non-Karnataka, and academic year (first to fourth years) differentiations were also taken into account to cover a cross-section of students representing all shades of opinion.

For the extensive sample, 19 colleges were selected from each of the three categories defined above; within each category also we selected representative colleges from different groups. Thus, from the first category of colleges run by dominant castes, eight colleges from both Lingayat- and Vokkaliga-managed colleges were studied. Similarly, from the second category, all types of minority groups, whether religious, linguistic or belonging to scheduled castes or scheduled tribes were covered—six such colleges were selected. From the last category of colleges run by private entrepreneurs, we selected five colleges being managed by family trusts because a majority of the colleges in this category belonged to this group. Different geographical regions were also considered to obtain a complete picture of capitation fee colleges in the State.

Thus, we selected the districts of Tumkur and Mysore where colleges run by a different Lingayat *mutt* in each case were located in order to examine the linkage between socio-religious organisations and education. Belgaum was chosen to obtain a picture of North Karnataka and also because it was the headquarters of the Karnataka Liberal Education Society which, as we mentioned earlier, was the first society of its kind to have initiated private enterprise in education in Karnataka. For similar reasons, the Kasturba Medical College at Manipal was chosen, being the first private medical college to be established in Karnataka. Chikmagalur and Nagamangala taluks in Mandya were selected because of their professed rural bias in the admission of students.

In addition to samples obtained from the 19 colleges detailed above, information was gathered from four government-run colleges for the purposes of comparison. These were Karnataka Regional Engineering College, Surathkal, University Vishvesvaraya College of Engineering, Bangalore, Mysore Medical College, and Bangalore Medical College.

Of the 19 colleges, four colleges were selected for intensive sampling to corroborate the reliability of data gathered from the earlier samples. Since the dominant caste managed colleges were larger in number, we selected one college each from the two dominant castes, the two being the Kempegowda Institute of Medical Sciences and the Siddaganga Institute of Technology. The Ambedkar Medical College was chosen as representing the scheduled caste group, while the M.S. Ramaiah Institute of Technology was selected from amongst colleges run by private entrepreneurs.

In addition to obtaining information from students of these colleges, some teachers, principals and management board members were also interviewed. Questionnaires were also circulated to the teachers. Some of the information provided in the previous chapter on 'The Management Process' and the following chapter on 'The Faculty' is based on these interviews and questionnaires. The following discussion is however focused on the students on the basis of data collected in our sample studies.

Socio-Economic Background

In this section, on the basis of the data gathered from 19 private colleges, we will examine the socio-economic background of the students, their caste and class dimensions, their rural or urban roots, and the kind of schooling they had. We will also study if, and how, these factors determined their attitude towards the capitation fee system.

It was observed that a majority of the students came from an affluent background. They belonged, in varying numbers, to the rural gentry or business groups, or whose parents were middle or higher level salaried professionals or government servants.

Of a total of 406 respondents in the initial sample (Sample I), 68 students (16.67 per cent) came from landed families (see Table 6.1). In S.S.I.T., for instance, nine of the 29 students, and in A.I.T. (Chikmagalur), five of the 20 respondents belonged to families engaged in farming. Considering that agricultural income was generally under-reported by the respondents, it was seen that most of the students who had an agricultural background were from middle and upper level income groups (Table 6.3). In a few

Table 6.1
Parents' Occupation—Initial Sample I

Name of college	Total no. of respondents in each college	Business	Farming	Profes-sionals	Other jobs/ services
1. B.I.T.	22	6	4	3	9
2. K.I.M.S.	23	7	3	7	6
3. A.I.M.S.	20	2	3	8	7
4. A.I.T. (Chikmagalur)	20	4	5	5	6
5. S.I.T.	21	5	3	3	10
6. J.S.S.M.C.	20	3	4	5	8
7. J.N.M.C.	23	10	2	5	6
8. K.L.E.S.E.C.	15	7	3	2	3
9. K.M.C.	22	5	2	10	5
10. M.I.T.	22	4	3	5	10
11. A.I.T.	21	5	4	4	8
12. A.M.C.	22	4	3	9	6
13. S.S.I.T.	29	5	9	9	6
14. I.I.T.	21	8	3	4	6
15. D.S.C.E.	20	6	3	3	8
16. M.S.R.I.T.	21	5	4	5	7
17. M.S.R.M.C.	18	3	3	6	6
18. M.V.J.C.E.	21	6	3	4	8
19. R.V.C.E.	25	6	4	5	10
TOTAL	406	101	68	102	135
Per cent Value		24.88	16.75	25.12	33.25

instances parents who possessed land had moved into urban areas and had their children educated in public schools. They were now sending their children to professional colleges. In some cases, this may have been owing to their desire, while retaining their hold on land, to see a change in their traditional occupation. In other cases this might have been because of insufficiency of income from land. Besides, having an engineer or a doctor in the family could always be an additional source of influence in society.

A similar trend was observed in the four colleges which were studied in detail. Of the 707 total respondents, an average of 17.24 per cent[1] of the parents were engaged in farming (see Table 6.2). The income level of over 12 per cent of the parents was above Rs. 50,000 per annum. An average of 4.45 per cent of the respondents

Table 6.2
Parents' Occupation—Detailed Sample II

Name of college	A.M.C. (Per cent)	K.I.M.S. (Per cent	S.I.T. (Per cent)	M.S.R.I.T. (Per cent)	Average (Per cent)
Total no. of students	1,074	1,096	2,287	2,718	—
Total no. of respondents	108	113	228	258	—
Students whose parents were in business	38 (35.19)	31 (27.43)	60 (26.32)	64 (24.81)	— 28.44
Students whose parents were in farming	14 (12.96)	21 (18.58)	50 (21.93)	40 (15.50)	— 17.24
Students whose parents were professionals	30 (27.78)	26 (23.01)	51 (22.37)	74 (28.68)	— 25.46
Students whose parents were in other jobs/ services	26 (24.07)	35 (30.97)	67 (29.39)	80 (31.01)	— 28.86

[1] While in the small sample actual numbers were quoted, here we have not mentioned them since these samples were of different sizes and would not reflect the actual figures. (In the smaller samples, the sizes were fairly uniform.)

were those whose family income was below Rs. 50,000 (see Table 6.3). Thus, it was largely the middle and rich farmers who were able to send their wards to capitation fee colleges.

In the intensive sample (Sample II), 28.44 per cent of the students belonged to the business group. The income level of 17.75 per cent of the parents in the group was between Rs. 50,000 and Rs. 1 lakh per annum and it was above Rs. 1 lakh for 6.03 per cent of the parents (see Table 6.3). A large number of these students hoped to become doctors and engineers with the aim of setting up private medical practice or their own industry, thereby enabling them to get maximum returns from the money invested in exorbitant capitation fees and other charges paid by their parents. A student whose parents had sent him to a private medical college (K.I.M.S.) stated that he would have 'no qualms in recovering the money spent on him' and that he had no intention of 'going into a rural area to serve the rural poor'. He only wished to gain some experience working in a hospital and then set up his own private practice. Amongst the more affluent students, there were some who admitted that they had joined these courses owing to family pressures and that they were actually not interested in pursuing medicine or engineering.

In Sample I, parents of 102 respondents (25.0 per cent) were professionals—they were either self-employed, having their own practice or employed in industry or government. Thus, these students also belonged to an affluent upper middle class background. A total of 135 respondents (33.9 per cent) stated that their parents were in various other jobs—in government, armed forces, private companies, etc.

A similar trend was observed in Sample II where, in 25.46 per cent of the cases, parents were from professional groups and 28.86 per cent of the parents were engaged in other jobs or services. A majority of such parents would not have faced any financial problems sending their wards to private colleges. The annual income of 20.43 per cent of the parents was found to be between Rs. 50,000 and Rs. 1 lakh, and of 4.28 per cent it was above Rs. 1 lakh. Parents of only 8.17 per cent of the respondents were earning less than Rs. 50,000 annually. However, from this group, some students stated that their families had difficulties in raising adequate funds for paying the capitation fee. Yet, acquiring an engineering or medical degree was seen as one way of getting decent employment,

Name of college	A.M.C. (Per cent)	K.I.M.S. (Per cent)	S.I.T. (Per cent)	M.S.R.I.T. (Per cent)	Average (Per cent)
Total no. of respondents	108	113	228	258	
Service Group					
Income between Rs. 30,000 and Rs. 50,000	8 (7.41)	15 (13.27)	15 (6.58)	14 (5.43)	8.17
Income between Rs. 50,000 and Rs. 1 lakh	16 (14.81)	14 (12.39)	45 (19.74)	60 (23.26)	17.55
Income above Rs. 1 lakh	2 (1.85)	6 (5.31)	7 (3.07)	0 (2.33)	3.14
Professional Group					
Between Rs. 30,000 and Rs. 50,000	2 (1.85)	—	—	3 (1.16)	0.75
Between Rs. 50,000 and Rs. 1 lakh	23 (21.30)	20 (17.70)	40 (17.54)	65 (25.19)	20.43
Above Rs. 1 lakh	5 (4.63)	6 (5.31)	11 (4.82)	6 (2.33)	4.27
Farming					
Between Rs. 30,000 and Rs. 50,000	4 (3.70)	5 (4.42)	15 (6.58)	8 (3.10)	4.45
Between Rs. 50,000 and Rs. 1 lakh	5 (4.63)	10 (8.85)	23 (10.09)	20 (7.75)	7.83
Above Rs. 1 lakh	5 (4.63)	6 (5.31)	12 (5.26)	12 (4.65)	4.96
Business					
Between Rs. 30,000 and Rs. 50,000	6 (5.56)	4 (3.54)	5 (2.19)	19 (7.36)	4.66
Between Rs. 50,000 and Rs. 1 lakh	23 (21.30)	20 (17.70)	42 (18.42)	35 (13.57)	17.75
Above Rs. 1 lakh	9 (8.33)	7 (6.19)	13 (5.70)	10 (3.88)	6.03

The percentages reflect the proportions from within the population of the same college.

and hence the families had somehow managed to pay the steep fees through loans or other sources. But such cases were few.

Referring again to the data in Table 6.2, we may observe that the largest component, 54.32 per cent students, were those whose parents were either professionals or holding some other jobs. Mishra[2] has termed professionals and other job-holders as 'the educated middle class' although he has recognised that this class did not emerge as a result essentially of an economic revolution as in the West. However, as the data presented is only a single-generation profile as revealed by students, we need to treat the socio-economic perception of students thus emerging with caution. Some respondents stated that they did not belong to a single nuclear family, and in many cases, although they did reveal the occupation of their parents, there were several sources of income for the family. An advocate's son, for example, may not reveal that his father was a landowner as well. In the group of 54.32 per cent, some respondents during the interviews had informally revealed that their families were still rooted in land. Hence, although from the data we may claim a middle class formation linked with industry and professions, we cannot conclude that there is a large middle class totally delinked from agriculture and land.

Rich businessmen and industrialists (28.44 per cent) constituted another significant group who were sending their wards to private colleges. The rural rich were also trying to diversify into other lucrative fields and build professional cadres of their own to acquire new channels of influence. The system of capitation provided them avenues to strengthen their dominance, and we can see this link between affluent groups and education.

In the government colleges examined, of the 60 respondents in U.V.C.E., S.K.R.E. and the Bangalore Medical College, parents of 36 students (60 per cent) were in government or private service; 14 (23.3 per cent) of the respondents had parents in the skilled professions; and only 10 students (16.6 per cent) belonged to the rural gentry and business group. Thus, the data gathered indicated that while students in both government and private colleges were from the middle class, i.e., whose parents were either professionals or in service; in private colleges, the proportion of students with a landed and business background was higher.

[2] B.B. Mishra, *The Indian Middle Classes: Their Growth in Modern Times*, Oxford University Press, London, 1961, pp. 162–210.

School Background

We found from the data that a little more than two-thirds of the students (68.47 per cent), whether those who had paid capitation fee or those from the merit quota, were from public schools. In Sample I, of the total of 406 respondents, 54 (13.30 per cent) were merit students and the remaining 352 (86.70 per cent) were students who had paid capitation fee. Of the 54 merit students, 21 (38.89 per cent) had attended government schools while the remaining 61.11 per cent public schools. In the case of non-merit students, 244 (69.32 per cent) of the 352 respondents had been educated in public schools, while 30.68 per cent had been to government schools (see Table 6.4). In Sample II on schooling, the non-merit students from public schools were found to be 64.36 per cent and the merit students 67.44 per cent. The non-merit respondents from government schools came to a total of 35.64 per cent and merit students from these schools 32.56 per cent (Table 6.4).

The data indicates that a large majority of students were from public schools, and as we have seen in Table 6.3, the parents of 81.97 per cent of the respondents belonged to the middle and higher income groups. Thus, the educational system being fostered through capitation fee continued to serve the higher income groups and the more affluent sections of society.

The ratio of government school vs. public school background was found to be similar in grants-in-aid colleges. Of the 22 respondents in S.J.C.E. and B.M.S. colleges, seven were from government schools and 15 from public schools. Again, of these 22 students, four were from rural areas and 18 from urban areas. However, in the case of the three government colleges studied, a difference was observed. Of the 60 respondents, 27 were from government schools. This indicated that students with a non-public school background were able to compete and find places for themselves in the few state colleges that were available.

Rural/Urban Dimensions

From among the 406 respondents in the initial sample (Sample I), 79 (19.46 per cent) were found to be from rural areas and the

Table 6.4
Schooling—Sample I

Name of college	Total no. of respondents in the college	Non-merit/Capitation students			Merit students		
		Total no. of capitation students	Public school	Govt. school	Total no. of merit students	Govt. school	Public school
1. B.I.T.	22	18	11	7	4	2	2
2. K.I.M.S.	23	19	14	5	4	1	3
3. A.I.M.S.	20	16	10	6	4	3	1
4. A.I.T.	20	20	10	10	—	—	—
5. S.I.T.	21	18	10	8	3	1	2
6. J.S.S.M.C.	20	18	13	5	2	1	1
7. J.N.M.C.	23	13	10	3	10	4	6
8. K.L.E.S.E.C.	15	12	9	3	3	1	2
9. K.M.C.	22	18	15	3	4	1	3
10. M.I.T.	22	19	14	5	3	1	2
11. A.I.T.	21	18	12	6	3	1	2
12. A.M.C.	22	19	15	4	3	1	2
13. S.S.I.T.	29	29	16	13	—	—	—
14. I.I.T.	21	21	15	6	—	—	—
15. D.S.C.E.	20	20	17	3	—	—	—
16. M.S.R.I.T.	21	17	11	6	4	1	3
17. M.S.R.M.C.	18	16	13	3	2	1	1
18. M.V.J.C.E.	21	21	13	8	—	—	—
19. R.V.C.E.	25	20	16	4	5	2	3
TOTAL	406	352	244	108	54	21	33
Per cent Value			69.32	30.68		38.89	61.11

Table 6.5
Schooling—Sample II

	Name of college				
	A.M.C. (per cent)	K.I.M.S. (per cent)	S.I.T. (per cent)	M.S.R.I.T. (per cent)	Average (per cent)
Total no. of students	1,074	1,096	2,287	2,718	
Total no. of respondents	108	113	228	258	
Total no. of non-merit students from govt. and public schools	83	83	188	224	
Non-merit students from govt. schools	21 (25.30)	23 (27.71)	68 (36.17)	94 (41.96)	35.64
Non-merit students from public schools*	62 (74.70)	60 (72.29)	120 (63.83)	130 (58.04)	64.36
Total no. of merit students from govt. and public schools	25	30	40	34	
Merit students from govt. schools	7 (28)	10 (33.33)	16 (40)	9 (26.47)	32.56
Merit students from public schools	18 (72)	20 (66.67)	24 (60)	25 (73.53)	67.44

* Non-merit students pay capitation fee as they are not covered under the merit quota of the State government.

remaining 327 (80.54 per cent) from cities or towns. In the larger samples obtained from four colleges, 25.03 per cent were from rural areas (see Tables 6.6 and 6.7). There were some private college managements who claimed that their institutions were meant to cater to the rural population, but this was not always true. In the case of the Adichunchanagiri Institute of Medical Sciences at Nagmangala, the main motivation in running the college (it was professed) was service of the rural poor. However, of the 20 students interviewed from this institute, three belonged to a rural background and none amongst them disclosed any intentions of going back to their respective villages to serve the rural poor; rather, two of them expressed a desire to set up their own private practice in urban areas. All the other respondents were from towns and cities. Of the urban students, a large number had attended public schools, while the rural students had mostly studied in government schools though there were some who had been to

Table 6.6
Rural–Urban Background—Sample I

Name of college	Total no. of respondents in the college	Respondents from rural areas	Respondents from urban areas
1. B.I.T.	22	5	17
2. K.I.M.S.	23	4	19
3. A.I.M.S.	20	3	17
4. A.I.T.	20	4	16
5. S.I.T.	21	5	16
6. J.S.S.M.C.	20	4	16
7. J.N.M.C.	23	3	20
8. K.L.E.S.E.C.	15	3	12
9. K.M.C.	22	3	19
10. M.I.T.	22	4	18
11. A.I.T.	21	4	17
12. A.M.C.	22	4	18
13. S.S.I.T.	29	11	18
14. I.I.T.	21	3	18
15. D.S.C.E.	20	2	18
16. M.S.R.I.T.	21	6	15
17. M.S.R.M.C.	18	3	15
18. M.V.J.C.E.	21	4	17
19. R.V.C.E.	25	4	21
TOTAL	406	79	327
Per cent Value		19.46	80.54

Table 6.7
Rural–Urban Background—Sample II

	Name of college				
	A.M.C. (per cent)	K.I.M.S. (per cent)	S.I.T. (per cent)	M.S.R.I.T. (per cent)	Average (per cent)
Total no. of students	1,074	1,096	2,287	2,718	
Total no. of respondents	108	113	228	258	
No. of students from rural areas	22 (20.37)	20 (17.70)	70 (30.70)	65 (25.19)	25.03
No. of students from urban areas	86 (79.63)	93 (82.30)	158 (69.30)	193 (74.81)	74.97

village-level public schools as well. In M.S. Ramaiah Institute of Technology, quite a number of non-Karnataka students from U.P. and Bihar had come from rural areas and belonged to wealthy landed families. They pointed out that it was not that their families could not afford public schools, but that they did not have access to any in their villages and rural areas. However, some of them had attended the new public schools that had sprung up in adjoining areas.

At S.I.T. again, 70 of the 228 respondents were from rural areas, mainly from South India. However, in both Samples I and II, the urban population was higher on an average.

In government institutions, the rural–urban dimension as compared to private capitation fee based colleges was found to be slightly different. Of the 60 respondents in government colleges, 18 were found to be from rural areas as against 19 per cent of rural representation in private colleges.

Thus, from the data we can see that it was mainly those urban students who had been through expensive public schools and could not make it to other institutions through merit, who now found a place for themselves in private professional colleges. However, some of these students had rural links. At the same time, the rural rich, who had been to public or government schools, realised the value and significance of professional degrees and gained admission to such colleges.

Caste Composition

Most of the Lingayat- and Vokkaliga-run professional colleges had been set up with the professed aim of promoting educational facilities for the youth of their own caste. However, amongst the dominant caste managed colleges studied in detail, it was found that, on an average, only about 20–25 per cent of the student population belonged to the particular caste running that college. At the Kempegowda Institute of Medical Sciences, 32 of the 113 respondents were of the Vokkaliga caste. At the Siddaganga Institute of Technology, of the 228 students, 36 were Lingayats. At the scheduled caste and scheduled tribe managed institutions, like the Ambedkar Medical College (A.M.C.), which was supposed to cater to the needs of scheduled castes, it was found that only 20 per cent of the seats went to scheduled caste students.[3] The majority of seats were allotted to those who had been in a position to pay the capitation fee. The dominant caste managed institutions projected a secular character by maintaining that the remaining seats were open to anyone. However, what they did not state was that seats went to the higher bidders. Thus, in the name of caste, they succeeded in promoting their own economic interests.

However, in a college run by a private entrepreneur, the M.S. Ramaiah Institute of Technology, there was a difference. Here a good mix of all castes and communities was found, including Vokkaligas, Brahmins, Lingayats, Kshatriyas, Bunts, Kurubas and Vysyas. There were Muslims and Christians as well amongst the respondents from urban Karnataka. Thus, in this college we observe the purely commercial nature of the enterprise where the admission of respondents was mainly dependent on how much capitation they could afford to pay.

Another significant fact noticed in the context of the caste background of the respondents was that, irrespective of which trusts managed the colleges, the dominant landed castes, namely the Vokkaligas and Lingayats, followed by the Brahmins, formed the majority of Karnataka students in private professional institutions. As we observed earlier in Chapter 2, although reservations had limited the opportunities for Brahmins to some extent, they enjoyed a pre-eminent position in education and state service in Karnataka despite their numerical weakness. These castes predominated professional education in engineering and medicine in Karnataka.

At K.I.M.S. again, of the 1096 students, the college maintained that 567 students were Vokkaligas, Brahmins or Lingayats. The breakup of the students as of June 1988 was given as follows:

---

[3] The A.M.C. authorities stated that 209/1073 seats were meant for SC/ST students (information as on 17 June 1988).

Vokkaligas	470
Brahmins	69
Lingayats	28
Others	300
Foreigners	21
Non-Karnataka	208
	1096

At the Ambedkar Medical College, the office did not maintain any caste-wise record of students, but of the 108 respondents, 40 were from Karnataka. Of these 40, only seven were scheduled castes. Amongst the others, there were eight Brahmins, six Vokkaligas, and six Lingayats. Thus, these three groups together formed a sizeable number.

At the Siddaganga Institute of Technology, of the 82 respondents from Karnataka, 37 were Lingayats, seven were Brahmins and eight were Vokkaligas. Even at the M.S. Ramaiah Institute of Technology, which was not a caste-based college, the proportion of these three groups was rather high. Of the 80 respondents from Karnataka, there were 12 Brahmins, 13 Vokkaligas and 15 Lingayats. Thus, we see a continuing Vokkaliga–Lingayat–Brahmin preponderance in capitation colleges.

Students' Perception of Admission Fee and Attitude Towards Capitation Fee System

From the data gathered from students, we observed a large difference between the capitation fee amounts most managements of private colleges claimed to collect from the students and what the students said they had actually paid. The managements tended to greatly understate this sum and reiterated only the fee laid down by the State government. However, through the interviews conducted it was found that in engineering colleges the amount paid by students varied between Rs. 25,000 and Rs. 60,000. The upper limit, according to the information gathered from the Directorate of Technical Education in June 1988, was raised to Rs. 80,000 (Rs. 90,000 in 1991) depending on the course opted for. In medical colleges, the rates varied from Rs. 3 to Rs. 5 lakh for Indians, and between 30,000 and 45,000 U.S. dollars for foreigners and non-resident Indians. Concessions in fees were noticed in some exceptional cases. Concessional seats were allotted on the basis of caste or political influence. For instance, as mentioned earlier, at the Siddaganga Institute of Technology, the Lingayat *mutt swamiji* permitted a Lingayat student to pay a sum of Rs. 8,000 as donation because he could not afford more. Another student at M.S. Ramaiah Medical College quoted her own case where, because of a personal favour from the then Chief Minister, she had to pay 'only Rs. 2 lakh'. Many students pointed out the arbitrariness in the management's collection of capitation fee and some of them also revealed that they were not issued receipts for the full amount paid.

As regards the capitation fee system itself, there were contradictory responses. In some cases we observed a dual response of students. They 'justified' the system, yet 'opposed' it. Different arguments were used for defending the system. Some felt that if they had the aptitude and the capacity to finance themselves, the capitation fee was justified. The system ensured the right to fulfil their 'dreams' to be engineers and doctors. If the college provided good teachers and facilities in return for what they had paid, then the money spent was worthwhile. Sometimes, capitation fee also proved useful in the case of students who were on the borderline of the merit cut-off point. Money, or some sort of influence, seemed the only two alternatives to these students to gain admission to these colleges. In Sample II, of the 32.96 per cent of the students who justified the capitation system (Table 6.9), there was a small number (6 per cent) who at the same time argued against it. For instance, one of the students at K.I.M.S. stated that although it was an unjust system helping only those who had money, yet since money was the only channel available to him, he had made use of it to 'educate' himself. In Sample I, of the 406 respondents from private colleges, 120 (34.48 per cent) spoke in favour of the system (see Table 6.8, Sample I).

An interesting finding of the study was that several students who had paid capitation fees were critical of the system. There were 266 respondents (65.52 per cent) (Sample I, Table 6.8) and 67.04 per cent respondents in Sample II (see Table 6.9) who spoke against the phenomenon on several counts. A large majority felt that

Table 6.8
Attitude of Students Towards Capitation Fee System—Sample I

Name of college	Total no. of respondents	No. who justified capitation fee system	No. who opposed capitation fee system
1. B.I.T.	22	6	16
2. K.I.M.S.	23	7	16
3. A.I.M.S.	20	6	14
4. A.I.T.	20	7	13
5. S.I.T.	21	7	14
6. J.S.S.M.C.	20	6	14
7. J.N.M.C.	23	8	15
8. K.L.E.S.E.C.	15	5	10
9. K.M.C.	22	9	13
10. M.I.T.	22	10	12
11. A.I.T.	21	8	13
12. A.M.C.	22	8	14
13. S.S.I.T.	29	9	20
14. I.I.T.	21	7	14
15. D.S.C.E.	20	4	16
16. M.S.R.I.T.	21	8	13
17. M.S.R.M.C.	18	6	12
18. M.V.J.C.E.	21	9	12
19. R.V.C.E.	25	10	15
TOTAL	406	140	266
Per cent Value	—	34.48	65.52

Table 6.9
Attitude of Students towards Capitation Fee System—Sample II

Name of college	Total no. of respondents	No. who justified capitation fee system	No. who opposed capitaion fee system
A.M.C.	108	38	70
K.I.M.S.	113	43	70
S.I.T.	228	64	164
M.S.R.I.T.	258	88	170
TOTAL	707	233	474
Per cent Value	—	32.96	67.04

although they had paid capitation fees it was a system which 'bred and regularised corruption'. Since performance at the school-level examination was given no importance and it was money that played a major role, it led to declining standards, which meant that their degrees would get devalued, thereby jeopardising the reputation of universities in their region. In fact, it was a sort of investment for the more prosperous because 'they make greater profits after passing from here'. Such a system helped only the rich and undermined brilliance. In most cases students felt that the money taken from them was not utilised for the development of the institutions and improving the facilities; instead, it was being used for non-educational purposes and other business ventures of the management. Two respondents from the government quota, commenting on the management quota students (those who had paid capitation fee), stated that many of their batch-mates had joined professional courses for either their glamour or because of parental pressure. 'Their disinterest is evident from the fact that many of them are constantly demanding the carry-over system and postponement of examinations,' remarked a merit student of the Bangalore Institute of Technology. The carry-over system meant an opportunity to repeat one course or paper several times. Their demands for postponements adversely affected the more sincere and dedicated students, as also stated by some respondents of government colleges.

Quality of Education

The Medical Council of India (M.C.I.) and the All India Council for Technical Education (A.I.C.T.E.)[4] have laid down certain norms

---

[4] The A.I.C.T.E. acquired a statutory status in December 1987. It had prepared only a rough outline of the guidelines for fulfilment by the private technical institutions in a letter issued on 12 July 1989 to the Directorate of Technical Education, Delhi Administration. Till 1990, the A.I.C.T.E. was still in the process of working out details of the guidelines for engineering colleges (information obtained from the A.I.C.T.E. Office, Ministry of Human Resources and Development, New Delhi). It therefore became necessary to go by the general guidelines for admission and other Central Government regulations. These were issued to all states in August 1990 whereby admissions were to be centralised by an entrance examination and a minimum of 60 per cent marks was necessary for entrance to engineering colleges. See *The Times of India*, New Delhi, 24 September 1990.

for maintaining quality education in medical and engineering colleges respectively. The students' perception of their colleges were reviewed in the light of these norms as well as the actual conditions to the extent possible.

As per our findings, the quality of education imparted in most government and private colleges was far from satisfactory and most of the students gave a poor rating to the faculty and the facilities available. However, there were some exceptions, such as the colleges at Manipal or the Jawaharlal Nehru Medical College at Belgaum, which were trying to maintain standards.

Many respondents confirmed the findings of the *White Paper on Professional Colleges and Institutions* (1983) and the *Report of the Review Commission* (1980). The latter report had pointed out that the growth in the number of engineering and medical colleges in the State had been unplanned, which in turn had affected the quality of education. Professional education had become purely 'commercial ventures' with many of the institutions being established with the lure of capitation fee.[5] It further stated:

> The facilities available for training are often inadequate and most of the instruction is in theoretical terms without much practical backing. This is often pointed out by employers, though they in turn do not seem to appreciate the need for on-the-job training and orientation of freshly inducted graduates, and want complete products who can be used directly on the job from the first day of employment. The students/graduates do not value the education imparted to them, and are showing their disillusionment and anger in several ways . . . .[6]

The *White Paper* on professional colleges had also stated that, in many instances, engineering colleges were started in Karnataka 'without the recommendations from the concerned university in the first instance regarding affiliation, or approval by the Medical Council of India in the case of medical college'.[7] It went on to observe: 'In terms of facilities only the four government and

[5] See Universities in Karnataka, *Report of the Review Commission*, Bangalore, 1980, pp. 81–89.

[6] Ibid., p. 82.

[7] Government of Karnataka, *White Paper on Professional Colleges and Institutions*, Department of Education and Youth Services and Department of Health and Family Welfare, March 1983, p. 4.

university institutions, eight aided private colleges and a few of the older unaided colleges appear to be satisfactory. In most of the unaided private colleges, facilities are very much below standard.'[8]

Private Medical Colleges

Amongst the private medical colleges, it was found that only four[9] had been granted permanent recognition by the Medical Council of India (M.C.I.). The students in private medical and engineering colleges largely echoed the findings of the *White Paper* and the *Report of the Review Commission.* At the S.S.I.T., some complained that the academic training was mostly theoretical, with little emphasis on practical knowledge, and did not encourage initiative to dwell on aspects outside the syllabus. Of the 406 respondents, 119 (29.31 per cent) felt that the faculties in their respective colleges were of poor quality, 202 (49.75 per cent) stated that they were average, and only 85 (20.94 per cent) expressed the view that some teachers were good (see Table 6.10). The M.C.I. norms laid emphasis on an 'adequate' number of teachers to enable 'practical instructions and demonstration in small groups' to be 'imparted effectively'.[10] However, several students remarked that the number of teachers was insufficient due to the high intake of students. This was true of engineering colleges as well. Teachers of one specialisation were made to handle classes of another. Some students studying instrumentation technology in a Bangalore college described the situation as 'pathetic' as there were no specialised teachers, and so the faculty in the electronics department taught them. Some respondents complained of a civil engineer specialised in environmental engineering teaching architecture. This happened when several colleges recklessly started new courses without bothering to provide the necessary infrastructure.

[8] Ibid., p. 6.

[9] These colleges were the M.R. Medical College, Gulbarga; Jawaharlal Nehru Medical College, Belgaum; J.J.M. Medical College, Davangere; and Kasturba Medical College, Manipal.

[10] *Minimum Standard Requirements for a Medical College for 100 Admissions Annually*, Medical Council of India, New Delhi, March 1973 (as revised up to December 1984), p. 15. These were approved as regulations under Section 30 of the Indian Medical Council Act, 1956 by the Government of India, Ministry of Health and Family Welfare.

Table 6.10

Quality of Education—Sample I

Name of college	Total no. of respondents	Facilities			Faculty		
		Good	Average	Poor	Good	Average	Poor
1. B.I.T.	22	2	12	8	2	11	9
2. K.I.M.S.	23	4	12	7	4	11	8
3. A.I.M.S.	23	4	12	4	3	13	4
4. A.I.T.	20	—	15	5	3	18	2
5. S.I.T.	21	5	13	3	4	14	3
6. J.S.S.M.C.	20	3	12	5	2	13	5
7. J.N.M.C.	23	16	7	—	17	6	—
8. K.L.E.S.C.E.	15	3	12	—	4	11	—
9. K.M.C.	22	20	2	—	19	3	—
10. M.I.T.	22	12	10	—	9	3	—
11. A.I.T.	21	—	11	10	—	9	12
12. A.M.C.	22	3	14	5	4	15	3
13. S.S.I.T.	29	5	16	4	4	15	10
14. I.I.T.	21	1	5	15	—	8	13
15. D.S.C.E.	20	—	1	19	—	3	17
16. M.S.R.I.T.	21	5	10	6	4	11	6
17. M.S.R.M.C.	18	5	13	—	3	13	2
18. M.V.J.C.E.	21	—	1	20	—	2	19
19. R.V.C.E.	25	5	12	8	6	13	6
TOTAL	406	93	190	123	85	202	119
Per Cent Value	—	22.91	46.80	30.29	20.94	49.75	29.31

The teaching staff of all departments in medical colleges was expected to work full-time and not have their own practice as per the M.C.I. regulations. However, in actual practice, part-time and honorary teachers had been appointed in many colleges. In engineering institutions, students stated that it was a practice to recruit retired persons from industries for teaching purposes. The management thus economised by giving such teachers only a consolidated salary. Some students of the Dayanand Sagar College of Engineering revealed that the teachers there seemed more interested in making money through private tuitions than in serious coaching in the classroom. Classes were not held regularly. For instance, at the M.V.J. College, many pupils remarked that they only went to classes for getting the required attendance to enable them to appear in the university examination.

Of the respondents in Sample I, only 93 (22.91 per cent) thought that the facilities in their institutions were good. The remaining 77.09 per cent considered the facilities as either average or poor.

In Sample II obtained from four colleges, 20.36 per cent of the respondents were of the view that the quality of education (in relation to facilities and faculty) was poor, 56.81 per cent stated it was average, while only 22.83 per cent said that it was good (see Table 6.11).

The M.C.I. has clearly laid down: 'The college shall be housed preferably in a unitary building and it should be located near the teaching hospital. The college grounds should have room for future expansion.'[11] It was only in August 1992 that the President of India promulgated an ordinance making it mandatory for new medical colleges to obtain prior approval of the Central government and the Medical Council of India.[12] However, before this, a number of colleges had been established in total disregard of M.C.I regulations. This was because recognition by the M.C.I. (till the promulgation of this ordinance) was never considered a precondition for starting a college since the Council was only a recommendatory body and was not vested with powers to derecognise colleges. Several colleges did not have a proper campus. The Ambedkar Medical College was housed in a corporation building for a few years; it had no hostel or teaching hospital of its own. As per the

[11] Ibid., p. 2.
[12] *Indian Express*, New Delhi, 30 August 1992.

Table 6.11
Quality of Education—Sample II

	Name of college				
	A.M.C. (per cent)	K.I.M.S. (per cent)	S.I.T. (per cent)	M.S.R.I.T. (per cent)	Average (per cent)
Total no. of students	1,074	1,096	2,287	2,718	
Total no. of respondents	108	113	228	258	
Quality of Education					
1. Good	20	23	48	81	
	(18.52)	(20.35)	(21.05)	(31.40)	22.83
2. Average	63	60	150	129	
	(58.33)	(53.10)	(65.79)	(50.00)	56.81
3. Poor	25	30	30	48	
	(23.15)	(26.55)	(13.16)	(18.60)	20.36

M.C.I. norms, the minimum number of teaching beds for a college having 100 admissions annually should have been 700, but the number of beds in the Bowring (government) hospital was insufficient for the students at the A.M.C. Many of the respondents of this college had gone on strike in April and August 1987 for eight weeks to press their demands for better hospital facilities and an increase in the number of staff. Students from the K.I.M.S. also stated that 14 other junior and degree colleges were located inside the same campus for several years. Part of the college was moved to a new campus only in 1988. Many respondents stated that they lacked their own clinical facilities and were using government hospitals. Several students had complaints about the insufficient number of books in the library and the lack of borrowing facilities. The seating capacity of the library was not enough because medical, dental and pharmacy students used it. In most medical colleges there were no departmental libraries.

In a medical college in the Nagamangala Taluka, what seemed an impressive edifice with a bold signboard of a large-sized library was only a massive concrete front with a few books and journals. A medical student of this college remarked that clinical facilities were nine kilometres away in the district. The college Principal stated that they had to often rush to Mandya to get hold of basic equipment like gas cylinders. Some respondents stated that the lecture theatres in their colleges were insufficient and their demonstration rooms lacked the necessary audio-visual aids. As per the M.C.I. norms, there should be four lecture theatres in a college, three with a seating capacity of 150 to 200 each, and one with a seating capacity of 350 to 400. The dissection halls were not spacious enough 'to accommodate 200 students at a time'.[13] Central workshops with facilities for repair of electrical and mechanical equipment were found to be lacking, and some respondents complained that there was no central gas plant in their colleges. The teacher–student ratio of 1:10 as laid down by the M.C.I. regulations was not maintained in some colleges.

Private Engineering Colleges

For engineering colleges, the All India Council for Technical Education (A.I.C.T.E.) has stated that 'admissions should be made strictly on merit and the institutions concerned should join the entrance test at the national or at the state level.'[14] However, the respondents in the management quota had all paid capitation fees to gain admission to the colleges, which in no way was governed by the results of any entrance examination.

As in the case of medical colleges, the library facilities were found to be inadequate by students in engineering colleges as well. Some respondents also pointed to the overcrowding and congestion in laboratories. While the central government has laid down general guidelines for laboratories, stating that they should 'provide an environment where the student can learn to take initiative in recognising and solving engineering problems',[15] students complained of lack of teaching staff and equipment. It has been further

[13] *Minimum Standard Requirements for a Medical College for 100 Admissions Annually*, op. cit., p. 3.

[14] Letter to the Directorate of Technical Education. Delhi Administration, *Guidelines laid down by the A.I.C.T.E. for Technical Education for Fulfilment by the Private Technical Institutions* for A.I.C.T.E.'s Approval, Ministry of Human Resources and Development, 12 July 1989.

[15] Government of India, *Four Year Degree Course in Engineering: A Model List of Laboratories, Experiments and Equipment*, Ministry of Education and Culture, New Delhi, April 1984. See Preface, p. 1.

outlined by the government that 'faculty efforts, the learning experience, scheduling, facilities and equipment should be designed so that the student can efficiently learn fundamental concepts and develop skills in the use of experimental techniques and in the analysis and presentation of data.'[16] However, in many institutions, the respondents stated that the machinery was outdated and unusable. The equipment was there, but it was not in running condition for want of upkeep and maintenance. Very often, the chairman or founder of the college assured the students that facilities and equipment would be soon provided, and some experiments conducted before the examination.

At the M.S.R.I.T., students remarked that the seating capacity in classrooms was just about adequate; some of the rooms were leaking and not well-ventilated. Noisy workshops in the vicinity disturbed the lectures. The number of lecturers was adequate but few were qualified or experienced. They were unprepared in the subject they were teaching and what was delivered by way of lectures was an exact reproduction of printed matter in textbooks. 'They are more busy in their private tuitions and granting attendance by accepting bribes', declared one respondent. A student of another engineering college, B.I.T., pointed out that what was meant to be an auditorium had been converted into a cinema theatre for the public by the management because that appeared a more lucrative proposition. At the M.V.J. College of Engineering, students complained of lack of basic amenities like toilets. In many colleges, there were no placement facilities; generally, one teacher was put in charge to provide the students some information, but there was no proper placement cell to be found anywhere. Many respondents revealed that no campus interviews were held in their colleges.

High Intake

Another important aspect adversely affecting the quality of education was that many of the private unaided colleges exceeded the intake fixed initially by the government, and later sought ratification for this. Hence, the intake increased enormously without any commensurate increase in either the teaching staff or facilities.

[16] Ibid.

As we can observe through Tables 6.12 and 6.13, the growth rates vis-à-vis intake were highest in private institutions, whether medical or engineering. Several respondents pointed out that the high intake affected the student–teacher ratio in their colleges and their combined staff strength was lower than in government colleges. In the 12 engineering colleges surveyed, the staff-student ratio varied between 1:15 to 1:35 as compared to government

Table 6.12
Intake of Students in Engineering and Medical Colleges, 1979–83

	Initially fixed (A)	Final/ actual (B)	Difference between A and B	Growth in actual intake over the previous year (per cent)
Government Engineering Colleges				
1979–80	922	1,138	216	—
1980–81	804	942	138	(−)17.2
1981–82	940	943	3	0.1
1982–83	942	1,001	59	6.2
Private Engineering Colleges				
1979–80	2,674	3,189	515	—
1980–81	4,184	4,928	744	54.5
1981–82	5,295	5,342	47	8.4
1982–83	5,885	6,790	905	27.1
Government Medical Colleges				
1979–80	400	405	5	—
1980–81	450	450	—	11.1
1981–82	450	454	4	0.9
1982–83	450	455	5	0.2
Private Medical Colleges				
1979–80	510	618	108	—
1980–81	685	725	40	17.3
1981–82	785	953	168	31.5
1982–83	785	978	193	2.6

Source: Government of Karnataka, *White Paper on Professional Colleges and Institutions*, op. cit., pp. 4 and 5 for intake figures. Growth rates have been worked out.

Table 6.13

Intake of Students in Engineering Colleges, 1986–88*

Type of Institutions	1986–87		1987–88		Growth in intake over the previous year (per cent)
	No. of colleges	Intake of students	No. of colleges	Intake of students	
Government	5	1,152	5	1,184	2.8
Private	34	9,660	34	10,895	12.8
Aided	11	3,797	11	4,329	14.0
TOTAL	50	14,609	50	16,408	12.3

* Based on information from the Directorate of Technical Education, Government of Karnataka, Bangalore, July 1988.

colleges where it did not exceed 1:10. At the Surathkal Karnataka Regional Engineering College, for instance, the teacher-student ratio during the academic year 1987–88 was 139:1450 (approx. 1:10). In most private medical colleges the staff–student ratio ranged between 1:10 and 1:15 compared to government medical colleges where it was 1:5.[17] According to the M.C.I. norms,[18] the ratio of the number of teaching staff to students should be 1:10.

A senior official in the Directorate of Technical Education stated that an intake of 700 students was authorised in engineering colleges. These institutions took 50 to 60 students more than the authorised figure. He added that in order to ensure some quality, not more than 300 students ought to be admitted.[19]

[17] Ratio verified in Government Medical College, Mysore, and Bangalore Medical College, June 1986 and November 1987 respectively.

[18] For every 50 additional admissions over 100, there should be two senior teachers and three junior teachers in addition to the number prescribed in the Standard Requirements for 100 admissions. The senior teachers had to be in the rank of Professor or Associate Professor and Reader or Assistant Professor. See *Minimum Standard Requirement*, op. cit., p. 26.

[19] Personal interview with the Joint Director, Technical Education, November 1987.

Government Colleges

While the study revealed a lack of infrastructural facilities in most private professional colleges, we found that not all government institutions in Karnataka were able to maintain minimum standards either. The *Report of the Review Commission on Universities in Karnataka (1980)*, commenting on medical education in the State had stated: 'The curriculum, methods of teaching practicals and clinical instruction in the medical courses are generally archaic and outmoded.'[20] At the Bangalore Medical College, where there was conformity to M.C.I. norms vis-à-vis the student–teacher ratio, lecture halls, clinical and library facilities and experienced and qualified teachers, of the 23 respondents, eight declared that equipment in their laboratories was inadequate and hospital facilities were not modern enough. They were still using age-old x-ray equipment in the hospital, and CAT scan and ultra-sound techniques were still not being frequently employed. There were complaints of overcrowding as well. 'Sometimes we have as many as 20 students for dissection of one body,' remarked a respondent.

Amongst the State engineering colleges, the Surathkal Regional Engineering College seemed to score high in terms of facilities and faculty. The students seemed satisfied with both. No shortage of staff was reported, the library was well-equipped and the laboratories and workshops met the needs of the students. However, the picture was different at the University Visesvaraya College of Engineering in Bangalore. Of the 19 respondents, nine felt that the facilities were inadequate. Laboratories were ill-equipped; the equipment was outdated, inadequate and not in working order. General maintenance and upkeep were found wanting. There was also a shortage of teaching staff as in the case of the Computer Science Department. Others complained of a lack of interest on the part of teachers.

Thus, not only were respondents at private professional colleges dissatisfied with the quality of education, but some students of government-run institutions also expressed their misgivings. We may observe that since state-run colleges have been unable to

[20] *Report of the Review Commission*, op. cit., p. 144.

maintain reasonable standards, they have given leeway to sub-standard private education. Private institutions have had no norms or standards to go by, and have been able to get away with poor and inadequate infrastructural facilities. It has thus been the inability on the part of the state to provide a sufficient number of good professional colleges and its failure to maintain the upkeep of equipment and to hire good teachers, specially in engineering colleges, that has been one of the major factors leading to the mushrooming of private institutions imparting substandard education.

Absence of Union Activity

A surprising fact noticed in private professional colleges was the absence of a students' body or union. Most managements argued against having unions. Such union activities, they said, led to rowdyism and indiscipline, distracted the students, and therefore colleges were better off without them. Of the 406 respondents, 335 (82.51 per cent) felt the need of a union for better representation and for having a forum to express their grievances. In the four colleges studied in detail (Sample II), 76.37 per cent of the students wanted a union of their own (see Tables 6.14 and 6.15). Students from the K.I.M.S., M.S.R.I.T. and S.I.T. and several other colleges stated that it was difficult to approach the college authorities or the Principal on every issue. They wanted a general upgrading of their faculty, better library facilities, better equipment, a better hostel mess, some emphasis on extra-curricular activities, and better interaction between students and teachers. But they had no forum to voice their demands. Students at the M.V.J. College said that the management not only denied them their money's worth by not providing them with adequate facilities and good teachers, but they were also denied the right to protest. Protest in any form was termed as indiscipline. A student of the A.M.C. stated that their boys' hostel was without mess facilities for three months. Even though a union could probably tackle some problems, the management did not want a union. It was also disclosed by some respondents that though there were no unions, in the previous few years the colleges had seen some strikes organised by restless

Table 6.14
Students' Union—Sample I

Name of college	Total no. of respondents	Do you want a union?	
		Yes	No
1. B.I.T.	22	19	3
2. K.I.M.S.	23	20	3
3. A.I.M.S.	20	17	3
4. A.I.T.	20	17	3
5. S.I.T.	21	17	4
6. J.S.S.M.C.	20	15	5
7. J.N.M.C.	23	17	6
8. K.L.E.S.E.C.	15	13	2
9. K.M.C.	22	13	9
10. M.I.T.	22	16	6
11. A.I.T.	21	20	1
12. A.M.C.	22	20	2
13. S.S.I.T.	29	27	2
14. I.I.T.	21	20	1
15. D.S.C.E.	20	19	1
16. M.S.R.I.T.	21	16	5
17. M.S.R.M.C.	18	12	6
18. M.V.J.C.E.	21	21	—
19. R.V.C.E.	25	16	9
TOTAL	406	335	71
Per Cent Value	—	82.51	17.49

Table 6.15
Students' Union—Sample II

	Name of college				
	A.M.C. (per cent)	K.I.M.S. (per cent)	S.I.T. (per cent)	M.S.R.I.T. (per cent)	Average (per cent)
Total no. of students	1,074	1,096	2,287	2,718	
Total no. of respondents	108	113	228	258	
Any students' union	None	None	None	None	—
No. of students who want a union	82 (75.93)	88 (77.88)	200 (87.72)	165 (63.95)	76.37
No. of students who do not want a union	26 (24.07)	25 (22.12)	28 (12.28)	93 (36.05)	23.63

students either for improvement of general conditions, or on other occasions, even for postponement of examinations. The remaining 71 students (17.49 per cent) were against having unions in their colleges because they led to strikes and caused closure of colleges. Further, they argued, another concern of unions was to secure limitless chances for students who had failed five or six times in a particular course to reappear for examination, and therefore unions, by and large, did not serve any constructive purpose. But while the students were opposed to the idea of strikes in their colleges, they agreed that some ways had to be found to curb the 'high-handedness' of 'authoritarian managements' running private institutions.

Students' Aspirations

We have already seen that most students seeking admission to private medical and engineering colleges were from an affluent background. Parents of 102 respondents were professionals—many of them doctors and engineers. About 101 parents had some business of their own (see Table 6.1). In most of these cases, their wards did not face any problems for a secure future. A majority of such respondents stated that they would join their fathers' industry or business after completing their training. A student at the M.S. Ramaiah Medical College, who had paid a large capitation fee and also used political influence to secure her seat, stated that hers was a family of doctors who had a chain of hospitals in Hyderabad. Some of the family members were also practising in the U.S.A. and so she would join the family profession after completing her course. A large number of students interviewed in engineering colleges spoke of their ambition to set up an industry of their own, or join their family business or enterprise. Of the 406 respondents, 240 (59.11 per cent) said that they would either set up their own private practice as doctors or join their parents. Others amongst them hoped that they would set up their own business or industry after gaining some experience in the public or private sector. A total of 133 respondents (32.76 per cent) stated that they would take up various jobs—only two amongst them wished to join

Defence Services like the Army. The others said that they had little choice and so would accept whatever jobs were available. Some students of engineering colleges wanted to take up a job to gain experience and ultimately set up their own industry.

Only 33 students (8.13 per cent) wished to continue further studies. Since the degrees of medical students were recognised by universities in Karnataka and if they wished to pursue post-graduate studies, they could apply to government colleges or even to private colleges offering post-graduate courses and pay capitation fees again. From the sample of engineering colleges, some of the more affluent students wished to pursue studies abroad and then settle down there. They said that their GATE (Graduate Admission Test for Engineering) scores would determine their future (see Table 6.16).

In the detailed sample obtained from A.M.C., K.I.M.S., S.I.T. and M.S.R.I.T., 62.92 per cent of the respondents wished to set up their own private practice, industry or business. An average of 29.92 per cent students wished to take up jobs and 7.16 per cent respondents wanted to study further (see Table 6.17).

From an analysis of data in Sample II (Table 6.17), we can observe that the aspirations of a large number of students were linked with the avenues available to them, which in turn were determined by their socio-economic status. Cross-tabulating data of Table 6.17 with Tables 6.2 and 6.3, we can arrive at some interesting derivations. About 63 per cent of the respondents stated that they wanted to be self-employed and set up their own business or private medical practice (Table 6.17). From Tables 6.2 and 6.3 we see that 19 per cent of the parents from various occupational categories were in the upper income group (over Rs. one lakh per annum). We may surmise then that 19 per cent of the students would have opportunities to set up their own factory or industry, to start private medical practice, or to enter business. Another 63.56 per cent of the parents whose income level was between Rs. 50,000 to Rs. one lakh would also be able to offer similar opportunities to their wards (Table 6.3).

Similarly, it was seen that 28.86 per cent of the parents were in government or private jobs (Table 6.3). The income level of 18.03 per cent of the parents was between Rs. 30,000 to Rs. 50,000 per annum. Students from such a background would have to look for jobs. Sample II of Table 6.17 revealed that 29.92 per cent of the

Table 6.16
Future Aspirations of Students—Sample I

Name of college	Total no. of respondents	Future		
		Business/ Own practice/ Industry	Service/ Job	Study further
1. B.I.T.	22	14	5	3
2. K.I.M.S.	23	16	5	2
3. A.I.M.S.	20	16	3	1
4. A.I.T.	20	9	11	—
5. S.I.T.	21	8	11	2
6. J.S.S.M.C.	20	13	4	3
7. J.N.M.C.	23	17	3	3
8. K.L.E.S.E.C.	15	8	6	1
9. K.M.C.	22	16	3	3
10. M.I.T.	22	8	12	2
11. A.I.T.	21	11	10	—
12. A.M.C.	22	14	6	2
13. S.S.I.T.	29	19	9	1
14. I.I.T.	21	14	5	2
15. D.S.C.E.	20	8	12	—
16. M.S.R.I.T.	21	13	6	2
17. M.S.R.M.C.	18	10	6	2
18. M.V.J.C.E.	21	11	9	1
19. R.V.C.E.	25	15	7	3
TOTAL	406	240	133	33
Per Cent Value	—	59.11	32.76	8.13

students were wanting to seek employment or enter some service. Some of them also stated that they would aspire for a higher degree later. To begin with it was important for them to get some employment. Thus, we can see the linkage between the parents' occupation, income level and students' aspirations. The placement of students according to the possibilities they saw for themselves also confirmed the advantage of their socio-economic background.

However, amongst students who would have to look for employment, there were some respondents at the Dayanand College of Engineering who seemed perturbed by the fact that a large number of advertisements, while asking for qualified engineers, clearly specified that graduates from Bangalore or other universities in

Table 6.17
Future Aspirations of Students—Sample II

	A.M.C. (per cent)	K.I.M.S. (per cent)	S.I.T. (per cent)	M.S.R.I.T. (per cent)	Average (per cent)
			Name of college		
Total no. of students	1,074	1,096	2,287	2,718	—
Total no. of respondents	108	113	228	258	—
Future plans					
Students who want to do business/ own industry/practice	81 (75.00)	73 (64.60)	123 (53.95)	150 (58.14)	62.92
Students who want to take up a job/service	17 (15.74)	28 (24.78)	93 (40.79)	99 (38.37)	29.92
Students who want to study further	10 (9.26)	12 (10.62)	12 (5.26)	9 (3.49)	7.16

Karnataka need not apply. This seemed to make their future most uncertain. Some other respondents were concerned about the low standards of the universities in Karnataka, especially in medical and engineering education. They spoke of the urgent need on the part of the university to act to ensure standards, or at least raise the minimum eligibility level.

In the case of medical education, there were only four private medical colleges permanently recognised by the Medical Council of India, as mentioned earlier in this chapter. The degrees from four other colleges were only temporarily recognised by the Council while the rest were not recognised at all. So, in these cases, students from outside Karnataka, unless their parents were in private medical practice, faced an uncertain future.

Some engineering students from outside Karnataka stated that unless they set up their own industries or joined their family business, they did not have bright prospects of employment outside the State. Thus, after spending four or five years in their training and acquiring a degree, at the end of it all, engineering graduates from Karnataka discovered that some of the best employment avenues categorically ruled out students from universities of that State. The employers gave a very low rating to such graduates. Therefore some students ended up getting absorbed in a small- or medium-size industry, where chances of progress or mobility were not too bright, or spent an extra year undergoing training in a public sector company.

There being no placement cells in most private colleges, no systematic investigation on placement could be made. However, we compared the students' aspirations in terms of what they foresaw for themselves as well as in terms of the actual possibilities available with views expressed by personnel officers of leading companies. Personnel managers of public and private sector companies were interviewed regarding the absorption of local engineering graduates in their concerns. Nearly all of them said that they had no faith in the degrees or the marks the applicants had obtained.

The H.M.T. Personnel Manager reported that for every 150 to 180 vacancies, they received over 1,000 applications. In the campus recruitment programme, they selected the very best from I.I.T.s, I.I.M.s and I.I.Sc. These select few formed the core group of their industry. In the open advertisement, they gave preference to candidates from regional engineering colleges (R.E.C.s) and other university and government colleges. Applicants from private colleges were their last preference. The selection was fairly stringent. Since they did not have much faith in the marks that the graduates from private engineering colleges secured, they had a cut-off point ranging between 65 and 70 per cent. After the final interview and selection, there was an induction period of only one year for the I.I.T. and I.I.M. boys, whereas the private college graduates had to be given training for at least two years. 'We have serious misgivings about these colleges and the training imparted there. It is for the government and the universities concerned to exercise a stringent quality control in such institutions. There must be a high level of unemployment also amongst these graduates,' the manager observed.[21]

The Personnel Officer of the Indian Telephone Industries also expressed his reservations about the standard of engineering graduates from private colleges. In their recruitment through campus interviews, they only went to premier institutions like the I.I.T.s and R.E.C.s and not to private colleges. But in the selection process through advertisements, they entertained applications

[21] Personal interview with the Personnel Manager of H.M.T., Bangalore, November 1987.

provided the students fulfilled the eligibility conditions. Then they made their selection after stiff interviews.[22]

The Branch Manager of Larsen & Toubro, Bangalore, stated that the private colleges lacked placement facilities, and they went to only well-known institutions. According to him, such boys did not apply there because they were aware of the stiff tests of filtering. They, at times, preferred government jobs in departments like the P.W.D. and Electricity Boards, 'where they could get back what they had invested (in the form of capitation) with compound interest multiplied'.[23]

Regarding unemployment amongst private college graduates, the Directorate of Technical Education revealed that about 5000 graduates from Karnataka qualified every year and only 3000 obtained employment within the State. The remaining 2000 were left stranded. The growth of private colleges in the region was not really 'need-based but vote-based' and the situation had been deteriorating since 1985.[24] In 1983 itself there were 2704 engineers (degree holders) seeking jobs through employment exchanges in Karnataka.[25] Even amongst the medical graduates, there were over a thousand of them who were unemployed in 1987.[26]

Summing Up

As regards the socio-economic origin of the students in private colleges we have seen that a large number (45.68 per cent) belonged to wealthier groups and families where their parents were rich or middle level farmers, or were running their own business or industry. There was also a 'middle class' formation associated with professions and other salaried groups (54.32 per cent) in private or government

---

[22] Personal interview with the Personnel Officer, I.T.I., Bangalore, June 1988.

[23] Personal interview with the Branch Manager, L. & T., Bangalore, July 1988.

[24] Personal interview with the Director, Technical Education, Government of Karnataka, June 1988.

[25] See Government of Karnataka, *Report on Assessment of Engineering Personnel during Sixth Five-Year Plan 1980–85*, Manpower and Employment Division, Planning Department, Bangalore, 1984, p. 17.

[26] Figures have been taken from the Directorate of Medical Education, Government of Karnataka, November 1987.

employment (though not all were totally delinked from land and agriculture) who were also expanding their ranks. Some amongst them viewed professional education as a channel for mobility. About two-thirds of the students in the colleges surveyed were from public schools and could afford a more expensive education.

Although some of the private colleges claimed to be running their institutions for the benefit of the rural youth, we observed through the intensive samples that only one-fourth of the students were from rural areas. Similarly, caste-based institutions were found to be promoting their economic interests in the name of caste by offering seats to those who could pay a larger capitation fee. Although the students were part of the capitation phenomenon and sustained the system, they were also critical of it, reacting against the arbitrariness on the part of the managements in collecting large capitation amounts and the money being utilised for purposes other than education. Hence, the quality of education imparted was adversely affected. The study also confirmed the entrepreneurial interests in education. In the light of the M.C.I. norms, the government's regulations vis-à-vis engineering colleges, the students' perceptions, and the poor placement possibilities for those seeking employment from private institutions, it was confirmed that the quality of education being imparted was poor. However, this aspect seemed of little consequence to those who were trying to seek these degrees as avenues for extending their socio-economic dominance in society.

7

THE FACULTY

In the preceding chapter we have observed that the quality of students who gained admission to private professional colleges was fairly mediocre. We have also seen that it was the general feeling of students that the teaching standards were poor. About 160 teachers were interviewed (through a cross-section of the same 19 private institutions identified in the previous chapter) to seek information on their personal background, their views on the capitation fee phenomenon and its socio-political linkages, and also to assess the causes for the poor quality of teaching in private colleges. Another important reason to study the faculty was to substantiate and check on the data gathered from the students and management.

Qualification and Recruitment

In general, it was seen that the teachers in private professional colleges were poorly qualified with a relatively small percentage possessing postgraduate degrees. To economise on the teachers' salaries, a large number of college managements appointed part-time teachers, retired personnel, teaching assistants, and tutors to make up their faculty strength. For a large number of teachers, the teaching assignment was their first job, and they were constantly on the lookout for better employment opportunities.

Over 30 teachers in government colleges were interviewed for comparison with their counterparts in private colleges. It was found that teachers in government medical colleges were, by and large, better qualified. But in the government-run engineering colleges like the U.V.C.E., the faculty, though qualified, was found to be disinterested in work. The students and teachers both pointed out that the State government could not be absolved of the responsibility for the ills that had crept into professional education in Karnataka. The State-run engineering institutions, in particular, were no model for private colleges, though the students there got good results relying on their own calibre and hard work.

Private Colleges

Barring a few old established private engineering colleges, the new ones, by and large, had a poorly qualified teaching faculty. Very often, the minimum eligibility conditions were waived by the management in the appointment of teachers. For a lecture's job, the qualification laid down by the Government of Karnataka is a master's degree. In practice, however, not only were there a large number of lecturers with merely a graduate degree in engineering, even some readers were not postgraduates. For instance, at the Ambedkar Institute of Technology, Bangalore, 35 teachers out of a total teaching staff of 62 were only B.E.s. At the Adichunchunagiri Institute of Technology, Chikmagalur, of the 63 members on the faculty, 43 were again only engineering graduates. At the Shree Siddhartha Institute of Technology (S.I.T.), Tumkur, 27 out of 57 teachers were B.E.s and at the Manipal Institute of Technology, 53 out of the 135 members of the teaching staff were graduates. At the S.I.T., of the 147 teachers, 75 were B.E.s, and there were only three who possessed doctorates. Institutions like the M.S. Ramaiah Institute of Technology had a number of lecturers who were post-graduates (62/78) and 12 of them were Ph.D.s.[1] The college authorities also seemed to have shown arbitrariness in the selection and

[1] Figures obtained from the respective college prospectuses (1986, 1987 and 1988) and college offices.

promotion of teachers. The Head of the Physics Department was a professor with an M.Sc. degree. Another reader in the Chemistry Department was also an M.Sc., while some lecturers were Ph.D.s.

Similarly, of the medical institutions in Karnataka, in the Ambedkar Medical College (A.M.C.), of the 119 full-time members of the faculty, 40 were junior lecturers or tutors with only an M.B.B.S. degree. At the J.S.S. Medical College, Mysore, 16 out of 25 teachers were tutors; at the Kempegowda Institute of Medical Sciences (K.I.M.S.), 67 of the 132 staff members were tutors with only a graduate degree, and at the Adichunchanagiri Institute of Medical Science (A.I.M.S.), 12 of the 19 teachers were again tutors with M.B.B.S. degrees. So, on an average, 60 per cent of the teaching staff consisted of tutors who were fresh graduates. There were only 20 Ph.D.s in all these colleges and very few teachers were involved in research. Some, who were keen to do research, stated that the teaching, supervision and administrative work allocated to them left them with very little time to engage in any satisfying academic activity.

Government Colleges

While the number of tutors was large in private medical colleges, in the state-run Bangalore Medical College, of the 296 faculty members, 157 (53.8 per cent) were professors or assistant professors, and 137 (46.2 per cent) were lecturers or residents. There were no tutors.

At the Surathkal Regional Engineering College (S.R.E.C.), of the 139 teachers, 79 (57.5 per cent) were assistant professors or professors. There were 60 (43.5 per cent) lecturers in the institutional who all held postgraduate degrees.

At the university-run engineering college in Bangalore (U.V.C.E.), the staff was fairly well qualified. The Civil Engineering Department had 45 teachers, all of who were postgraduates, with about half of them also possessing doctorates. The Electrical Engineering Department, consisting of 45 faculty members had 10 teachers with doctorate degrees and 17 postgraduates. There were 20 members in the Mechanical Engineering Department; 10 were postgraduates and five had doctorate degrees. Thus, of a total of 110 faculty members in the above three departments, 45.5 per cent were postgraduates, 33.6 per cent had Ph.D.s, while 21 per cent held a bachelor's degree. The overall picture that emerged of the qualifications of the faculty (545 members) in the three government colleges studied was as follows:

Lecturers—all postgraduates	36%
Professors/Assistant Professors/Readers—Ph.D.s	55%
Tutors and teachers with only graduate degrees	9%

The private colleges presented a different profile as regards the qualifications of their teaching members. Of the 645 teachers on whom information was gathered vis-à-vis their educational background, 333 held a bachelor's degree in engineering or medicine. There were 35 Ph.D.s and the rest were postgraduates. The picture that emerged was as follows:

B.E.s or M.B.B.S.s	51.5%
Ph.D.s	5%
Postgraduates	43.5%

Thus, we can see that the staff was much better qualified in government colleges. While the majority of teachers in the three government colleges studied were Ph.D.s, in the 10 private colleges from where data was obtained 5 per cent of the teaching community had this qualification.

Some teachers in government colleges, like the head of the Electrical Engineering Department at the U.V.C.E., stated that the faculty in the Computer Science Department had not been appointed, and although there were some teaching assistants available, temporary staff had also been recruited. He added that there was difficulty in getting qualified staff; owing to lack of job satisfaction and poor emoluments, less people were opting for teaching. They preferred to be absorbed in industry because of better career prospects. The minimum qualification for a lecturer was an M.E., but in some cases this qualification had been relaxed in view of the shortage of staff. He also stated that the teachers were asked to complete their master's degree programme within five years of their appointment. However, when a university relaxed terms and conditions in the appointment of faculty, private college managements did not hesitate to appoint many more under-qualified teachers and pay them less emoluments.

The selection committee for the appointment of teachers comprised some members from the management or the board of trustees, the college principal, the chairman of the governing council, the head of the concerned department, and generally one or two university experts. But, as was revealed by some of the younger teachers, it was the management which mainly influenced the selection of teachers and got them to work on their own terms. In certain colleges, like the medical college in Nagamangala Taluk, the Principal stated that no university experts were involved in the selection process and 'a lot was left to the discretion of the management,' which meant that the management could even waive aside the minimum eligibility conditions and recruit teachers not adequately qualified. This did not happen in government colleges and university experts were always involved at the selection level. The management kept a minimum number of teaching staff and a low teacher-student ratio as compared to government colleges. At the U.V.C.E. and S.R.E.C., both government colleges, the teacher-student ratio was 1:12 and 1:10 respectively, while in some private engineering colleges like S.I.T. and M.S.R.I.T., it was 1:20. At the Bangalore Medical College and the Government Medical College at Mysore the teacher–student ratio was 1:5, while in private medical colleges like the A.M.C. and K.I.M.S., it was 1:10. Since profit considerations remained uppermost, a larger intake of students was not followed by the appointment of an adequate number of teachers in private institutions.

Reasons for Joining

For 84 respondents (52.50 per cent) out of 160, the teaching assignment in their respective colleges was their first job (see Table 7.1). Apart from four of these teachers who had joined service some years earlier, the rest were fresh graduates, not particularly interested in teaching. They were biding their time, looking for better avenues while working in these colleges.

There were 28 respondents (17.50 per cent) who stated that they

Table 7.1
Reasons for Joining Private Colleges

Reason	No. of respondents	Percentage
Total respondents	160	—
First job	84	52.50
Dislike transfers/want to stay in one place/native place	28	17.50
Joined after retirement	18	11.25
Joined for monetary incentive or as deputies/promotion from government colleges	15	9.37
From industry/preferred teaching	15	9.37

had taken up their present job owing to their desire to stay in their native place. Others, particularly doctors, said that they did not like the idea of transfers and therefore 'preferred to work for even less money in private colleges'. There were four government medical colleges in Karnataka, and there was a fear among faculty members of being transferred to any of these institutions. Some teachers stated that transfers brought about many domestic inconveniences. Therefore, some chose to teach in a private medical college so that they could remain in one place. Being in the same town also meant extra income for working couples. There were 15 (9.37 per cent) other teachers who said that they had come to teaching from industry because they preferred it.

A total of 18 (11.25 per cent) respondents had taken up jobs after their retirement, and received only a consolidated salary. However, there were cases where some capable retired people had been employed on a good salary. A few good teachers were also brought over from government colleges with offers of better remuneration, thus creating a false image of quality to attract capitation fee students.

There were 15 respondents (9.37 per cent) who stated that they had come from government to private medical colleges as deputies. The strike in the summer of 1987 by the government-run Bangalore Medical College students pertained to the issue of many of their better faculty members being lent as deputies to a private medical college in Bangalore. However, six respondents stated that they chose deputation because they either wished to be in their native place, or came on promotion as they were given an opportunity to act as principals or heads of departments. This also meant better remuneration for them. Some government college teachers were also found to be simultaneously teaching in private institutions so as to supplement their incomes.

Background

Of the 160 teacher respondents, 120 (75 per cent) had obtained their education in Karnataka. 132 (82.5 per cent) had attended government colleges and were in a position to compare the situation in private institutions. 28 (17.5 per cent) had studied in private medical or engineering colleges and nine (5.62 per cent) were also teaching in colleges where they had studied. Of the private institutions surveyed, five colleges had employed their old students. Some of them stated that they did not believe in employing their old students as a matter of policy. The administrator of S.S.I.T., Tumkur, stated that they did not want to encourage inbreeding.

As Table 7.2 reveals, only 5.62 per cent of the students were teaching in the same private colleges where they had been trained. This confirmed the fact that the managements were not willing to trust their own products as teachers, and in fact, recruited more teachers (82.5 per cent) who were trained in government colleges. Again, 75 per cent of the faculty members had been educated in Karnataka, the balance 25 per cent had had their education outside the State. We also observed that local people (about 80 per cent) were employed by the private entrepreneurs. Of the remaining 20

Table 7.2
Background of Faculty

		Percentage
Total number of teacher respondents	**160**	
Educated in Karnataka	120	75
Educated outside Karnataka	40	25
From government colleges	132	82.5
From private colleges in Karnataka	28	17.5
Those teaching in the private colleges where they had studied	9	5.62

per cent teachers, a large number came from the neighbouring states in south India. This indicated the regional character of entrepreneurship as the college managements were not willing to offer attractive salaries to recruit the best available national talent.

Caste

In the four colleges where we carried out a detailed survey, we found that in the dominant-caste (Vokkaliga-managed) college, namely the Kempegowda Institute of Medical Sciences (K.I.M.S.), of the 132 teachers, 85 (63.39 per cent) were Vokkaligas. In the Lingayat-run college, S.I.T., over 60 per cent of the teachers were Lingayats. Again, at the Ambedkar Medical College (A.M.C.), run by a scheduled caste trust, about 60 per cent faculty members were scheduled castes. In these cases we observe a heavy bias in the appointment of teachers having a similar caste background— the majority of teachers belonged to the same caste as that of the management. The M.S. Ramaiah Institute of Technology presented a different picture. Here it was found that teachers were appointed from all castes. This being a college run by a private entrepreneur, it was enterprise which seemed to have overcome caste consider- ations.

Salaries and Other Benefits

We observed that managements of most private professional col- leges made several temporary appointments in the form of tutors and lecturers. By keeping the vacancies temporary, the rules of appointment could be circumvented and the teachers could also be held on a tight leash. Unlike government colleges where teachers felt secure about their jobs, the fear of insecurity loomed large in private institutions. When the temporary teachers left, the vacancies took about four to five months to be filled, and so the students, during that period, were left in the lurch. The salaries of many teachers were lower than what the managements claimed they paid. In one engineering college, a faculty member with a bachelor's degree stated that he received only Rs. 1,000 per month for the first year of teaching. After a year, a raise of Rs. 350 was given to him. Those with a master's degree were getting only Rs. 2,100 per month. In government engineering colleges, at the time this study was conducted (November 1987), the pay scales of the teachers were as follows:

Professors : Rs. 1500–60–1800–100–2000–125–2500
Readers : Rs. 1200–50–1300–60–1900
Lecturers : Rs. 700–40–1100–50–1600

These scales have now been revised as given below:[2]

Professors : Rs. 4500–150–5700–200–7300
Readers : Rs. 3700–125–4950–150–5700
Lecturers : Rs. 2000–75–2800–100–4000

Although most privately managed engineering colleges professed that they followed the A.I.C.T.E. and Government of Karnataka scales, in reality they did not, as was reported by some teachers at the Ambedkar Institute of Technology. However, there were faculty members from only a few private colleges like the M.S.R.I.T. and R.V.C. who maintained that their remuneration was on par with that of teachers from government colleges.

In medical colleges, the revised scales as revealed by the Directorate of Medical Education were:[3]

Professors : Rs. 3650–4550
Associate Professors : Rs. 3170–4430
Readers/Asst. Professors : Rs. 2450–4190
Lecturers : Rs. 2200–4070

In this case again, private medical colleges did not follow any uniform practice in relation to payment of salaries. There were only a few instances where the teaching staff of some private medical colleges, like the K.M.C. in Manipal or the J.S.S. Medical College in Mysore, seemed satisfied with their salaries. But this was not the picture in most other institutions where the demand of the faculty for good salaries had not been met. Towards the end of 1991, teachers in medical colleges were on strike for better scales.

[2] Information regarding revised pay scales provided by the Directorate of Technical Education, Bangalore, 1991.
[3] As on July 1988; the scales are still operative (1992).

It was no wonder, then, that so many of the private college teachers took private tuitions and were really not interested in teaching in the classroom. Some students from an engineering college revealed that regular classes were held only for the sixth, seventh and eight semester students because they had to face an examination. But there were practically no classes for the earlier batches. Most of the teachers seemed interested in making money through private tuition, and therefore, regular classes suffered in the process.

Facilities

As was stated by a majority of students (see Chapter 6), most teachers in private medical and engineering colleges also felt that the facilities for teaching were inadequate in their institutions. Of the total number of 160 respondents, only 26 (16.25 per cent) felt that the facilities in their colleges were good and were meeting the M.C.I. and central government norms.[4] Another 80 (50 per cent) felt that the equipment and library facilities for students were just average, while 54 (33.75 per cent) others said that the conditions were poor in their institutions (see Table 7.3). Although there was no lack of funds (considering the capitation fees charged and donations collected), to purchase good equipment, books and journals, yet no allocations were made for these items by the managements. A faculty member of a private medical college observed that even though the request for new instruments had been placed four years earlier, nothing had been bought. It was the middle management here which was to be blamed for this. A teacher at S.I.T. complained of non-availability of staff, especially for computer science and electronics, since the managements were not willing to offer good salaries. All the private medical colleges that were studied (except K.M.C. Manipal) did not have hospital facilities of their own and had to rely on government hospitals. Some teachers at K.I.M.S. and A.M.C. stated that they lacked sophisticated equipment and modern teaching aids. They needed to equip themselves more by way of specimens (for pathology) and they required a wide hospital base. Laboratory facilities and teaching

---

[4] These norms have been discussed in Chapter 6.

Table 7.3
Facilities for Teaching and Research

			Percentage
Total number of teacher respondents		160	
Facilities for teaching:	Good	26	16.25
	Average	80	50.00
	Bad	54	33.75
Facilities for research:	Good	15	9.37
	Average	20	12.50
	Bad/Nil	125	78.13

rooms were also stated to be inadequate at K.I.M.S. At the Bangalore Medical College, we observed that five students were attached to one hospital bed, whereas in A.M.C. and K.I.M.S., 20 students were attached to one bed in the hospital.

The work of the teachers in these colleges entailed mainly teaching, laboratory work, guidance, and supervision of projects. According to one respondent from R.V. College of Engineering, there was no time and no facilities available for their individual development. Another faculty member from the Kasturba Medical College (K.M.C.) remarked that much time had to be devoted to the large number of students they had, which was about 45 in a class at the postgraduate level and 240 at the graduate level. In a college like K.M.C., facilities were certainly available for research in some departments, but as one staff member stated, 'research is not a priority. So research facilities suffer and there is not much scope for most of us to grow.' Some teachers at M.S.R.I.T. said that more equipment was required for project work and research in the Civil Engineering Department in their collge. Manpower assistance in laboratories was also inadequate according to some staff members. Most of the private managements were operating with low investments and were interested in high profits.

As Table 7.3 shows, a total of 125 respondents (78.12 per cent) in the private medical and engineering colleges surveyed stated that faciltiies for research in their colleges were either inadequate or non-existent. Only 9.37 per cent of the teachers viewed these facilities as good. At M.S.R.I.T., some faculty members felt that their equipment and apparatus were much better than at U.V.C.E., the university-managed college. The teachers at U.V.C.E. also pointed out these deficiencies.

Besides the lack of adequate facilities for teaching or for personal academic development, the general apathy and lack of motivation on the part of the teachers was heightened by the fact that they had very little to look forward to by way of students, a majority of whom lacked initiative and diligence. Some faculty members felt that the accountability of teachers was higher in private colleges, and teaching was regular. Although they worked hard with average students, the latter, because of the inadequate facilities, were not able to show good results and the output was poor even from those 'who had almost to be spoon-fed'. Of the 1,000 odd students at the A.M.C., 300 were 'repeaters' (those who had failed in previous examinations).[5] At M.S.R.I.T., about 50 per cent students were 'repeaters'.

'Only 40 of the 160 students in the Mechanical Engineering Department had passed,' remarked a teacher.[6] Due to the high intake and inadequate staff, the pass percenrage was low at S.I.T. also.

One of the teachers said that to study an engineering course, 'analysis and conceptual skills are required and so it is difficult to deal with students who come with a notion that it is some kind of a fault-and-repair programme.' Very often students did not grasp what was taught. One teacher at S.I.T. observed that government colleges like the U.V.C.E. attracted the 'cream of intelligence'. There the faculty put in much less effort with the students. Some also felt that the students in private colleges were not really interested. A majority of them were from fairly affluent families with a business or landed background or form upper middle class families. About 50 per cent of them seemed to have been pushed into these courses. Communicating with the students was also a problem felt by some teachers. Those who had come from a regional language medium were unable to follow English which was the medium of instruction. Others felt that students only wanted to scrape through the examinations and did not want to really acquire knowledge. They approached the teachers for attendance or for postponement of a test but rarely for help in academic work.

Those who supported the practice of charging capitation fee (27.5 per cent) argued mainly in terms of platitudes and their

---

[5] Figures obtained from the A.M.C. office, July 1988.
[6] Interview in July 1988.

critique was confined to how education should be available to those who could pay for it. There were some who felt that when these institutions received no aid from the government there seemed no other recourse but to charge capitation fee, which should be prescribed by the government. Interested students with an aptitude should not face disappointment because the state was not in a position to finance professional education. 'Since everything else in our society works through influence, or money, why ban only one type of influence, namely money?' asked one faculty member. Some teachers at A.I.M.S. also stated that the state should ensure that money collected by private institutions was properly utilised for the prescribed purpose and was accounted for. The government should be responsible for ensuring standards and should de-recognise colleges which did not meet the requisite norms. Some teachers suggested that to ensure quality, private collges could raise the eligibility conditions like a higher cut-off point (minimum percentage) for students entering private institutions.

Although the faculty was fully integrated into the capitation fee system and was sustaining it by lending its teaching skills to the system, there were 63.75 per cent of the teachers who showed their disapproval with this growing phenomenon. While many amongst them felt that this kind of private enterprise in higher professional education ought to be banned, they were quick to admit that it would not be possible to do so in practice. It was the government which talked of banning the system for securing votes but actually it was not interested in this. 'Ministers and MPs are all interested in their own kith and kin; caste-based colleges are interested in their caste votes for the caste leaders, and such institutions cater to the rich,' remarked a faculty member, thereby indicating the dynamics of caste, class and politics in the operation of the capitation fee phenomenon. He thus felt that a ban on capitation fee would not succeed.

Ineffective Teachers' Forum

Nearly all the faculty members interviewed stated that they would have liked a forum to express their grievances. However, no teachers' organisation existed in these colleges. There were no teachers' union in the unaided medical or engineering institutions which could take care of their problems, and hence, there was no outlet for expresion of their grievances. There existed in some institutions club-like associations, but these were generally defunct organisations and only functioned in a limited way, for example to welcome a new teacher, or engage themselves in a cultural programme together with the students. College councils, where they existed, as in Manipal, were formed by professors and heads of departments, who were generally the mouthpiece of the management. The teachers could approach the management only through their Principal. The college councils or associations were supposed to attend to academic or disciplinary matters or departmental difficulties.

Thus, in private engineering and medical colleges in Karnataka, the teaching faculty faced serious problems of inadequate facilities, lack of motivation to teach because of disinterested students, no monetary incentive, and a general feeling of insecurity. Hence, under these circumstances it was difficult to expect the quality of teaching to be anything but mediocre. The absence of college-level union activity also indicated the tight control of teachers by the managements.

Although there were 10 organisations of university and college teachers in Karnataka, all of them did not represent private college teachers. However, the Bangalore University College Teachers Association (B.U.C.T.A.) was in effect, an organisation of private college teachers. When it started in 1965, it was primarily a 'cultural organisation' conducting teacher seminars, organising social service camps and arranging film shows. It was only around 1971 that the Association shifted its focus to teachers' issues.[7] But many teachers enrolled simply to oblige their active colleagues and their involvement in the activities of the Association was dismal.

While the B.U.C.T.A. directed its agitation against the government and the university and even boycotted examination work, it shied away from any direct confrontation with the managements of private colleges. As Jayaram and Sivaramakrishnan have reiterated in their study, 'no teachers' organisation in Karnataka has ever struck directly against the private colleges.'[8] Private managements

[7] N. Jayaram and G. Sivaramakrishnan, 'Teachers and Unionism,' in N. Jayaram, *Sociology of Education in India*, Rawat Publications, Jaipur, 1990, pp. 150–76.

[8] Ibid., p. 161.

were also irregular in the payment of salaries to teachers. Retrenchment of temporary faculty members often took place before summer vacations, many remained unconfirmed and they often had excess teaching load. Although in a large number of cases, the condition of teachers was pathetic, they did not venture to fight private managements. The B.U.C.T.A. was careful to ensure that while their actions attracted public attention, they should not invoke any punitive action from the management because the service conditions of teachers did not accord them adequate statutory protection.

Views on Capitation Fee

Of the 160 respondents, there were 44 (27.5 per cent) who supported the system of capitation fee, 102 (63.75 per cent) were against it, and the remaining 14 (8.75 per cent) withheld their views on the subject.

Table 7.4
Teachers' Views on Capitation

No. for capitation	44	27.50
No. against capitation	102	63.75
Indifferent	14	8.75
Total no. of respondents	160	100.00

Those against the system argued that it led to a deterioration in the standards of professional education and degrees could be purchased. It was a strain on the average parent and it also commercialised the attitude of students who wished to recover quickly the amount spent on them.

Some teachers felt that merit should be an important criterion for selection of students. When government allotment stopped at 85 per cent, a student with 80 per cent was not given admission, but one with 50 per cent and who could pay capitation got a seat. Hence the quality of education was bound to suffer. Other teachers observed that the difference in the calibre of students from the merit pool and those from the capitation fee or management quota was quite pronounced, the former showing greater aptitude, more interest, and a better level of performance. But the responsibility of the teachers towards students who paid money for a seat in a college increased.

Some faculty members remarked that granting sanction to so many engineering colleges without giving due consideration to manpower requirements seemed illogical. The inspection committees of the universities needed to perform their role of inspecting the infrastructural facilities with greater vigilance. Faculty members who disapproved of the capitation fee system strongly felt that the system needed to be curbed since several of these colleges had become business propositions.

Summing Up

In this chapter we have examined the background of the teachers and their working conditions in private engineering and medical institutions. In the caste- and community-based colleges, it was found that a large number of teachers belonged to the same caste or community as the management, thus reinforcing the sectional base of the education system. While many of faculty members condemned the capitation fee system, they placed the onus on the government and the university for lack of strict vigilance in their institutions. The reason pointed out by them for the poor standards in private colleges was that government intervention and university inspection were ineffective. Even where the conditions were unsatisfactory, private colleges were granted affiliations to universities in Karnataka. They expressed dissatisfaction about the lack of adequate facilities and sophisticated equipment, low emoluments, and deteriorating standards. 'The choice is limited. Even in government colleges, standards are similar. The universities formulate the syllabus and conduct examinations,' remarked some faculty members. Many of them were working in private colleges for lack of employment opportunities. Much of the apathy and frustration among the teachers could be attributed to the indifferent attitude of the government, relatively poorer salaries, inadequate facilities, incongenial working atmosphere and unmotivated students.

The capitation fee phenomenon, when viewed in the light of the data gathered from the faculty, demonstrated contradictory features in private enterprise in education. Modern professional education was being imparted by a largely poorly qualified faculty. The low salary of the teachers and the inadequate facilities in colleges were not commensurate with the high capitation fees charged from the students. The expectation of the entrepreneur to make the entreprise profitable and yield high returns with low investment was itself an indication of how much such a system could acheive.

The demand for professional education was so large that private professional institutions which were mushrooming over the years could get away with providing minimum facilities, and thereby substandard education continued to be imparted. The caste origin of the teachers, their mode of recruitment and the low-investment/high-profit parameter within which most private managements operated, all reflected the socio-economic and political dynamics of the capitation fee phenomenon.

8

CONCLUSION

In the preceding chapters we have analysed the complex character of the capitation fee phenomenon, and how the interplay of various social, economic and political factors has led to its emergence and growth. We have also related the evolution of the phenomenon to agrarian reforms after Independence. These reforms have led to the emergence of new social forces in the form of rich peasants and intermediate castes. Mohanty has observed that this new landed gentry 'is not totally devoid of the social basis of its power in land, caste and culture. In addition, it now uses the new capital entering the village. It is linked with the political party, and manipulates both the old and new instruments of power.'[1]

In the specific case of Karnataka, we have seen how the rich peasants and landlords belonging to the dominant intermediate castes, the Vokkaligas and Lingayats, have exercised their influence to set up capitation fee colleges. These colleges have become economic channels for diverting some of their agrarian surplus in the shape of finances for their establishment.

We have also seen in our study that the dominant castes set up

[1] See Manoranjan Mohanty, 'Duality of the State Process in India: A Hypothesis' in Ghanshyam Shah (Ed.), *Capitalist Development: Critical Essays*, Popular Prakashan, Bombay, 1990, p. 154.

these colleges as part of the process of seeking greater educational opportunities for their caste members. The process, which began with the non-Brahmin movement, further buttressed their desire for social mobility. They saw the economic and social advantages of professional cadres and skill structure generated through these colleges and the political leverage that would accrue as a result. Thus, educational societies and caste associations were made use of to achieve this objective, and greater opportunities were sought through reservations.

This brings us to the moot question: Can the capitation fee phenomenon be viewed as a possible channel of mobility for the backward and underprivileged sections? The special privileges provided in the Constitution for various groups, particularly through protective discrimination, and the process of modern democratic politics have afforded new educational opportunities as channels of social mobility.[2] As a result of reservations by the State, intermediate castes and backward groups have emerged as serious contenders, and education has not remained wholly confined to the upper castes. Caste- and community-based institutions have been sought to be established with an eye to social status, mobility, power and pelf. While this has been so, all the contending groups have not been equally placed in this competition. For instance, the capitation fee colleges run by scheduled castes have been a relatively more recent phenomenon — the first such college was established only in the early 1980s. Since they started late, they have not been on an equal footing with other colleges and not as well established in terms of recognition and infrastructural facilities. Thus, the capitation fee system as an avenue of mobility for the underprivileged has been too narrow to meet the egalitarian objectives. In fact, the whole notion of mobility has been criticised by some as one that weakens the path of the really poor because opportunities at the top become privileges of a few.[3] Thus, to say that private capitation fee institutions have served as an avenue of social mobility would only be taking a myopic view of the phenomenon.

The capitation fee phenomenon can be better understood when

[2] Suma Chitnis, *A Long Way To Go*, Allied Publishers, New Delhi, 1981. Chitnis has argued that as a result of protective discrimination, the scheduled castes 'are not only equal, but better situated, with respect to facilities like education, than their non-scheduled caste counterparts'.

[3] See Harold Entwistle, *Class, Culture and Education*, Methuen, London, 1978.

it is seen as an interplay of caste, class and power. While the elites of the dominant castes have viewed it as an avenue for building their own professional cadres, other backward castes, religious minorities and scheduled castes have also come into the fray, seeing it as an assertion of their caste and community rights. These institutions charging capitation fees have thus become spheres for caste competition and conflict, where different interest groups vie with one another in the race for setting up an engineering or medical college. Inasmuch as it has become a domain of elite competition and patronage, the phenomenon has also acquired a political dimension. That a political or caste leader is able to secure a college for his area gives him social prestige and gets him the electoral support of his caste members, and caste structures serve as convenient mechanisms for mobilising electoral support and building 'vote banks'. Such leaders also rely on financial support for themselves from such institutions during elections.

More specifically, our study of the management of private institutions in Karnataka has revealed the close nexus between caste, money power and politics. The managers of several caste- and community-based colleges were found to be rich landlords, businessmen, industrialists, bureaucrats or even lawyers. Often, they were also caste leaders or political leaders (M.L.A.s) and hence with the support of caste, political party and their financial strength, they were able to influence the government for permission to start an institution. Later, they were able to exert pressure on the government to ensure that the admission policy was so framed as to be conducive to their own political interests. The composition of the managing bodies of the Vokkaliga-run Bangalore Institute of Technology depicted a single caste or community dominance. The election to the Vokkaligara Sangha in the B.I.T. college campus and the involvement of the managing committee members there, some of whom were also contenders for the Sangha seats, revealed how politics was pervading the affairs of the college.

The procedure for selection of faculty members of many private colleges was biased in favour of appointing teachers of the caste that managed the institutions. At the Vokkaliga-managed Kempegowda Institute of Medical Sciences, 63.39 per cent of the teachers were Vokkaligas; at the Lingayat-run Siddaganga Institute of Technology, 60 per cent of the faculty members were Lingayats. Urban-based students who paid large donations to gain admission came from affluent groups. 78 per cent of the students came from towns and cities. About 50 per cent of the respondents belonged to families where their parents were rich or middle-level farmers or were running their own industry or business. And as Bardhan has observed, it is the educated children of the rich farmers and industrialists and traders who are now increasingly invading the professional class. 'For a long time in India', he has remarked, 'the professionals almost exclusively came from the traditional literate groups which unlike in Europe, had little organic relationship with trade or industry, with social origins that did not have much stake in the fortunes of private capital. This is changing and has already started influencing the flow of state services and subsidies and policy implementation in favour of some groups at the local level.'[4]

However, as has been observed in our study, the capitation fee phenomenon has essentially become an elite enterprise and an instrument for commerce and profit. Private entrepreneurs have also joined the race, looking for alternative lucrative sources. The charging of high fees from students, the poor and inadequate facilities, the appointment of under-qualified staff where 51.5 per cent of the teachers were found employed with a B.E. or M.B.B.S. degree, and the low salaries of faculty members indicates that the managements did not want to spend on the infrastructure and were more interested in making profits.

When there is such intermeshing of social, economic and political forces in the domain of education, there are bound to be serious repurcussions.

Implications

We will now discuss the implications of the phenomenon in the light of its contradictions with the Constitutional objectives inasmuch as it is a reflection of persisting inequalities and the elitist base of the education system. We will also try to show that it has sought to reproduce dominant structures, has been anti-secular and has also led to the lowering of educational standards.

[4] Pranab Bardhan, 'The Third Dominant Class,' *Economic and Political Weekly*, Vol. XXIV, No. 3, 21 January 1989, pp. 155–56.

Reflection of Persisting Inequalities

Education is an important input in the process of development for any developing society. In the Indian context, an important assumption of the education system has been the principle of equality of opportunity as indicated in the Constitution. The University Education Commission Report had stated: 'In a democratic society, the opportunity of learning must be open not only to the elite but to all those who have to carry the privilege and responsibility of citizenship.'[5] Explaining the concept of equality of opportunity, it has observed that the system must provide education to every young person to the extent that he or she can profit from it. Education should be of a character best designed to assure the maximum development of individual nature. However, the fundamental right to equality is itself ridden with contradictions. 'In the contemporary Indian social situation, the promise of political equality has been frustrated by the denial of social and economic equalities.'[6] This dilemma has also been manifest in the Indian education system.

The concept of equal opportunities also implies equal access to the channels of mobility. While there is no assurance that with education one can always move to higher positions, it is even more unlikely that one can do so without education.[7] In fact, Bottomore has pointed out that equality of opportunity means the opportunity to rise to a higher level in a stratified society. It also implies that the inequalities of the stratified system have to be counteracted in every generation so that individuals can develop their abilities—in this sense it presupposes equality. He has added, however, that the influence upon 'individual life chances of the entrenched distinctions of social class is strong and pervasive.'[8] In India we find that besides the stratification based on class, there has been a stratification based on caste as well, which has also an influence on educational opportunities. It is the status acquired through both

[5] Government of India, *Report of the University Education Commission, 1948–49*, Publications Division, New Delhi, p. 50.

[6] Manoranjan Mohanty, 'Towards a Political Theory of Inequality' in Andre Beteille (Ed.), *Equality and Inequality: Theory and Practice*, Oxford University Press, Delhi, 1983, p. 248.

[7] See M.S. Gore, *Education and Modernisation in India*, Rawat Publications, Jaipur, 1982, pp. 25–39.

[8] T.B. Bottomore, *Elites and Society*, Penguin Books, London, 1964, pp. 148–49.

caste and income which determines one's chances of receiving education. The overall effect of such a system has been that access to the 'privileged sector through the portals of education'[9] has become more and more restrictive.

In this context, Karlekar has stressed the 'role of education in the perpetuation of inequality.'[10] Bhatia and Seth in their study on private schooling in Delhi have also pointed out that the economic status of a parent is a significant determinant of school selection.[11] At the level of primary education itself the drop-out rate of students of poorer parents has been high.[12] Thus, we find weaker sections dropping out much before they reach the level of higher education. And, as Bottomore has stated: 'The differences which originate in economic inequalities are enhanced by educational differences.'[13] The expansion in higher education has also led to the emergence of sharp hierarchies in terms of courses and institutions. Courses such as medicine and engineering have been considered more prestigious since they lead to high income and high status occupations. Admission to such courses has been based on stiff competition, and as Chitnis has pointed out, children from poor families are likely to lose out in this competition.[14] At the level of higher education, again, the weaker sections have been poorly represented. B.V. Shah, in a study of Baroda University in the 1960s,[15] had observed that the students there came largely from upper-caste families residing in urban areas. Their parents were generally better educated and were largely occupied in high status occupations. Kamat has also referred to the class cleavages present in the

[9] See J.P. Naik, *The Education Commission and After*, Allied Publishers, New Delhi, 1982, p. 171.

[10] Malavika Karlekar, 'Education and Inequality' in Andre Beteille, op. cit., p. 193.

[11] See C.M. Bhatia and V.K. Seth, 'Hierarchy in the System of School: Political Economy of Education,' *Sociological Bulletin*,, 24: 1, 1975, pp.13–28.

[12] Naik has pointed out in a study that of the children who enter schools, nearly half drop out by class V; only about 15 per cent reach class XII, and less than one per cent get the degree. See J.P. Naik, op. cit., p. 170.

[13] T.B. Bottomore, op. cit., p. 123.

[14] Suma Chitnis, 'Education and Social Stratification: An Illustration from a Metropolitan City' in R. Ghosh and M. Zachariah (Eds.), *Education and the Process of Change*, Sage Publications, New Delhi, 1987, pp. 81–82.

[15] B.V. Shah, *Social Change and College Students of Gujarat*, University of Baroda, Baroda, 1964.

system of education being strengthened by the 'social selection process'.[16]

Thus we can see that owing to the inability of the weaker sections to provide education to their wards for a longer period, their elimination takes place much before they reach the level of higher education.[17] When there has been little equality at the elementary level, it is hard to conceive of equality at the higher level of education. At the higher level, the rhetoric of equal opportunity can only benefit those sections of society who have already benefited from the state's inegalitarian policies. In our context, the capitation fee phenomenon has only enabled the wealthier and propertied classes to further expand their options and opportunities. In fact, it has reinforced an unequal system and brought into focus more sharply the inequalities of the social and educational reality.

As we have seen in the chapter on students (Chapter 6), competition at the higher level of education has been largely between different strata of the better-off sections. From the sample on students, we have seen that 17.24 per cent of the students came from the landed gentry while about 29 per cent were from business families. The remaining respondents were from families where the parents were either professionals or in various other jobs. It was also seen in the intensive sample that the annual income level of 50.18 per cent of the parents sending their wards to these colleges was between Rs. 50,000 and Rs. 1 lakh. For nearly 12 per cent of the parents, the income level per annum was above Rs. 1 lakh. Thus, our study of capitation fee colleges has revealed a sharp reflection of persisting inequalities and the narrow social base of the Indian education system. In such a situation the Constitutional commitments of equality and equal opportunity seem statements of aspirations, far removed from the socio-economic reality.

[16] A.R. Kamat, *Education and Social Change in India*, Somaiya Publications, Bombay, 1986, pp. 139–204. Tilak, in a study of the East Godavari district of Andhra Pradesh, has maintained that the rates of return to education are lower for the weaker section. Also, the weaker sections are subject to labour market discrimination in employment and wages. See J.B. Tilak, *The Economics of Inequality in Education*, Sage Publications, New Delhi, 1987.

[17] A.M. Nalla Gounden, 'Investment in Education in India', *Journal of Human Resources*, No. 2, Summer 1967, pp. 345–58.

The Elitist Base of Education

As we have observed in Chapter 6, the economic status of parents has been an important determinant in the selection of students to private professional colleges. Amongst the dominant middle castes, such as the Vokkaligas and Lingayats who have been utilising such higher education facilities to advance their interests in the social structure,[18] it has been mainly students from more affluent backgrounds who have been the beneficiaries of the capitation fee based colleges. The growth of such colleges can be explained by the demand that has been generated for them year after year. But it is indeed remarkable that this domain of education has been left largely to the vegaries of unplanned consumer demand. That this has led to a reinforcement of the elitist character of the Indian education system cannot be undermined. Through exclusive access to capitation fee private instituions, a limited number of priviledged students are prepared for particular elite positions in society. Since the state-aided facilities in higher education have not expanded in the last 30 years or so, such education has been effectively turned into the private perserve of a few, with hardly any chance for the vast number of first generation learners to get into it.[19]

As has been observed earlier, in the absence of accompanying social and political changes education, far from becoming an instrument of social mobility, can very well have the reverse effect. As Richards and Leonar have stated, 'promotion of education which simply means its expansion, may equally well lead to the opposite of the effect intended, i.e. greater inequality in incomes and overall well-being.'[20]

In the case of capitation fee institutions, even where there is provision for government merit-quota seats (20 per cent in engineering colleges, for instance, as per the data collected from this study), and a few students from not very affluent backgrounds do

[18] See Chitra Sivakumar, *Education, Social Inequality and Social Change in Karnataka*, Hindustan Publishing House, Dehi, 1982.
[19] J.V. Deshpande, 'Boom in Teaching Shops,' *Economic and Political Weekly*, Vol. XXVI, No. 30, July 27, 1991 p. 1787.
[20] Cited in Dinesh Mohan, 'Science and Technology Policy in India' in R. Ghosh and M. Zachariah (Eds.), op. cit.

get admitted, these students suffer on account of poor teachers and inadequate facilities. And, as Dinesh Mohan has remarked; 'In a very tight job market and an over-inflated supply situation, those with poor backgrounds end up where they started after having wasted time and effort in an endeavour that was supposed to help them in upward mobility.'[21] By legitimising institutions motivated mainly by the pursuit of profit and where only a few manage to gain admission largely on the strength of their money power, the state has in fact strengthened the duality in the system of education and made it more elitist in nature.

It was in the 1960s that the Kothari Commission had maintained that if social transformation and 'change on a grand scale is to be achieved without violent revolution (and even then it will still be necessary), there is one instrument, and one instrument only, that can be used—education.'[22] How this change can be realised by maintaining a parallel system of education which has been the exclusive preserve of a privileged few is something open to question. 'The private sector in education is not an aberration. It is accepted as a legitimate means of expanding and improving education. It fits well in the contradiction that has characterised Indian educational thought and policy on the question of equality versus merit.'[23] The dominant concern of maintaining quality has been put forward as the rationale for encouraging competitive enterprise in education. However, this purpose has also not been served through private capitation fee colleges. It is only the capacity to sell a seat that has assumed importance, and not the maintenance of quality education. The sample in our study has revealed that the annual income level of over 62 per cent of the parents sending their wards to private engineering and medical colleges was over Rs. 50,000. The performance of the respondents at the school-level examination was of little consequence in their gaining admission to a college nor was any aptitude test evolved for their selection. Thus, their pre-selection (depending on their capacity to pay) has clearly meant the bottlenecking of opportunities for the majority. As has been seen earlier, since it is largely the propertied classes who are the

[21] Dinesh Mohan, op. cit., p. 43.
[22] *Kothari Commission Report*, 1964–66, p. 4.
[23] Krishna Kumar, 'Reproduction or Change? Education and Elites in India,' *Economic and Political Weekly*, Vol. XX, No. 30, 27 July 1985.

beneficiaries of such a system of education, it would not be wrong to go along with Navlakha when he states that the process contributing to the formation of the educated-professional elite continues to be linked to the dominant strata.[24] This select education enables them later to achieve positions of power, pelf and prestige in technocracy, industry, business and medicine,[25] and join, what Kamat calls, the 'super elite'.[26]

The elitist character of private enterprise in education was reflected in the members of the management of the capitation fee colleges as well. In Chapter 5 it was seen that the management committees had a mix of businessmen, industrialists, landlords, politicians, bureaucrats, and advocates. The dominant-caste colleges, in particular, had this kind of composition; these being the three Vokkaliga-run and five Lingayat-run colleges studied. About 50 per cent of the management board members were politicians in addition to being landlords or businessmen. Then there were institutions managed by private entrepreneurs like the M.V.J. College of Engineering and the Ramaiah colleges which were run more along the lines of a family enterprise. The Manipal colleges were being run by a business house, although they had managed a minority status for themselves. Bureaucrats and lawyers figured on some managements in larger numbers, as in the case of the Islamiah Institute of Technology. Thus it may be seen that the members of the managements in these colleges belonged to the powerful elite group and were in a position to influence any government in power through their community, caste and political support as well as their financial strength.

The pre-selection of the privileged few can be seen as a 'reproductionist' force in the system of education. A class reproduction perspective suggests somewhat divisive results. Students come to

[24] Suren Navlakha, *Elite and Social Change: A Study of Elite Formation in India*, Sage Publications, New Delhi, 1989, pp. 172–75.

[25] See A.D. King, 'Elite Education and the Economy,' *Economic and Political Weekly*, Vol. V, No. 35, 29 August 1970.

[26] A.R. Kamat, 'Education and Social Change' in A.B. Shah, *The Social Context of Education*, Allied Publishers, New Delhi, 1978, pp. 254–69. According to Kamat, the 'super elite' is devoid of a feeling of social commitment. Their only interest is their professional prospect (namely, acquiring money, influence and connections), and their social life which is one of affluence.

believe in the appropriateness of their class position in society.[27] About 33 per cent of the students in the study sample felt that the capitation fee system was justified because the advantage of wealth enabled them to buy an opportunity. By being exposed to social distinctions on a daily basis, students come to accept such inequality as necessary, inevitable and just.[28] This privatised form of education has only succeeded in reproducing inequality by legitimitising the allocation of individuals to professionally high status positions. With the help of their monetary power, many students have been able to secure degrees from private colleges which have served as passports to prestigious professions in society. A large number of students (62.82 per cent) interviewed in the course of this study stated that after getting their degrees they would either set up their private medical practice or an industry or enter their own business. Also, as has been seen in the earlier chapters on students and the managements, such a system replicates the relationships of dominance in the socio-economic sphere because only a few can benefit from it. Bourdieu and Passeron have argued that appropriation of knowledge is a function of class position and the family's basic socialisation in such traditions.[29] Their theory is significant in the Indian context where the system of dominance characterises the educational and wider socio-economic spheres. The capitation fee system has evolved ways that intensify and politicise the basic contradictions and conflicts of Indian society. The existence of such private institutions has only resulted in strengthening the existing class differentiation of the student clientele who, as was seen in the data gathered, came either from business groups (29 per cent) or from the feudal landed groups and the emerging class of rich peasantry (17.24 per cent).

[27] See Pierre Bourdieu and Jean-Claude Passeron, *Reproduction in Education, Society and Culture*, Tr. Richard Nice, Sage Publications, London, 1977; Samuel Bowles and Herbert Gintis, *Schooling in Capitalist America*, Routledge & Kegan Paul, London, 1976; Robert V. Robinson, 'Reproducing Class Relations in Industrial Capitalism,' in *American Sociological Review*, Vol. 49, April 1984, pp. 182-96. The point emphasised is that education usually reproduces the prevailing social and economic order.

[28] Also see Peter W. Cookson and Caroline H. Persell, 'English and American Residential Secondary Schools: A Comparative Study of the Reproduction of the Social Elites' in *Comparative Education Review*, August 1986, pp. 284–98.

[29] Pierre Bourdieu and Jean-Claude Passeron, op. cit.

Anti-Secular

The granting of permission to private interests to run community-based colleges in Karnataka has also contravened the secular basis of the Indian Constitution. The Constitution in order to provide educational opportunities to certain groups has included certain provisions which would specially benefit them. This was meant to provide a material basis for secularism in the country. However, in Karnataka it was found that almost every community had been granted permission to run capitation fee colleges. The Constitution has been based on the modern liberal concept of the individual securing liberty, equality and justice. This involves liberating individuals from traditional bondages like those of caste. For, as Beteille has remarked: 'The individual has been from times immemorial stamped with the identity of his caste or subcaste with very little scope to move out of the niche assigned in the social order to his ancestors.'[30] In electoral politics, however, support and power are drawn from various groups. Elites with resources at their disposal have been able to mobilise various groups by appealing to caste, religious, regional and other sentiments. The domain of education has become ridden with institutions based on such appeals. As was seen earlier, capitation fee colleges have become arenas for caste politics. It was also observed that other sectional interests based on religion have dominated the scene as well. Thus, the capitation phenomenon has been showing anti-secular trends.

While such institutions ostensibly profess a secular and liberal outlook, they have essentially been based on fragmentary interests, such as caste, religion and language. Owing to their parochial nature, these institutions can sometimes become centres of tension and rivalry and lead to explosive situations. This was seen in the September 1988 Bidar riots in Karnataka. Hostility between the Hindus and the Sikhs was sparked off by an incident in a private-run engineering college. Since the consequences of this incident are of vital concern, we will go into some of its details.

The State's Janata government granted permission in mid-1988

[30] Andre Beteille (Ed.), *Equality and Inequality; Theory and Practice*, Oxford Univesity Press, Delhi, 1983, p. 22.

to the Guru Nanak Dev Foundation to establish a medical college. This was apparently resented by the other communities and groups in the area. The affluence of the Sikh students who were flaunting their wealth—'an island of prosperity in an ocean of poverty',[31] as one newspaper chose to describe it—also contributed to the resentment of the local population. Trouble began during the Ganesh Chaturthi festival when some Shiva Sena volunteers were reported to have tried to force Sikh students to give donations for the festival. This eventually exploded with the killing of six Sikh students on September 14–15, 1989.[32] Over a hundred others were injured.

Besides the clashes at Bidar, there have occurred an increasing number of 'outsider'–local clashes in other capitation fee colleges as well. Incidents occurred at the Adichunchanagiri Medical College and at the Bhalki Engineering College in November–December 1988 where once again the fashionable and aggressive lifestyle of the 'outsiders', particularly students from the north, had irked the local population. In Kodagu, at around the same time, much before an engineering college of a Kerala-based Malankara Orthodox Church Education Trust could start functioning, local groups who had been trying to get their own projects sanctioned launched a bitter agitation.[33]

The incidents in Bidar, Bhalki and Kodagu revealed that the imposition of free-wheeling and free-spending urbanite students amid semi-rural communities can have disastrous consequences. The clashes further brought to surface the fact that the local caste- and community-based institutions have also been encouraging the forces of regionalism and parochialism. Kothari has also observed that it is in such trends, spurred by a leadership that has lost confidence in its own 'secular' and 'socialist' credo, that the 'turn around towards the communalisation of the Indian state is to be

[31] *Indian Express*, New Delhi, 3 October 1988.

[32] The carnage took place against the backdrop of the dominant Lingayat community's leaders' apprehension of losing their hold on the town if the Lingayat educational trust lost out in the race for the medical college. The object of the carnage was to scare away a Sikh businessman, Joga Singh, from the race for a medical college and the Sikhs in general from coming to Bidar for educational purposes. See the study conducted by the Delhi-based Peoples' Rights Organisation reported in *The Times of India*, 25 November 1988.

[33] *The Week*, 11–17 December 1988, pp. 22–23.

found . . . . By providing greater play to vested interests and to new "power brokers" at the grassroots and intermediate levels, it has further opened the fields to local mafias and professionals in violence at the cost of the poor in all communities.'[34] The communal temper has to be kept alive either for electoral or monetary gains. It is unfortunate that capitation fee colleges in Karnataka have been used as channels to sustain communalism, casteism and regionalism.

Denial of Right to Protest

In the course of this study several students registered complaints regarding inadequate facilities, upkeep and maintenance in their colleges. As there was lack of students' unions in the private institutions, students had to approach the management directly for their demands and few dared to do that. Such a situation subverts any open political process or dialogue. As Bowles and Gintis have remarked, 'an educational system can be egalitarian and liberating only when it prepares youth for fully democratic participation in social life and an equal claim to the fruits of economic activity.'[35] In the private institutions studied, the students were not prepared to learn or gain by participating in a democratic process. Not only this, such a system also amounted to a violation of the fundamental rights of any citizen to protest for safeguarding his interests.

Lowering of Standards

The existence of the system has also led to a disorientation of the roles of teachers and students. Minimum educational qualifications and requirements of practical experience are important for recruitment and promotion of teachers. However, the managements of private institutions have flouted university regulations and even legislation in this regard. They have considered these stipulations

[34] Rajni Kothari, 'The Death of Secularism,' *Illustrated Weekly of India*, 18 June 1989, pp. 29–31, excerpted from Rajni Kothari, *Politics and the People*, Ajanta Publications, Delhi, 1989. Also see Rajni Kothari, 'Cultural Context of Communalism in India,' *Economic and Political Weekly*, 14 January 1989, p. 84.

[35] Bowles and Gintis, op. cit., p. 14.

as too harsh and interfering with their right to administer their colleges. At the same time, the managements have not demanded of the teachers adherence to university regulations in regard to a minimum of classroom and laboratory work, qualifications, etc.

As we have seen in Chapter 6, besides a few old established private colleges, most of the colleges had a poorly qualified teaching faculty. The qualification laid down by the Government of Karnataka for a lecturer's job is a master's degree. But, in practice, several lecturers were merely graduates. For instance, at the Ambedkar Institute of Technology, 35 teachers out of 62 were found to have only B.E. degrees. At the Kempegowda Institute of Medical Sciences, of the 132 members of the staff, 67 were tutors with only an M.B.B.S. degree.

The teachers also found themselves in an exploitative position; they were thrown into a market situation totally favourable to the management.[36] The Karnataka State government scales being followed in medical colleges were not at par with the UGC scales (for details see Chapter 6). Most engineering college managements professed that they followed A.I.C.T.E. scales, but this was not borne out by the teachers who were interviewed. Although many amongst the faculty seemed disenchanted with the existing state of affairs, there were no effective forums or teachers' unions to voice their grievances.

As for the students, the rush for admissions to private professional institutions had created conditions of a seller's market.[37] The authorities could have used this to impose higher academic standards for admissions as, for instance, in Manipal colleges where the cut-off percentage for admission was higher than in many other colleges in the region.[38] However, by and large, they have opted for imposing minimal academic merit conditions, yielding monetary gains

[36] See Nirmal Singh, *Education Under Siege*, Concept Publishing Company, New Delhi, 1983, pp. 212–16. Singh's study on private colleges in Kanpur has also pointed out that the teachers there were at the mercy of the buyer and therefore undersold themselves. Also see, M. Jha, 'Relations with the Management of Colleges: A Note' in S.C. Malik (Ed.), *Management and Organisation of Indian Universities*, Indian Institute of Advanced Studies, Simla, 1971, p. 184.

[37] See Amartya Sen, 'The Crisis in Indian Education' in S.C. Malik (Ed.), op. cit., pp. 251–52.

[38] Also being an older institution (the medical college was set up in 1953) it has had time to develop facilities. But the capitation fee here has remained very steep. The Pais have sought a minority status for their institutions and do not offer any open or merit seats.

for themselves. This situation has permitted the private managements to further lower the educational facilities. Of the 160 teacher respondents in the study, 80 felt that the equipment and library facilities for students were just average, while 50 others stated that these were poor. The rush for engineering and medical courses and the managements filling their quota of seats for monetary, political or other non-academic considerations has made this situation worse. In the case of university examinations, attempts to prevent 'mass copying' under heavy police patrolling have also been sometimes foiled by connivance between student and management representatives. Such a situation disorients even an honest student who then begins seeking short-cuts to a professional degree, which naturally results in the production of degree holders without sound professional training.

Employment and Health

According to the Labour Ministry, over 300 million people are registered with the employment exchanges in India. Although not all of them are necessarily unemployed, an interesting statistic that emerges is that the tally includes 27,000 medical graduates and 57,900 engineers, the most envied professions in the country.[39] It takes about Rs. 3 lakh to train a doctor and a little less to train a first-rate engineer. Because the training imparted to doctors and engineers is specific, expensive and deteriorates fast with disuse, unemployment among them could represent a tremendous waste of resources and lead to social distress.

In the course of this study, as has been stated earlier, the extent of unemployment among engineers and doctors was openly admitted by the Director of Technical Education, Karnataka, and also by a member of the Legislative Council. It was revealed that there were over a thousand unemployed engineering graduates in Karnataka alone.[40] A proliferation of private institutions and the increasing unemployment amongst students graduating from here is bound to lead to frustration and increase strife in society. Qualified scientists,

---

[39] *Business India*, 17–20 April 1989.
[40] Figures quoted by B.K. Chandrashekar, M.L.C. (Janata), November 1987, from the live registers of the employment exchange in Karnataka.

engineers and medical personnel occupy a pivotal position in society, and at any given point of time, the higher the degree of malutilisation, the higher is the volume of social disaffection generated by the sections affected by imbalances. As Nandy and Chowdhury have remarked, the impact of social tension is that 'students who constitute the would-be entrants into the labour force tend to develop a morbid attitude towards social goals and practices . . . .'[41] A large number of student respondents seemed to have imbibed the values of a profit-oriented society and stated that they were interested in earning a good living and making good the amount that had been spent on their capitation fees.

Many medical students interviewed in these institutions stated that they did not want to work in villages because they would not be able to recover the cost of their own investment in education. Thus, the setting up of several private medical colleges has not really contributed to mass health services. For a total population of 371.36 lakh in Karnataka, there were only 388 hospitals.[42] Although there has been a ten-fold increase since Independence in the number of doctors, and today there is a doctor for every 2,500 persons in the country, 80 per cent of them practise in urban areas. Only 27 per cent of the country's hospitals are in rural areas, and according to figures quoted by the Medical Council of India, of the 4.5 lakh doctors, only 21,000 are working in the countryside.[43] A situation like this does not allow the benefits of the professional cadres being created to be distributed where they are really needed.

Possible Alternatives

Today India is passing through a period of political instability and economic crises. Recent agitations such as those protesting against

[41] P.N. Chowdhury and R.K. Nandy, 'Scientific and Technical Personnel' in Amrik Singh and Philip G. Altbach (Eds.), *The Higher Learning in India*, Vikas Publishing House, Delhi, 1974, p. 105 (pp. 103–18).

[42] Government of Karnataka, *Karnataka at a Glance 1989–90*, Directorate of Economics and Statistics, Bangalore, pp. 14, 61.

[43] Padma Prakash and Amar Jesani, 'Do We Need So Many Doctors?' *Indian Express*, New Delhi, 14 September 1986. See also *Imprint*, March 1988, pp. 26–31, Veeranarayana Kethineni, 'Political Economy of State Intervention in Health Care,' *Economic and Political Weekly*, Vol. XXVI, No. 42, 19 October 1991, pp. 2427–33 and *The Times of India*, New Delhi, 22 September 1992.

reservations based on the Mandal Commission Report and the demands of the dalits for more rights are indicative of the frustration of the people and their increased political consciousness. These have accentuated the existing contradictions in society, furthered the political divide and intensified the crises. In this scenario it has become necessary for education to assume a key role in bringing about greater democratisation in the socio-political sphere. When we examine the implications of the capitation fee phenomenon in this light it becomes important to search for possible alternatives. Until some corrective measures are taken and interventions made, the consequences could assume serious proportions. We have briefly indicated below a few possible directions in which alternatives can be sought.

There are two levels at which intervention can possibly be made. First, at the level of the state where it exercises effective controls, and second, at the grassroots level where social forces actively participate. It is activisation at the latter level which can exercise pressure on the state for taking greater initiatives.

State Intervention

With the National Policy on Education (1986) and the emphasis of Narasimha Rao's government (1991) on privatisation and the Indian economy 'clearly moving towards greater reliance on market forces'[44] it has become all the more necessary to ensure that such initiatives do not run counter to the objectives of providing opportunities to the weaker sections and ensuring that minimum quality criteria are met.

While the Indian state has retained its ideological commitment to the goal of equality, it has also been dependent on the support of dominant groups in society for its political survival. This is reflective of the contradictory trends in the process of state functioning.[45] The 'coercive' and 'repressive' state has also been 'responsive', and as Rao has observed, it would indeed be a

---

[44] Amartya Sen's interview, *Indian Express*, New Delhi, 22 December 1991.
[45] Manoranjan Mohanty, 'Duality of the State Process in India: A Hypothesis', op. cit.

mistake to write off the 'liberal democratic potentialities'[46] of the Indian state. Moreover, as we observed in Chapter 1, the class configurations in the Indian situation have not crystallised, and hence, the state has enjoyed a certain degree of autonomy.[47] It has exercised its autonomy by taking a number of positive measures to maintain its legitimacy. In trying to seek legitimacy, the state has also tried to understand the aspirations of the people and develop a programme that appears 'to demonstrate an intention to implement it'.[48] It has ensured minimum ameliorative measures and plans for development. This being the case, once sufficient pressure is exerted on it, the state can intervene in a more positive way. For any developing society, mobilisation of resources through state initiative is important. However, in the case of India, such state initiatives have been vitiated by the operation of the nexus of dominant interests. Private initiative in the form of the capitation fee system has encouraged a nexus among entrepreneurs, caste interests and politicians. To counter the serious consequences that follow, the state in its interaction with private interests in education needs to exercise more effective controls.

Specific Measures

Some specific measures where the state could intervene immediately in the existing situation are given below.

Let us take the case of the private corporate sector in India. In a way it is being subsidised by the state by making available to them trained engineering graduates from state-funded institutions such as the Indian Institutes of Technology. For this facility, the state

[46] Raghavendra Rao, 'Understanding the Indian States: A Historical Materialist Exercise' in Zoya Hasan, S.N. Jha and Rasheed-ud-din Khan (Eds.), *The State, Political Processes and Identity*, Sage Publications, New Delhi, 1989, pp. 88–89.

[47] See Susanne H. Rudolph and Lloyd H. Rudolph, *In Pursuit of Lakshmi: The Political Economy of the Indian State*, Orient Longman, Hyderabad, 1987. The Rudolphs have argued that the state is able to act as a 'self-determining third actor', independent of both private capital and organised labour, these being the other two actors.

[48] Jayant K. Lele, 'The Legitimacy Question' *Seminar*, March 1990, pp. 21–5. Also see Jayant K. Lele, *Elite Pluralism and Class Rule*, Popular Prakashan, Bombay, 1982, p. 205.

could possibly levy a cess on industry employing such engineering graduates. It would leave the state with more funds at its disposal to be able to run more professional institutions or provide them with better facilities.

Another possibility would be for the state to invite the industry to sponsor meritorious students and see them financially through their academic training. While getting the industry to pay for their education, the students could in turn be asked to sign a bond to serve that particular sponsoring corporate organization for a certain minimum specified number of years. For the selection of such students, a system of pre-recruitment could be adopted at the initial part of their academic training. Such a system is already prevalent in the case of the state-owned Railways, for instance.

The state and industry could also join hands and evolve some innovative cooperative systems of education, as is presently in vogue at the Thapar Institute at Patiala, a private institution imparting engineering education. This institute has introduced a system whereby the students participate in work-terms in industry and academic-terms in the institute. During a work-term the students are paid wages on par with the employees and therefore can support themselves through the academic term.[49]

For ensuring quality standards, qualifying examinations could be evolved for admissions to engineering and medical institutions. Although the States of Karnataka and Andhra Pradesh have evolved such an entrance examination, in practice the situation has been different. For instance, in Karnataka a student who has only secured 50 per cent marks can get a seat in private professional college if he has the wherewithal to pay capitation, while those with even 80 per cent go abegging.

Private initiatives in education have not functioned as commerical ventures alone. The Indian Institute of Science (I.I.Sc.) at Bangalore was the first institution set up in India with the objective of furthering advanced research work in pure and applied sciences. The Institute owes its establishment in 1886 to the munificence of the late Jamshedji Tata who gave an endowment of two hundred thousand pounds for setting it up.[50] Hennessy in his study of the

[49] Navin C. Nigam, 'Technical Education Dilemma', *Indian Exprerss*, 14 October 1992.
[50] E.V. Ganapati Iyer, *Indian Institute of Science: 1938–1948*, Bangalore, 1948. Also see, B. Subarayappa, *In Pursuit of Excellence: A History of the Indian Institute of Science*, Tata McGraw-Hill, New Delhi, 1992.

work of the Birla Education Trust has glorified its services in the educational sphere.[51] The Birla Institute of Technology and Science (B.I.T.S.) at Pilani, for instance, has built up a reputation for itself. The admission criteria for institutions such as I.I.Sc. Bangalore and B.I.T.S. Pilani are stiff and based purely on merit. Such philanthropic interest in education does keep an alternative alive.

Menefee's[52] study on Manipal has also revealed that the colleges which were established there were initially inspired by altruistic motives. While these colleges have continued to maintain minimum standards, their objectives have become more entrepreneurial and they now charge very high capitation fees.

Where students have to pay steep college fees, an alternative could be to evolve a system of granting loans by the state to the needy and deserving. The loans could cover tuition fees and other charges and their repayment could be spread over a student's career span. While some loan schemes are available, they are too meagre to fulfil the requirements of needy students, especially those belonging to the weaker sections. Under the 'selective pricing' scheme suggested in some studies,[53] fees paid by students ought to be related to the cost of courses and the ability of the students to pay; there would be different rates of fees for students belonging to different socio-economic strata. However, here also the state would have to ensure necessary controls to make this type of privatisation more efficient and equitable.

Justice Venkataramiah has suggested more stringent laws for controlling the mushrooming of sub-standard private colleges. He has proposed that in case some trust or society wishes to start a medical college, the government should enact a law that provides that only if the trust or society first builds a hospital with 500 beds and keeps a deposit of Rs. 2 crore with the government should it be permitted to start a medical college, provided the teaching staff and other facilities satisfy the prescribed standards. He has further suggested that the Parliament enact a law in exercise of its powers under Entry 25 of List III of the VII Schedule to the Constitution

[51] Jossleyn Hennessy, *India, Democracy and Education*, Orient Longman, Bombay, 1955.
[52] Selden Menefee, *The Pais of Manipal*, The Academy of General Education, Manipal, 1984.
[53] See Jandhyala, B.G. Tilak, 'The Privatisation of Higher Education' in *Prospects*, Vol. XXI, No. 2, 1991; also see E. Jimenez, *Pricing Policy in the Social Sectors*, Johns Hopkins, Baltimore, 1987.

of India 'prohibiting collection of capitation fees and laying down reasonable conditions which the private managements should satisfy before establishing technical and medical colleges'.[54]

Universities need to exercise greater autonomy without interference from the government so that they can ensure more effective controls.[55] One possibility would be to have professional experts and Local Inspection Committees carefully scrutinize the infrastructural facilities available in colleges before universities grant them affiliation. So far, no private medical or engineering college has been disaffiliated or derecognised by universities in Karnataka on grounds of non-compliance of any laid-out stipulations.

Community Initiatives

One of the major reasons why state initiatives so far have not really succeeded in ameliorating the problem may be explained by the fact that governments representing the dominant coalition of forces yield to pressures of various caste, entrepreneurial and political interests. As Apple has observed, education has become one of the spheres in which 'forms of domination and subordination are being built and rebuilt', and therefore, 'the politics of education at all levels provides one crucial arena in which the struggle for a democratised economy, a democratised culture and a democratised polity will be carried out'.[56] What is required therefore are democratic and secular initiatives which can transform narrow sectarian interests and not those based on the concerns of a particular caste or community for making profit. These could stem from the public or the community at large. In recent times, some voluntary organisations like Eklavya and Kishore Bharti in Madhya Pradesh, and others in Maharashtra and Bihar have made community interaction with education possible. Kishore Bharti, established in Hoshangabad

[54] See E.S., Venkataramiah, 'Higher Learning in India—Legal and Social Aspects,' *Fourteenth J.N. Tata Lecture*, Indian Institute of Science, Bangalore, 27 September 1991, pp. 18–19.

[55] See Sumit Sarkar, 'Autonomy for Whom?' *Social Scientist*, Vol. XVII, Nos. 9–10, September–October 1989. Also, *Universities in Karnataka*, Report of the Review Commission, Bangalore, 1980.

[56] Michael W. Apple, 'Critical Introduction' in Roger Dale, *The State and Education Policy*, Open University Press, Milton Keynes, 1989, pp. 2 and 18.

district of Madhya Pradesh, was a voluntary agency committed to rural transformation. It carried out the Hoshangabad Science Teaching Project (H.S.T.P.) in collaboration with the government where the effort was to impart science education to rural children. Now the H.S.T.P. has become Eklavya.[57] Eklavya has made an intervention in the governmental educational system, and has been concerned with pedagogical materials, teacher orientation, educational objectives and administration of education in interior areas. It has also redesigned the curricula of Classes I to VIII for schools.

In Bihar, organisations like the Nav Bharat Jagriti Kendra (Hazaribagh) and Prayas have been involved in popular mobilisation and have undertaken developmental and educational work. The Xavier Institute of Social Science (Ranchi), participating with the Jan Vikas Mandal (a consortium of voluntary agencies), has been concerned with the promotion of adult education and rural development in Chotanagpur.[58] In Maharashtra, voluntary organisations in Wardha and Nagpur have been involved in educational programmes which emphasise vocational education. Although such experiments and some in Orissa and West Bengal have been partly state-funded and have been primarily at the levels of primary and school education, similar initiatives in the sphere of higher education could also be attempted.

The capitation fee phenomenon continues to grow unabated even though the education it provides is sub-standard. But once the demand for quality education is widespread, there would be checks on such private colleges. Student and teacher bodies in these institutions require to be more vigilant and resist any pressures from politicians and those running the colleges to admit students who do not fulfil minimum standards.

Quality is one aspect, but receiving education at a reasonable cost is another. Again, it is the deprived groups and backward sections who are losing out on education. Attempts for securing the privilege of education for more and more people have always been resisted by the socially and economically advantageous groups.[59]

[57] Krishna Kumar, 'Dialogues: On the Teaching of Science,' *Lokayan Bulletin*, 4:1, 1986, pp. 38–58.

[58] See Philip Eldridge and Nil Ratan. 'Voluntary Organisations and Popular Movements in Bihar,' *Lokayan Bulletin*, 6:4, 1988, pp. 3-44.

[59] See Maurice Levitas, *Marxist Perspectives in the Sociology of Education*, Routledge and Kegan Paul, London, 1974, pp. 72–98.

Instead of self-seeking entrepreneurs, there have to be more dedicated groups taking greater interest and seeing that private initiative does not become an instrument for perpetuating inequalities.

Given the complex character of the Indian state, measures such as those suggested above can only be transitional steps to a full-fledged policy on education. Such a policy must necessarily be people-focused and go beyond the markets.[60] And, as Amartya Sen has remarked, in India, so far, the emphasis has been on negative state intervention, regulations or restrictions; what is really needed is 'positive policy intervention',[61] specially in spheres like education and health to benefit the underprivileged sections of society. However, it is only with greater participation of the people that the democratic process can be activised and the state pressurised effectively to act as an enabler or facilitator of development.

[60] See Ranganath Bhardwaj and K.K. Balachander, 'Social Investment in Education and New Economic Policy,' paper presented at a meeting on New Economic Policies and Financing Education, NIEPA, New Delhi, 28–30 September 1992. Also see Vinod Thomas, 'Lessons from Economic Development—What have We Learnt about the Path to Successful Development?' Finance and Development, Vol. 28, No. 3, September 1991.

[61] Amartya Sen, op. cit.

SELECT BIBLIOGRAPHY

Books and Articles

Acharya, Poromesh, 'Development of Modern Language Text-books and the Social Context in the Nineteenth Century Bengal,' *Economic and Political Weekly*, Vol. XXI, No. 17, 26 April 1986, pp. 745–51.

——————, 'Is Macaulay Still Our Guru?' *Economic and Political Weekly*, Vol. XXIII, No. 2, 28 May 1988, pp. 1124–30.

Altbach, Philip G. and **Gail Kelly** (Eds.), *Education and Colonialism*, Longman, New York, 1978.

Altbach, Philip G., *Higher Education in the Third World: Themes and Variations*, Radiant Publishers, New Delhi, 1987.

Balachander, K.K., 'Higher Education in India: Quest for Equality and Equity,' *Mainstream*, Vol. XXIV, No. 48, 2 August 1986, pp. 11–14.

Bardhan, Pranab, *The Political Economy of Development in India*, Oxford University Press, Delhi, 1984.

——————, 'The Third Dominant Class,' *Economic and Political Weekly*, Vol. XXLV, No. 3, 21 January 1989, pp. 155–56.

Basu, Aparna, *The Growth of Education and Political Development in India: 1898–1920*, Oxford University Press, Delhi, 1974.

——————, *Essays in the History of Indian Education*, Concept Publishing Company, New Delhi, 1981.

Beteille, Andre, *Castes: Old and New*, Asia Publishing House, New Delhi, 1969.

——————, (Ed.), *Equality and Inequality: Theory and Practice*, Oxford University Press, Delhi, 1983.

——————, 'Millstone of Reservations: Liberation with Caste Quotas,' *The Times of India*, New Delhi, 12 October 1991.

——————, 'Access to Medical Education: Matter of Right and Policy,' *The Times of India*, New Delhi, 1 September 1992.

Bheemappa, S., 'Analysis of Elections,' *The Times of India*, Bangalore, 25 April 1987.

Bottomore, T.B., *Elites and Society*, Penguin Books, London, 1966.

Bourdieu, Pierre and Jean-Claude Passeron, *Reproduction in Education, Society and Culture*, Sage Publications, London, 1977.

Bowles, S. and H. Gintis, *Schooling in Capitalist America*, Routledge and Kegan Paul, London, 1976.

Bowles, S., H. Gintis and J. Simmons, 'The Impact of Education on Poverty: The U.S. Experience,' in S. Shukla and Krishna Kumar (Eds.), *Sociological Perspective in Education: A Reader*, Chanakya Publications, Delhi, 1985, pp. 102–11.

Chitnis, Suma, *A Long Way to Go*, Allied Publishers, New Delhi, 1981.

Dale, Roger, *The State and Education Policy*, Open University Press, Milton Keynes, 1989.

Deshpande, J.V., 'Business and Politics of Universities,' *Economic and Political Weekly*, Vol. XXLL, No. 3, 17 January 1987, p. 74.

————, 'Boom in Teaching Shops,' *Economic and Political Weekly*, Vol. XXVI, No. 30, 27 July 1991, p. 1787.

Desai, A.R., *India's Path of Development*, Popular Prakashan, Bombay, 1984.

————, 'Trends of Change in Indian Society since Independence,' *Economic and Political Weekly*, Vol. XXIV, No. 33, 19 August 1989, pp. 661–67.

Dharampal, *The Beautiful Tree: Indigenous Education in the Eighteenth Century*, Biblia Impex, New Delhi, 1983.

Dhavan, Rajeev, 'Constitutional Rhetoric and Right to Education,' *Indian Express*, New Delhi, 10 August 1992.

Dushkin, Lelah, *The Non-Brahmin Movement in Princely Mysore*, Unpublished Ph.D. Dissertation, University of Pennsylvania, 1974.

————, 'Backward Class Benefits and Social Class in India: 1920–1970,' *Economic and Political Weekly*, Vol. XIV, No. 14, 7 April 1979, pp. 661–67.

————, 'Caste Associations in Bangalore,' *Economic and Political Weekly*, Vol. XV, No. 37, 13 September 1980, pp. 1551–57.

Engineer, Asghar Ali (Ed.), *Mandal Commission Controversy*, Ajanta Publications, Delhi, 1991.

Entwistle, Harold, *Class, Culture and Education*, Methuen, London, 1978.

Frankel, Francine R., *India's Green Revolution: Economic Gains and Political Costs*, Princeton University Press, New Jersey, 1971.

Frankel, Francine R., and M.S.A. Rao (Eds.), *Dominance and State Power in Modern India: Decline of a Social Order*, Oxford University Press, Delhi, 1989.

Galanter, Marc, *Competing Equalities*, Oxford University Press, Delhi, 1984.

Ghosh, R. and M. Zacharia (Eds.), *Education and the Process of Change*, Sage Publications, New Delhi, 1987.

Gounden, Nalla A.M., 'Investment in Education in India,' *Journal of Human Resources*, Summer 1967, pp. 345–58.

Haragopal, G., 'Dimensions of State Politics: A Political Economy Perspective,' Paper presented at ICSSR Seminar on 'India since Independence,' New Delhi, 26–30 December 1988.

Hennessy, Jossleyn, *India, Democracy and Education*, Orient Longman, Bombay, 1953.

Hettne, Bjorn, *The Political Economy of Indirect Rule: Mysore 1881–1947*, Ambika Publications, New Delhi, 1978.

Holmstrom, Mark, *South Indian Factory Workers: Their Life and Their World*, Cambridge University Press, London 1976.

Horio, Turuhisa, 'Towards Reform in Japanese Education: A Critique of Privatization and Proposal for the Re-creation of Public Education,' *Comparative Education*, Vol. 22, No. 1, 1986, pp. 31–36.

Jayaram, N., *Sociology of Education*, Rawat Publications, Jaipur, 1990.

Joglekar, P.J., 'The Case for Capitation Fees,' *The Times of India*, New Delhi, 6 June 1985.

Joshi, P.C., *Land Reforms in India: Trends and Perspectives*, Allied Publishers, New Delhi, 1975.

Kamat, A.R., *The Educational Situation and Other Essays*, People's Publishing House, New Delhi, 1973.

——————— 'The Emerging Situation: A Socio-Structural Analysis,' *Economic and Political Weekly*, Vol. XIV, Nos. 7 and 8, February 1979, pp. 349–54.

———————, *Education and Social Change in India*, Somaiya Publications, Bombay, 1985.

Kashyap, Subhash (Ed.), *National Policy Studies*, Tata McGraw-Hill, New Delhi, 1990.

Kohli, Atul, *The State and Poverty in India: The Politics of Reform*, Cambridge University Press, Cambridge, 1987.

Kothari, Rajni, *Caste in Indian Politics*, Orient Longman, New Delhi, 1970.

———————, *State Against Democracy*, Ajanta Publications, Delhi, 1988.

———————, 'Cultural Context of Communalism in India,' *Economic and Political Weekly*, Vol. XXIV, No. 2, 14 January 1989, pp. 81–85.

Kothari, V.N., 'Private Unaided Engineering and Medical Colleges: Consequences of Misguided Policy,' *Economic and Political Weekly*, Vol. XXI, No. 14, 5 April 1986, pp. 593–96.

Krishna, Raj, 'Piece-rate Education,' *Seminar*, May 1981, pp. 34–36.

Kumar, Krishna, 'Reproduction or Change? Education and Elites in India,' *Economic and Political Weekly*, Vol. XX, No. 30, 27 July 1985, pp. 1280–84.

–——————, 'Colonial Citizen as an Educational Ideal,' *Economic and Political Weekly*, Vol. XXIV, No. 4, 28 January, 1989, pp. 45–51.

Kumar, Ravinder, *Western India in the Nineteenth Century: A Study of the Social History of Maharashtra*, Routledge and Kegan Paul, London, 1968.

Kusumakar, H., 'The Name-tag Tells All in the South,' *The Times of India*, New Delhi, 1 September 1985.

Lele, Jayant K., 'The Legitimacy Question,' *Seminar*, March 1990, pp. 21–25.

Levitas, Maurice, *Marxist Perspectives in the Sociology of Education*, Routledge and Kegan Paul, London, 1974.

Mahajan, Krishna, 'Right to Education: Implications of the Verdict,' *Indian Express*, New Delhi, 9 August 1992.

Manor, James, *Political Change in an Indian State: Mysore 1917–1955*, Manohar, New Delhi, 1977.

———————, 'The Evolution of Political Arenas and Units of Social Organization: The Lingayats and Okkaligas of Princely Mysore,' in M.N. Srinivas et al. (Eds.), *Dimensions of Social Change in India*, Allied Publishers, New Delhi, 1977, pp. 170–87.

———————, 'Blurring the Lines between Parties and Social Bases: Gundu Rao and the Emergence of a Janata Government in Karnataka, 'Economic and Political Weekly, Vol. XIX, No. 37, 15 September 1984, pp. 1623–32.

Manor, James, 'Caste, Class, Dominance and Politics in a Cohesive Society,' in Francine R. Frankel and M.S.A. Rao (Eds.), Dominance and State Power in Modern India: Decline of a Social Order, Oxford University Press, Delhi, 1989, pp. 322–61.

Menefee, Selden, The Pais of Manipal, The Academy of General Education, Manipal, 1984.

Mohanty, Manoranjan, 'Duality of the State Process in India: A Hypothesis,' Paper presented at the XII Indian Social Science Congress, Mysore, 14–17 July 1987.

————, 'University and the State,' PUCL Bulletin, Vol. II, No. 2, February 1982, pp. 8–10.

Misra, B.B., The Indian Middle Classes: Their Growth in Modern Times, Oxford University Press, London, 1961.

Mukherjee, Haridas and Uma Mukherjee, The Origins of the National Education Movement (1905–1910), Jadavpur University, Calcutta, 1957.

Murthy, Sachidananda, 'Campus Battlefields: Increasing "Outsider"–Local Clashes in Many Capitation Fee Colleges,' The Week, 11–17 December 1988, pp. 22–23.

Naik, J.P., Equality, Quality and Quantity: The Elusive Triangle, Allied Publishers, New Delhi, 1975.

————, The Education Commission and After, Allied Publishers, New Delhi, 1982.

Nair, Janaki, 'Fighting for Backwardness: Venkataswamy Commission Report and After,' Economic and Political Weekly, Vol. XXI, No. 42, 18 October 1986, pp. 1837–38.

Nair, Kusum, Blossoms in the Dust, Gerald Duckworth and Company, London, 1961.

Nataraj, Lalitha and V.K. Nataraj, 'Limits of Populism: Devaraj Urs and Karnatak Politics,' Economic and Political Weekly, Vol. XVII, No. 37, 11 September 1982, pp. 1503–06.

Nataraj, Lalitha, 'Twists and Turns of Caste Politics,' Economic and Political Weekly, Vol. XVIII, No. 5, 29 January 1983, pp. 139–40.

Nataraj, V.K., 'Backward Classes and Minorities in Karnataka Politics,' in Ramashray Roy and Richard Sisson (Eds.), Diversity and Dominance in Indian Politics, Vol. II, Sage Publications, New Delhi, 1990, pp. 170–86.

Navlakha, Suren, 'Self-Legitimacy of Indian Higher Education,' Contributions to Indian Sociology, New Series, Vol. XVIII, No. 2, July–December 1984, pp. 244–65.

————, Elite and Social Change: A Study of Elite Formation in India, Sage Publications, New Delhi, 1989.

Omvedt, Gail, Cultural Revolt in a Colonial Society: The Non-Brahmin Movement in Western India—1873–1930, Scientific Socialist Education Trust, Bombay, 1976.

————, (Ed.), Land, Caste and Politics in Indian States, A Project of Teaching Politics, Department of Political Science, University of Delhi, Delhi, 1982.

————, 'Twice-Born Riot Against Democracy,' Economic and Political Weekly, Vol. XXV, No. 39, 29 September 1990, pp. 2195–01.

Pani, Narendra, *Reforms to Preempt Change: Land Legislation in Karnataka*, Concept Publishing Company, New Delhi, 1983.
——————, 'Backtracking on Capitation,' *Economic Times*, Bangalore, 29 June 1987.
Paranjape, H.K., 'Where Do We Go from Here?' *Mainstream*, 15 August 1987, pp. 9–13.
Puttaswamaiah, K., *Economic Development of Karnataka: A Treatise in Continuity and Change*, Oxford and IBH, New Delhi, 1980.
Radhakrishnan, P., 'Karnataka Backward Classes,' *Economic and Political Weekly*, Vol. XXV, No. 32, 11 August 1990, pp. 1749–54.
Raghavan, Veera J. (Ed.), *Higher Education in the Eighties*, Lancer International, New Delhi, 1985.
Rajan, M.A.S., *The Land Reform Law in Karnataka*, Government of Karnataka, Bangalore, 1979.
Ram, N.. 'Dravidian Movement in its Pre-Independence Phases,' *Economic and Political Weekly*, Vol. XIV, Nos. 7 and 8 February 1979.
Ramakrishna, G., 'Higher Education: A Perspective from the Periphery,' *Journal of Higher Education*, Vol. VII, No. 1, Monsoon 1981, pp. 51–58.
——————, (Ed.), *Towards a Redefinition of the Education Policy*, Madhu Printers, Bangalore, 1992.
Rao, Raghavendra, 'Understanding the Indian State: A Historical Materialist Exercise,' in Zoya Hasan, S.N. Jha and R. Khan (Eds.), *The State, Political Processes and Identity*, Sage Publications, New Delhi, 1989, pp. 88–98.
Rao, V.K.R.V. (Ed.), *Planning in Perspective: Policy Choices in Planning for Karnataka, 1973–74 to 1988–89*, Allied Publishers, New Delhi, 1978.
Robinson, Robert V., 'Reproducing Class Relations in Industrial Capitalism,' *American Sociological Review*, Vol. XXXXIX, April 1984, pp. 182–96.
Rudolph, S.H. and L.I. Rudolph, *Education and Politics in India: Studies in Organization, Society and Polity*, Oxford University Press, Delhi, 1972.
——————, *In Pursuit of Lakshmi: The Political Economy of the Indian State*, Orient Longman, Hyderabad, 1987.
Sardesai, Rajdeep, 'New Education Barons: Profiteering Begins Where Welfare Ends,' *The Times of India*, New Delhi, 1 October 1992.
Sarkar, Sumit, *Modern India: 1885–1947*, Macmillan India Limited, Delhi, 1983.
——————, 'Autonomy for Whom?' *Social Scientist*, Vol. XVII, Nos. 9–10, September–October 1989, pp. 27–33.
Seetharamu, A., 'Education in Karnataka State,' *Journal of Educational Planning and Administration*, Vol. II, January and April 1988, pp. 129–46.
Sethi, J.D., 'Privatisation of Higher Education,' *Indian Express*, New Delhi, 3 January 1986.
Shah, A.B., *The Social Context of Education*, Allied Publishers, New Delhi, 1978.
Shah, B.V., *Social Change and College Students of Gujarat*, University of Baroda, Baroda, 1964.
Shah, Ghanshyam, 'Caste, Class and the State,' *Seminar*, March 1990, pp. 31–35.
——————, (Ed.), *Capitalist Development: Critical Essays*, Popular Prakashan, Bombay, 1990.
Shakir, Moin, *State and Politics in Contemporary India*, Ajanta Publications, Delhi, 1986.

Shatrugna, M., 'Privatising Higher Education,' *Economic and Political Weekly*, Vol. XXIII, No. 50, 10 December 1988, pp. 2624–25.

Sheth, D.L., 'Caste and Politics: A Survey of Literature' in Gopal Krishna (Ed.), *Contributions to South Asian Studies*, Vol. I, Oxford University Press, Delhi, 1979, pp. 161–97.

Shukla, S.C., Educational Development in British India (1854–1904), *Ph.D. Thesis*, Faculty of Education, University of Delhi, 1959.

Singh, Amrik and Philip G. Altbach (Eds.), *The Higher Learning in India*, Vikas Publishing House, Delhi, 1974.

Singh, Amrik, *Redeeming Higher Education*, Ajanta Publications, Delhi, 1985.

Singh, Amrik and G.D. Sharma (Eds.), *Higher Education in India: The Social Context*, Konark Publishers, Delhi, 1988.

Singh, Nirmal, 'A Perspective on Higher Education in India: The Case of Private Control,' *Journal of Higher Education*, Vol. V, No. 1, Monsoon 1979, pp. 21–31.

—————, *Education Under Siege: A Sociological Study of Private Colleges*, Concept Publishing Company, New Delhi, 1983.

Srinivas, M.N., *Caste in Modern India and Other Essays*, Asia Publishing House, Bombay, 1962.

—————, *India: Social Structure*, Hindustan Publishing House, Delhi, 1980.

Srinivas, M.N. and N. Panini, 'Politics and Society in Karnataka,' *Economic and Political Weekly*, Vol. XIX, No. 2, January 1984, pp. 69–75.

Tawney, R.H., *Equality*, Allen Unwin Books, 1964.

Thimmaiah, G. and Abdul Aziz, *Political Economy of Land Reforms*, Ashish Publishing House, New Delhi, 1987.

Tilak, Jandhyala B.G., *The Economics of Inequality in Education*, Sage Publications, New Delhi, 1987.

—————, 'The Privatization of Higher Education,' *Prospects*, Vol. XXI, No. 2, 1991.

Vattam, Krishna, 'Lack of Facilities: Bane of New Engineering Colleges,' *Deccan Herald*, Bangalore, 28 June 1982.

Vedantam, Vatsala, 'Mess in Technical Education,' *Deccan Herald*, Bangalore, 11, 14, 18 and 21 February 1983.

—————, 'Medicos Hard Options: Perspectives in Education,' *Deccan Hearld*, 21 June 1987.

Venkataraman, K., M.Prahladachar and R.S. Deshpande, *Dynamics of Rural Transformation in Karnataka: 1956–76*, Institute of Social and Economic Change, Bangalore, 1985.

Watson, Kieth (Ed.), *Dependence and Inter-dependence in Education*, Croom Helm, London, 1984.

Weiner, Myron, *The Indian Paradox: Essays in Indian Politics*, Sage Publications, New Delhi, 1989.

Zaidi, Askari H., 'Doctors in Distress,' *The Times of India*, New Delhi, 22 August 1987.

Government Reports, Documents and Other Publications

Government of India, *Report of the University Education Commission 1948–49*, Publications Division, Delhi, 1951.

Government of India, *Education Commission: 1964–66*, Ministry of Education, New Delhi, 1966.

——, *Trends of Expenditure on Education: 1968–69 to 1979*, Ministry of Education and Culture, New Delhi, 1978.

——, *Four-Year Degree Course in Engineering: A Model List of Laboratories, Experiments and Equipment*, Ministry of Education and Culture, New Delhi, 1984.

——, *Analysis of Budgeted Expenditure on Education: 1984–85 to 1986–87*, Ministry of Education, New Delhi, 1985.

—— ——, *Challenge of Education: A Policy Perspective*, Ministry of Education, New Delhi, 1985.

——, *National Policy on Education*, Ministry of Human Resource Development, New Delhi, 1986.

——, *Guidelines Laid Down by the AICTE for Technical Education for Fulfilment by Private Technical Institutions*, Ministry of Human Resource Development, New Delhi, July 1989.

Government of Karnataka, *The Havanur Report*, Bangalore, 1975.

——, *Karnataka State Gazetteer*, Bangalore, 1982.

——, *Draft Five-Year Plan: 1978–83*, Planning Department, Bangalore, 1983.

——, *The Karnataka Education Bill 1983*, Karnataka Legislative Assembly, Seventh Assembly, Third Session, Bangalore, 1983.

——, *Report of the Joint Select Committee on the Karnataka Education Bill*, Karnataka Legislature, Bangalore, 1983.

——, *White Paper on Professional Colleges and Institutions*, Department of Education and Youth Services and Department of Health and Family Welfare, Bangalore, March 1983.

——, *Report on Assessment of Engineering Personnel During Sixth Five-Year Plan: 1980–85*, Manpower and Employment Division, Planning Department, Bangalore, 1984.

——, *Rules for Selection of Candidates to M.B.B.S. Course in Government/Private Medical Colleges 1984–85*, Bangalore.

——, *Report of the Second Backward Classes Commission*, Bangalore, 1986.

——, *Economic Survey 1986–87*, Planning Department, Bangalore.

——, *Karnataka's Economy in Figures*, Directorate of Economics and Statistics, Bangalore, 1987.

——, *Karnataka at a Glance: 1989–90*, Directorate of Economics and Statistics, Bangalore, 1990.

——, *Report of the Karnataka Third Backward Classes Commission*, Vols. I and II, Bangalore, 1990.

——, *Economic Survey 1990–91*, Planning Department, Bangalore.

Karnatak Liberal Education Society, *Diamond Jubilee Souvenir 1916–1976*, Belgaum, 1979.

Legislative Assembly Debates, Karnataka Vidhan Soudha, Bangalore, 11 July 1972, 17 June 1978, 24 June 1977, 13 July 1978, 9 July 1980.

Sree Siddaganga Mutt, *A Brief Note on Sree Siddaganga Mutt and Its Activities*, Tumkur, 1982.

INDEX

absence of students' body or union in private colleges, 215–17

Adichunchanagiri Institute of Medical Sciences (A.I.M.S.), 149, 163, 226

Adichunchanagiri Institute of Technology, Chikmagalur (A.I.T.), 162, 163, 190

Adichunchanagiri Shikshana Trust, 162

agrarian interests and private colleges, 103–5

agricultural economy in Karnataka, 43–45

agriculture–industry link in Karnataka, 53

All India Council for Technical Education (A.I.C.T.E.), 96, 97, 98, 204; guidelines, 210–11

alternatives to capitation, 258

Ambedkar Institute of Technology (A.I.T.), 92, 149, 168, 172, 225

Ambedkar Medical College (A.M.C.), 92, 123, 127, 149, 151, 168, 169, 172, 181, 189, 201, 208, 209, 226, 233, 234, 235

Ananda Social and Educational Trust, 168–69

Anti-Capitation Act, 138

Apple, Michael, 32

Banerjee, Albion, 94

Bangalore Institute of Technology (B.I.T.), 159, 160–61, 204, 211, 243

Bangalore Medical College, 98, 137, 189, 214, 226, 229

Bangalore University College Teachers Association (B.U.C.T.A.), 237–38

Bangarappa, 139–40

Bardhan, Pranab, 19, 244

Beteille, Andre, 18, 39, 252

Birla Institute of Technology and Science (B.I.T.S.), 261

Bommai, 77, 106, 186

bottlenecking of opportunities for the majority, 249

Bottomore, T.B., 246

Bourdieu, Pierre, 251

Brahmin representation in education and services in Karnataka, 74, 81

capitation fee, 15; its political dimensions, 105–9; and Devraj Urs phase, 117–19; and Gundu Rao phase, 119–27; and Hegde phase, 127–37; and post-Hegde phase, 137–39; colleges used as channels to sustain communalism, casteism, regionalism, 254; phenomenon showing anti-secular trends, 252

capitation fee colleges, types of, run as family enterprise, 250; as instruments for commerce and profit,

244; by private entrepreneurs, 158; by religious and linguistic minorities, 158; by scheduled castes, 158
caste associations, 20, 28, 58, 242; Karnataka Liberal Education Society, 89, 147, 150, 153, 165, 168; Karnataka Lingayat Education Society (K.L.E.S.), 28; Mysore Lingayat Educational Fund Association (M.L.E.F.A.), 28, 159; Vokkaliga/Vokkaligara Sangha, 29, 76, 143, 145, 146, 159, 185, 243
caste–class–power configuration/interplay, 17–21, 37, 83, 90, 169
caste–money power politics nexus, 243, 259
Chitnis, Suma, 242, 246
colonial system of education, 21–26
commercialisation of education, 103, 119, 137, 152
community initiatives in education, 262–63
constitution and education, 29–32
controlling the mushrooming of substandard private colleges, 261–62
cooperative systems of education, 260

Dale, Roger, 262
Dayananda Sagar College of Engineering (D.S.C.E.), 179, 208, 219
democratisation in the socio-political sphere, 258
Desai, A.R., 35–36
Dewans of former Mysore State, 51, 93
dominant castes, 39, 40, 56, 109, 144, 184, 241; see also Lingayats, Vokkaligas
dual fee structure in private colleges, 145
Dushkin, Lelah, 69, 79, 92

effective controls, 262
Eklavya, 262–63; see also voluntary organisations
eligibility conditions for entrance to government and private colleges, 153, 157

elitist character, of the Indian education system, 248; of private enterprise in education, 250
engineering colleges in Karnataka, 85
entrepreneurship in education, 57; see also private enterprise in education
equality of opportunity, 245, 247
executive committee of private colleges, 143, 144, 158

facilities for teaching inadequate, 233–35
faculty in private colleges, caste background, 230; educational background, 230; fear of insecurity in private jobs, 231; pay-scales 232; poorly qualified teachers, 225–26, 255
fee structure for private colleges, 117–39
First Backward Classes Commission, 73–74
Frankel, Francine, 18, 53

Galanter, Marc, 30
Gokula Education Foundation, 177
governing councils of private colleges, 143–44
Government Order of 1981, 121–22
Gundu Rao, 75, 119–27, 139, 169, 181

Hardgrave, Robert, L., 28
Havanur, L.G., 73, 74, 76
Hegde, Ramakrishna, 16, 75, 108, 127–37, 139
Hennessy, Jossleyn, 260–61
Hettne, Bjorn, 40, 51, 53, 65, 93–95
Holmstrom, Mark, 56–57

Inam lands, 45–47
increase in student intake in private colleges, 126, 127, 132, 156, 211–13
Indian Institute of Science, Bangalore, 260
industrial enterprises in Mysore, 95
industrial sector in Karnataka, 51–53
ineffective teachers' forum, 236–38
interaction between government and private colleges, 111–42

Islamiah Institute of Technology, 150, 172, 174, 185
Ismail, Mirza, 94, 95

Janardhan Reddy government, 16, 88
Janata–Congress clash, 186
Janata government/party in Karnataka, 76, 107, 127, 162, 180–81, 183
J.N. Medical College, Belgaum (J.N.M.C.), 119, 123, 165, 170–71, 205
J.S.S. Medical College, Mysore, 164, 226

Kamat, A.R., 247
Karnataka Educational Bill (1983), 113, 143, 150
Karnataka Educational Institutions Act (1984), 16, 135–37
Karnataka Liberal Education Society, see caste associations
Karnataka Regional Engineering College, Surathkal (K.R.E.), 189, 194, 213, 214, 226, 228
Karnataka State Universities Act (1976), 115, 116
Kasturba Medical College (K.M.C.), 84, 86, 91, 97, 127, 151, 174, 176, 189, 234
Kempegowda Institute of Medical Sciences (K.I.M.S.), 122, 144, 145, 150, 151, 159–61, 199, 200, 201, 215, 218, 228, 231, 243
K.L.E. Society's Engineering College, Belgaum (K.L.E.S.E.C.), 165, 170–71
Kohli, Atul, 72
Kothari, Rajni, 252–53
Kothari Commission Report, 249
Kumar, Krishna, 27, 61, 249

lack of autonomy in universities, 116
lack of facilities in private colleges, 152–53, 254
lack of students' unions in private colleges, 254
Land Reforms Amendment (1974), 72

land reforms in Karnataka, 45, 47, 51
Lele, Jayant, 259
Lingayat, 41, 46, 47, 50, 56, 57, 62, 65, 66, 69; chief ministers, 67; dominance in rural leadership, 77; occupational groups, 73; representation in civil services, 77; representation in engineering and medical colleges, 80, 82; representation in the Legislative Assembly, 74, 78; -run colleges, 90, 142, 145, 159, 163–68, 188; see also dominant castes
linkage between parents' occupation, income level and students' aspirations, 219
linkage between state, society and education, 142, 158
loan schemes, 260
lowering of standards, 254–56
low-investment/high-profit parameter, 240

Managing board(s), of private colleges, 142; socio-economic profile, 159–87
Mandal Commission, 16, 17, 258
Manipal Institute of Technology (M.I.T.), 175, 176, 225
Manor, James, 40, 41, 46, 57, 67, 72, 73, 140
Medical Council of India, 87, 108, 204, 206; regulations/norms, 207–9, 214, 220, 223, 233
medical education, British period, 24–26; in Karnataka, 85–86; post-independence period, 32–34
middle castes, 27, 28, 31, 57
Miller Report, 64, 79, 80
minimal academic merit conditions, 255
minority institutions, 150, 181
Mohanty, Manoranjan, 241, 245
Mohini Jain vs. State of Karnataka, 140
Moily, Veerappa, 138–39
M.S. Ramaiah Institute of Technology (M.S.R.I.T.), 177–78, 189, 211, 215, 218, 225, 231

M.S. Ramaiah Medical College (M.S.R.M.C.), 123, 126, 151, 178, 200, 201, 202, 217

M.V.J. College, 168, 179–80, 208, 211, 215

Mysore Lingayat Educational Fund Association (M.L.E.F.A.), see caste associations

Mysore Medical College, 90, 93, 97

Nagan Gowda Committee, 68, 70

Naik, J.P., 66

National Front Government and capitation, 141

National Policy on Education, 36

nationalist initiatives in education, 26

New Education Policy (1986), 36, 258

Nijalingappa, 184

Non-Brahmin movement, 27, 48, 62–66, 91, 242

Omvedt, Gail, 18, 20, 22

operation of finance in private colleges, 145–50

opportunities to weaker sections, 258

organisational hierarchy in private colleges, 144

other backward classes in Karnataka, 42, 70–72; representation in professional colleges, 81

Pais of Manipal, 151

Panchajanya Vidhya Peetha Welfare Trust, 168

Passeron, Jean-Claude, 251

policy perspectives in respect of engineering and medical personnel, 110, 140

Praja Mithra Mandali, 62

private 'initiative/enterprise in education, 31, 32, 35, 84, 97, 98, 148, 151, 158, 168, 249, 260, 264

profit motives, 103, 249

quality of education in private colleges, 204–13, 223

Radhakrishnan Commission, 32, 245; see also University Education Commission

Rame Gowda Committee, 138

Rashtriya Shikshana Samiti Trust, 179

reflection of persisting inequalities, 247

Reddy, Chinappa O., 76

relationships of dominance, 251

Report of the Review Commission on Universities in Karnataka, 205–6, 214

reproductionist force in education, 250

reservations, 68, 73, 76, 89, 242, 258

Rudolphs, 105–6, 107, 108

R.V. College of Engineering (R.V.C.E.), 145, 146, 152, 153, 179

Second Backward Classes Commission in Karnataka, 76–77; see also Venkataswami, T.

Second Education Commission, 35

selective pricing scheme, 261

Sen, Amartya, 264

Shah, Ghanshyam, 21

Siddaganga Education Society, 164

Siddaganga Institute of Technology (S.I.T.), 148, 150, 164, 166–67, 188, 189, 199, 202, 235, 243

Siddaganga mutt, 147, 185

single caste or community dominance, 243

Sree Adichunchanagiri mutt, 162

Sree Siddhartha Institute of Technology (S.S.I.T.), 143, 149, 172–73, 181, 190, 206, 225, 230

Sri Suttur Veera Sinhasana mutt, 164

Srinath Committee, 138

Srinivas, M.N., 20, 31, 38, 39, 57, 59, 90

state initiatives in education, 262, 258–59

stratification based on class/caste, 245

students, aspirations of, 216–21; caste profile, 199–201; pre-selection of, 249, 250; proportion whose parents came from: landed and business background, 194; private corporate sector, 259; professional background or other jobs, 194; rural–urban background 195–98; school background, 195–97; who justified capitation, 202; who wanted to set up their own business or private medical practice, 218

Supreme Court judgement on capitation fee, 15, 141, 142

teacher–student ratio, 99, 210, 213, 228

technical education, British period, 22–23; in Karnataka, 85; post-independence phase, 32–34

Telugu Desam Party, 88

Third Backward Classes Commission Report, 78, 79, 81; *see also* Reddy, Chinappa O.

Tilak, Jandhyala B.G., 37, 53

T.M.A. Pai Trust, 175

types of capitation fee colleges, *see* capitation fee colleges

unemployment, consequences of, 256–57

University Education Commission, 32, 245

University Visvesvaraya College of Engineering (U.V.C.E.), 189, 194, 214, 225, 226, 228, 234, 235

Urs, Devraj, 50, 71–75, 106, 117–19, 139

Veer Shaivya cult, 41

Veerendra Patil's government, 79

Venkataswamy, T., 76

Venkatesha Education Society, 180

Visvesvaraya, 51, 93, 94

Vokkaliga, 40, 46, 47, 50, 56, 57, 62, 65, 66, 69; chief ministers, 67; dominance in rural leadership, 77; representation in civil services, 77; representation in medical and engineering colleges, 80, 81, 82; representation in the Legislative Assembly, 74, 78; -run colleges, 90, 142, 145, 159, 160–61, 188; Sangha, *see* caste associations

voluntary organisations in education, 262–63

vote-bank, 243

weaker sections, representation in higher education, 246–47

welfare state, 32

White Paper on Professional Colleges and Institutions, 205–6

zamindari system, 19